Northwestern University
STUDIES IN *Phenomenology &*
Existential Philosophy

Tragic Wisdom
and Beyond

Gabriel Marcel

Translated by

Tragic Wisdom and Beyond

including

Conversations between
Paul Ricoeur and Gabriel Marcel

STEPHEN JOLIN

and PETER McCORMICK

NORTHWESTERN UNIVERSITY PRESS

EVANSTON   1973

B
2430
.M253T7

The first part of this book was originally published in French under the title *Pour une sagesse tragique*, © Librairie Plon, 1968. The second part was originally published in French under the title *Entretins: Paul Ricoeur, Gabriel Marcel*, © 1968 by Editions Aubier-Montaigne.

Stephen Jolin is Assistant Professor of Philosophy at the University of Portland; Peter McCormick is Associate Professor of Philosophy at the University of Ottawa.

Contents

Acknowledgments / xi
Translator's Preface / Peter McCormick / xiii
Translator's Introduction / Stephen Jolin / xix
Author's Preface / xxxi

TRAGIC WISDOM AND BEYOND

1 / What Can Be Expected of Philosophy? / 3
2 / The Responsibility of the Philosopher in Today's World / 16
3 / Authentic Humanism and Its Existential Presuppositions / 33
4 / The Questioning of Being / 45
5 / Truth and Freedom / 80
6 / Truth and Concrete Situations / 91
7 / Life and the Sacred / 104
8 / My Death / 120
9 / The Encounter with Evil / 132
10 / Man and His Future / 147
11 / Philosophical Atheism / 158
12 / Philosophy, Negative Theology, and Atheism / 171
13 / Passion and Wisdom in the Context of Existential Philosophy / 187
14 / Toward a Tragic Wisdom and Beyond / 199

CONVERSATIONS BETWEEN PAUL RICOEUR AND GABRIEL MARCEL

Conversation 1 / 217
Conversation 2 / 223
Conversation 3 / 230
Conversation 4 / 237
Conversation 5 / 244
Conversation 6 / 251

Acknowledgments

THE TRANSLATORS WISH TO THANK Gabriel Marcel for his help in the early stages of this translation, when they were both in Paris and had the opportunity for many long visits with him. Thanks are also due to Hubert L. Dreyfus for his encouragement throughout the project. A special debt of gratitude is owed to Claudine Fisher for her help in sorting out some of the knottiest translation problems. Thanks also to the University of Notre Dame, the University of Portland, and Denison University for their support at crucial moments.

Stephen Jolin takes primary responsibility for the translation of chapters 1, 2, 4, 5, 6, 10, 12, 13, and 14, and Peter McCormick for the remaining chapters and the "Conversations."

Chapter 4 was originally presented as a lecture before the Société française de philosophie on January 25, 1958. The permission of the following publishers for the use of quotations in this book is gratefully acknowledged: the Citadel Press for permission to quote from *The Philosophy of Existentialism*, by Gabriel Marcel, trans. Manya Harari (New York: Citadel Press, Philosophical Library, 1956), and Penguin Books Ltd for permission to quote the English translations of selections from Gerard de Nerval, *Vers dorés*, and Paul Claudel, *Tête d'or*, from *The Penguin Book of French Verse*, Vols. III and IV, trans. and ed. Anthony Hartley (Harmondsworth and Baltimore, Md.: Penguin, 1957, 1959), translations copyright © Anthony Hartley, 1957, 1959, 1966.

Translator's Preface

THIS IS NOT THE PLACE to attempt what Gabriel Marcel himself has neither wanted nor accomplished—a synoptic presentation of his philosophical concerns. What may be worthwhile, however, is to call attention briefly to several features of this book which may not be immediately evident and which do enhance its philosophical interest.

In one sense, Marcel's philosophy requires little introduction now. For a number of American philosophers have first-hand acquaintance with much of his work, which has been available in translation since before the Second World War. Moreover, some have heard him present the William James Lectures at Harvard, which were later published under the title *The Existential Background of Human Dignity*. Some years previously his two-volume Gifford Lectures, *The Mystery of Being*, had already reached a large audience. Since then, with the deepening understanding of Merleau-Ponty's work (which the Northwestern Studies in Phenomenology and Existential Philosophy has helped immeasurably), the importance of Marcel's work has only grown. For Marcel's early conceptual struggles with the idealism of Schelling, Royce, and Bradley (he has written a book on Schelling as well as one on Royce) and his analyses of sensation and objectivity not only made possible some of the central arguments Merleau-Ponty groped toward in *The Structure of Behavior* and then masterfully delineated in *Phenomenology of Perception;* they were contributions in their own right.

In another sense, however, his work requires much more than an introduction: it invites what an introduction cannot provide, extensive and thoughtful criticism. That is why this translation presents two works together. The first is a translation of Marcel's later writings which show throughout the impact of his encounter with Heidegger's later writing; the second is a series of six conversations between Marcel and his best-known student, Paul Ricoeur. Since this second work might be considered the most satisfactory introduction to the first, it may be helpful to supply some idea of its contents in summary form.

Published as a separate volume in France in 1968, almost simultaneously with the essays collected in *Tragic Wisdom*, these conversations carefully review six major thematic clusters in Marcel's work. The conversations provide some authoritative help in situating Marcel's later reflections in the context of his work as a whole. The major themes, as Marcel sees them, might be roughly summarized as the following: (1) the dialectical analysis of the concept of existence and the development of a descriptive account of sensation; (2) the conceptual analysis of the term "being," with the distinction between primary and secondary reflection and the articulation of the concept of "ontological *exigence*"; (3) the abiding concern with literature, especially poetry and drama (Marcel has written more than twenty-five plays) as one kind of secondary reflection which enables the philosopher to deal with what is not yet sayable for him in a philosophical way; (4) the analysis of the distinction between problem and mystery and the concept of "ontological mystery"; (5) the speculative and practical problem of justice and the ideas of both philosophical commitment and philosophical responsibility; and finally (6) the need to construe philosophy, not skeptically yet not systematically either, as centrally concerned with determining the conditions for what Marcel calls "a higher empiricism."

The strangeness of these terms and distinctions, however, is not entirely cleared up when they are studied in the fuller context of the "Conversations" themselves. A word may be in order, then, about the other of the two books, *Tragic Wisdom*.

These essays are striking, I think, in two ways. The first is the distinctive use of argument, and the second is the recalcitrance of the questions these essays are concerned with exploring. We need no more than the familiar dichotomy, rough as it is, between "how" and "what."

To begin with, it is important to notice that Marcel does argue. He is not content with describing what he likes to call "concrete situations." He is more concerned with recommending his descriptions, rather than completing them. He urges his views; he adduces reasons why our understanding of some concepts require new descriptions. And then he elaborates examples of the specific point he is arguing, whether from imagined situations such as those to be found in his plays, from personal experiences which have marked the stages of his own philosophical development, or from social and political events of his own times —the Dreyfus affair, the world wars, the uprisings in Hungary, the Algerian war and its atrocities, the war in Vietnam, the invasion of Czechoslovakia. Marcel argues, then, mainly with examples taken from contemporary history rather than from the various ways we use language. And his informal arguments serve precisely formulated purposes.

Another characteristic of his thought that deserves some notice is the extraordinary number of objections Marcel continually develops to his own views; the dialectical method is essential to his purpose. Marcel's dialectic can be seen mainly in his use of counterexamples. His thought characteristically develops from initial incisive formulations, across a series of extended and converging (but not always) examples, through the construction of counterarguments, to the reformulation of his initial views as a final series of questions requiring further investigation. The various uses this dialectic is put to in these essays becomes more apparent to the degree one has followed Marcel's remarks in the "Conversations" about his earlier use of nondialectical methods of conceptual analysis against the idealist views of both Hegel and Schelling.

Besides these methodological aspects of Marcel's essays, their second striking feature is their unusual content. Once the essays are read against the backdrop of Marcel's formulations of his general philosophical concerns in the "Conversations," they might be viewed as falling into three groups. First, there are four essays (chapters 3, 4, 6, and 10) on the nature of man and his social and political situation today, essays which are specifically concerned with clarifying some of the conceptual blurs between such opaque notions as truth and freedom. Another set of four essays which, significantly, are grouped in pairs at the beginning and the end of the book (chapters 1, 2, 13, and 14), attempt to describe a particular view of philosophy Marcel sees as required today by man's situation. These essays are difficult to appreciate without some effort at working out the connections (some of a logical nature) between them and the first series. And third, the remaining essays, not all of them equally successful in my opinion, are devoted to questions which philosophers have traditionally found almost intractable. The question, for example, not of God's existence but of the intelligibility and consistency of the concepts of God and of evil, the question of death and immortality which arises at the very beginnings of Western philosophy in the trial of Socrates, or the question of man's future and the concept of progress—these are some of the problems Marcel is intent on examining here.

Or, more generally and in another order, it might be helpful to organize these essays around the idea of a progression: from a series of detailed views of man's nature and situation today, through a consideration of what these views would seem to entail for an interpretation of how philosophy ought to be construed in our times, to a series of exploratory and interrogatory essays aimed at trying out this construction of philosophy on some questions for which philosophers are not even sure what satisfactory answers would look like—evil, death, the sacred, immortality, the divine.

No attempt at critical appraisal and reconstruction of Marcel's essays is appropriate here; this is not to deny that the task is a necessary one, as Marcel himself has repeatedly insisted. But such a task is secondary to a more immediate and more demanding one, of resisting the temptation to quarrel with a philosophical style now somewhat out of fashion, and of comprehending sympathetically the intention of Marcel's thought, especially the reasons this philosophy chooses to struggle with what, for many philosophers, seem such unpromising questions. On this level of comprehension, from which all instructive criticism finally flows, we need to ask: just what are the central questions for which these essays offer, not answers, but explorations? Can these questions be stated plainly? If not, can the reasons *why not* be stated plainly? And again, if not, must those who would persist in pursuing such concerns take some other way than the path of philosophy?

"As soon as reflection has reached a certain level," Marcel writes, "questioning is brought to bear on truth itself, by which I mean that one is led to ask what this word signifies, and what are the conditions and the limits in which the aspiration for truth can be satisfied."[1] Philosophy, as Kant and his most thoughtful

1. *Infra*, pp. 20–21.

readers, Heidegger and Wittgenstein, have taught us, brings us to the limits of both reason and language without stilling our aspiration to articulate, finally, just what is the case. Marcel is asking in these essays whether there may not be converging concerns at the very limits of post-Kantian philosophy, at the limits of what can be said and thought, which strongly suggest the necessity that philosophy undergo one more of its tiresome "revolutions," one more of its metamorphoses. That is why Marcel in his own preface to these essays closes with Nietzsche.

PETER MCCORMICK

Translator's Introduction

FOR A READER TO UNDERSTAND this or any other book, it would seem to be necessary that he appreciate to some extent the experience lying behind its claims, and that he grasp the universal (as opposed to merely private) import of what it says.

But Marcel views experience and universality in a way that is quite original, and the manner in which he philosophizes in this book and his other works is accordingly uncommon. Because his views on universality and experience are interesting in themselves for their originality, and because an explicit awareness of them may help the reader to receive the present volume (in which, indeed, these subjects are discussed) in the spirit in which the author offers it, the following brief remarks seem worthwhile.

THE PHILOSOPHER

THE NOTIONS of experience and universality arise in the early chapters of *Tragic Wisdom*, where Marcel takes up the questions "What can be expected of the philosopher?" and "What is the responsibility of the philosopher?" He focuses on the expression "the philosopher" in these questions, and argues that the kind of generality it implies is not what might at first be expected. It makes no sense to use this expression in the same way one could say, legitimately, "the scientist." [1] The meaning of the latter expression can presumably be fixed by reference to certain

1. *Infra*, p. 3.

objective traits (such as a mastery of the hypothetico-deductive method, a certain competence at mathematical evaluation, the fact of having done actual work in one of the recognized branches of science, and so on), possession of which would be the necessary and sufficient condition for a man to be rightly called a scientist. With at least implicit reference to such traits, then, it would be meaningful to speak of "the scientist in general," or "any scientist whatever."

Now Marcel claims that it would not be meaningful to speak of "the philosopher in general" or "any philosopher whatever," precisely because fulfillment of certain general, objective criteria is not what makes a philosopher. The philosopher's situation is in this respect akin to that of the artist—the poet or musician—of whom it would also be fundamentally improper to speak in purely general terms because his uniquely personal contribution is essential to his being a true artist.[2]

Must we then always use only proper names—Aristotle, Kierkegaard, Renoir, Debussy—when we wish to speak of the philosopher or the artist? Must we always stubbornly insist "whose philosophy?" and "whose art?" when we are asked about philosophy or art? It may at first seem that this is the only alternative we have to speaking in general terms, and Marcel, with his highly personal, existential style of philosophizing, is peculiarly sensitive to the criticism he would have to admit as justified if this alternative were accepted: the criticism that what *he* is saying about the nature or responsibiliy of philosophy (or any other philosophical question) has no objective bearing, no universal applicability, and represents instead only the isolated opinion of a single man, based on his observation of himself.[3] Marcel the philosopher finds himself faced with a dilemma when he sets out to speak about philosophy: either he must betray philosophy's kinship with poetry and music by speaking in general terms, or else he can speak about his own individual philosophy but must admit that what he says has no universal bearing.[4] His manner of dealing with this dilemma reveals his conception of philosophy as *vocation*, and at the same time throws into relief the importance of the two ideas, experience and universality, that particularly concern us here.

2. *Ibid.*, pp. 3, 5, 178–79.
3 *Ibid.*, pp. 4–5.
4. *Ibid.*, pp. 10, 18, 184–85.

In brief, his position is that we need not choose between the horns of the dilemma, as a logic rooted in the traditional opposition between individual experience and universal significance would seem to demand. Philosophy (like poetry or music) ought to be defined by reference to a "third" which is properly speaking a vocation, and the philosopher true to this vocation is the one who succeeds in

> preserving in himself a paradoxical equilibrium between the spirit of universality on the one hand, inasmuch as this is embodied in values which must be recognized as unalterable, and on the other hand his personal experience . . . for it will be the source of whatever individual contribution he might make.[5]

EXPERIENCE

THE PHILOSOPHER'S VOCATION consists in his personal response to a "call," which demands of him that, in paradoxical cooperation with the spirit of universality, he have and pay attention to *experience*. It thus becomes important to know what is meant by experience. Indeed Paul Ricoeur remarks to Marcel, in the "Conversations," that his interpretation of experience is a key to the underlying unity of his work. Marcel agrees, and affirms that his effort has been to "rediscover experience, but at a level beyond that of traditional empiricism." He invites a comparison of his thinking with what he calls the "higher empiricism" of Schelling, and he approves the name his friend Henry Bugbee has given his philosophical work: "experiential thinking."[6]

The traditional empiricism Marcel rejects is especially that of Locke and Hume, in which the primary meaning of experience, the foundation of all knowing, is individual sense data.[7] In the "experiential thinking" Marcel advocates and represents, the most intense effort of attention must be directed to experience, but certainly this effort must not be squandered on what he would regard as the highly special, largely automatic, noetically neutral, and personally indifferent form of experience represented in pure sense data. The philosophically important sense of experience is that in which it is taken as a global encounter

5. *Ibid.*, p. 31.
6. *Ibid.*, pp. 253, 228–29.
7. *Ibid.*, p. 253.

with situations in which one is personally involved and in which one's destiny is somehow at stake, an encounter which itself founds meaning, and which requires a special ability and effort to engage in fully.

Thus Marcel speaks of the necessity for a philosopher to develop an "ear" for experience, much like the ear of the musician or connoisseur of music. The philosopher's ear, however, will be especially attuned to power, to value, and to being itself, as these are suggested in the situations he encounters.[8] The philosopher must learn to appreciate experience, says Marcel.[9] He will then be able to find and perhaps articulate the significance inherent in the encounter with himself, with historical situations, and above all with other persons. Thus we see Marcel struggling to express the meaning of the "inner demand" he finds animating (as a power?) his personal response to the vocation of philosophy.[10] He calls on us to experience, that is, to be aware of, to recognize (*reconnaître*), to see into, to appreciate the Hungarian uprising, where we might discover (as a value) the meaning of truth. And finally, in response to the adept questioning of Paul Ricoeur, he acknowledges the central role of experience as recognizing others, particularly in situations of intersubjectivity such as love and hope which, in virtue of their inexhaustibility, provide the philosopher with concrete approaches to being.[11]

Experience understood in this way includes understanding. Clearly it is not something *opposed* to understanding, no mere affectivity which needs to be overcome by some Platonic inspiration before understanding can occur. Marcel insists on the intimate bond between affectivity and knowledge.[12] Nor can experience here be taken simply as the "building blocks" of understanding, as might be done in a pure empiricism, though again understanding would no doubt be impossible without the contribution of the five senses. Finally, experience here should not be taken in a narrowly Kantian sense, though it would certainly be appropriate to see Kant's influence in Marcel's insistence on the

8. *Ibid.*, pp. 6, 182–83.
9. *Ibid.*, p. 229.
10. *Ibid.*, pp. 11–12.
11. *Ibid.*, pp. 253–54. Cf. Gabriel Marcel, *Being and Having*, trans. Katherine Farrer (New York: Harper Torchbooks, 1961), p. 119.
12. *Infra*, p. 150.

role imagination must play in reflection.[13] For Marcel, such interpretations of experience would be abstractions, reductions which may serve interesting theoretical purposes but which nonetheless essentially violate the integrity of experience as we first live it in such global acts as becoming aware, recognizing, encountering, "seeing," and appreciating.

In this original and philosophically most important sense, experience *is itself understanding,* so that the event of "coming to an understanding," whether it be of a piece of music or a historical event or a person, is described most adequately not as an intellectual abstraction *from* experience, but rather as a deepening of experience itself. For science, no doubt, abstraction can legitimately be regarded as the primary methodological tool, but that is because the purposes of science are more special than those of philosophy. For philosophy understanding is first of all the sympathetic experiential penetration of the essential structures of the situation. Comprehension is above all compassion, says Marcel.[14]

It remains true that reflection, especially what Marcel has called "second" or "secondary" reflection, is held up throughout his work as the kind of thinking peculiar to philosophy, the "special high instrument of philosophical research." [15] But two remarks are in order here. First of all, in Marcel's actual work reflection is almost never found divorced from experience of the most concrete sort. "Let me begin with an example . . ." or "As is my usual procedure, I shall start by trying to articulate an experience . . .": such announcements are trademarks of Marcel's style, and if it is proper to speak of progress in the "spiral" or "winding" analyses he offers, it is most often progress toward a deepening or enhancing of experience. It is true that this deepening is achieved through reflection (not, for example, through prayer, exhortation, or ritual acts), but the reader of Marcel need never fear that he will find reflective thought independently spinning its own web of distinctions and relations remote from the core of concrete experience.

A second observation has to do with Marcel's own stated rea-

13. *Ibid.,* p. 133.
14. *Ibid.,* p. 150.
15. Gabriel Marcel, *The Mystery of Being,* trans. G. S. Fraser (Chicago: Regnery, 1960), I, 102; cf. *Being and Having,* pp. 100–101; cf. also *infra,* p. 235.

son for keeping reflective thought intimately tied to experience. In a crucial but often overlooked passage in *The Mystery of Being,* Marcel expresses his fundamental conviction that reflection itself ultimately belongs to experience.

> The more we grasp the notion of experience in its proper complexity [says Marcel], in its active and I would even dare say dialectical aspects, the better we shall understand how experience cannot fail to transform itself into reflection, and we shall even have the right to say that the more richly it is experience, the more, also, it is reflection.[16]

Of course it is here if anywhere that Marcel may be open to the charge of a deep-seated irrationalism. But a more interesting meditation on this passage would focus on the statement of the dialectical character of experience. Without following up this line of thought here, it is appropriate at least to remark that there are intriguing possibilities in the idea of understanding as a dialectical process in which experience, ever enhanced by more penetrating reflection, offers itself thus ever anew and ever more richly to the probing of further reflection.

UNIVERSALITY

MARCEL'S VIEW of the nature of understanding is interesting in its own right, and the sympathetic reader of Marcel's work may be inclined to examine it more fully in the interest of better appreciating how the author might wish his work to be understood. But for our present purposes the foregoing discussion is meant primarily to serve as a bridge from the notion of experience to that of universality. For while experience is perhaps most commonly regarded as being at the opposite pole from the universal, universality and understanding are for most people intimately connected. Now, just as we have found understanding involved in concrete experience, so shall we find universality, in Marcel's view, primarily a form of experience.

Marcel's notion of universality can best be examined against the background of the traditional view, which can be recalled sufficiently by a brief review of the persistent "problem of universals." This problem has two main phases. The first is the

16. *Mystery of Being,* I, 102.

effort to explain the fact that developed human languages are made up almost entirely of general terms, and that we are aware of resemblances between things, whereas our immediate experience is always of discrete particulars. The standard answer is that, besides particulars, which we experience concretely and directly, there are also universals, related in some way to the particulars. These correspond not to experience but to the structures of understanding and language by which what is common to different particulars is apprehended and expressed. The second phase of the problem is dominated by the concern to establish the status of these universals, and sometimes to explain their relationship to particulars. One who, like Plato, holds that there are universals independent of both particulars and human minds is traditionally called a realist. One who holds, like Locke, that there are independent universals but that they are the product of a mind is a conceptualist. Finally, one who holds, with Abelard, that there really are no independent universals, but only particulars (including words which are applicable to many other particulars) is a nominalist. These designations have rough equivalents in, respectively, the logicism, intuitionism, and formalism of contemporary philosophy of mathematics.[17]

In his own efforts to explain and achieve universality, Marcel does not, of course, enter the discussion of universals in its usual form. He would regard this discussion as abstract and secondary, admittedly of value for a theoretical epistemology or perhaps metaphysics, but failing to touch the question of universality in its existential dimension, which is primary.[18] Nonetheless, by examining the assumptions inherent in the traditional discussion and certain notions implicitly or explicitly associated with it, it is possible to bring out, largely by contrast, Marcel's view of the universal, which fits in well with what we have seen of his views on experience and understanding.

First of all, in the traditional view universality may fairly be regarded as a kind of victory, whether of understanding or of language taken as the equivalent of understanding, over the discrete and particular matter of experience. For Marcel, however, as we have seen, understanding is actually a form of experience,

17. See Richard Van Iten, ed., *The Problem of Universals* (New York: Appleton-Century-Crofts, 1970), especially W. V. O. Quine, "On What There Is," pp. 224–25, and Thomas Reid, "Of Abstraction," pp. 101–4.

18. *Infra*, p. 40.

but experience taken as the global affective and intellectual encounter with a situation. Likewise universality, insofar as it is linked to understanding, must be viewed as an achievement involved in and enhancing experience itself, not simply overcoming it and leaving it behind.

The emphasis in the traditional treatment of universality is most often on the generality of the universal. But for Marcel the universality the philosopher is most interested in is that represented in "unalterable" values to be discovered in experiential encounter. The spirit of universality is characterized by a search for an "exalting truth" which is unconditional.[19] Marcel is primarily interested in what might be called an intensive, rather than extensive, universality, and it is in this connection that he regards his work as a revival of concern with essence.[20] What is encountered as unalterable and unconditional ought, no doubt, to be generally applicable, and the encounter with it sharable. But with the truths that matter, those in which one is personally involved, general applicability merges into sharing, which is itself not given, but rather a task to be carried out in the spirit of fraternity, as we shall see below.

Just as the traditional discussion focuses on the general applicability of the universal to objects of experience, so is it most often concerned with perception of resemblances and the use of general names, insofar as these acts can be carried out by anyone above a certain age who is endowed with normal intellectual and linguistic powers—by "anyone whomever," as Marcel might say. Again, while he would no doubt admit the epistemological value of such a focus, Marcel is primarily interested in universality as it can only be achieved by a certain elite who have developed what amounts to an "ear" for experience, as we have discussed above. The universal in the most fundamental sense is not what can be seen by anyone to be generally true of many things, but rather what requires a difficult and even courageous effort to see, perhaps in the depths of a single experience. It is not what the masses can appreciate but what holds unconditionally, *de jure*, and may well be appreciated, if at all, by a single person.[21]

Generally speaking the traditional discussion bears on the

19. *Ibid.*, pp. 30–31, 187.
20. *Ibid.*, p. 5.
21. *Ibid.*, pp. 86–87.

universal as expressed in abstract concepts or terms that lend themselves to theoretical precision as their natural development. Marcel's concern with the universal in the depths of experience leads him to warn against the subtle betrayal of experience that takes place in conceptualization, and to declare that "the function of abstract thought is above all the recognition of its own insufficiency and thereby the preparation of new modalities of thought which transcend abstract thinking without repudiating it." [22] He recognizes music, poetry, and even the concrete lives of certain exemplary witnesses as appropriate vehicles for the expression of the universal. His advice to the philosopher dedicated to the true spirit of universality is to pay attention to Walt Whitman, Mozart, Claudel, Gerard de Nerval.[23] It is not in some theoretical tract of political speculation, for example, but in Whitman's poetry that American democracy "in its purest and most universally human intention has found an organ for expressing itself, that is, for existing." [24]

Whereas the traditional treatment most often regards universality as closely allied to objectivity, Marcel stresses the personal involvement and personal commitment required in the achievement of universality in its most fundamental sense. Anyone familiar with Marcel's notion of person, however, will be ready to see at once that personal involvement or commitment could not mean preoccupation with the individual self taken as an isolated entity. On the contrary, personhood for Marcel is characterized precisely by an openness to and involvement with others.[25]

Accordingly, the universal is to be found especially in the "existential assurances" encountered in experiences of love, hope, fidelity, and other related ones, such as belonging. These require personal involvement of the most intense kind if they are to be experienced in all their significance, but they can by no means be lived in isolation. They are experiences of intersubjectivity.[26]

Similarly, the sharing involved in the idea of universality becomes a matter of personal involvement and commitment. The

22. *Ibid.*, p. 38; cf. p. 39.

23. *Ibid.*, pp. 30, 40, 192, 207.

24. *Ibid.*, p. 40.

25. See "The Ego and Its Relations to Others," in Gabriel Marcel, *Homo Viator*, trans. Emma Craufurd (New York: Harper Torchbooks, 1962), pp. 13–28.

26. *Infra*, p. 39.

philosopher's vocation is a call to "fraternal comprehension," [27] which means in practice the brotherly attempt to share with other persons the deepest insights that experience enhanced by reflection can provide. The fraternal spirit of universality means not only speaking *with* others, however, but prophetically speaking *for* them, as Marcel finds Whitman speaking "for innumerable beings incapable of expressing themselves." [28] Marcel himself claims to have first responded to his philosophical vocation with the determination to "take in charge the doubts and anxieties of other persons," particularly on the question of personal immortality.[29]

The model for the sharing implied in the universality most worthy of the philosopher's attention and devotion is to be found, says Marcel, in art and art appreciation. The sharing that goes on between the artist and his audience, or between art lovers with a sufficiently developed "ear," is far from the objectivity that characterizes, say, the communication of the results of a chemical experiment. Yet it is a true sharing, perhaps of some eminently important apprehension of life's meaning. As Marcel puts it in a key passage: "In art subjectivity tends to pass over into an intersubjectivity which is entirely different from the objectivity science honors so much, but which nonetheless completely surpasses the limits of the individual consciousness taken in isolation." [30]

Finally, in its traditional treatment, the universal can be taken as a relatively fixed, permanent achievement, once and for all representing the features common to certain parts of experienced reality. But for Marcel universality is to be found primarily in the most inexhaustible of interpersonal experiences, and expressed under the sign of fraternity, itself a phenomenon of uncommon richness. Thus universality cannot be regarded as a possession, so much as an ongoing task. Even the unalterability and unconditionality encountered in the universal is to be taken as a direction for a journey, not as a resting place.[31] And since it is after all the achievement of the universal which makes a wise man, a sage, we can see why Marcel insists that one *is*

27. *Ibid.*, pp. 182–83; cf. p. 32.
28. *Ibid.*, p. 40.
29. *Ibid.*, p. 20; cf. p. 185.
30. *Ibid.*, p. 6.
31. *Ibid.*, pp. 252–53.

not a sage but is rather always *becoming* a sage.[32] Wisdom based on a universality that refuses to abandon its home in the inexhaustibility of concrete experience is inevitably an unfinished and to that extent an agonizingly insecure wisdom—a tragic wisdom.

STEPHEN JOLIN

32. *Ibid.*, p. 211.

Author's Preface

THE BOOK I AM PRESENTING here is in the image of my work as a whole. This means first of all that it is a collection of inquiries, and it would be a mistake to look for the outlines of a system in its pages. Of course this does not mean that the inquiries are wholly disconnected. Perhaps this book could best be compared to a magnetic field. Indeed I think the reader will notice that he is in the presence of a kind of field, but a field which cannot be circumscribed, because it opens onto the infinite. This opening, in fact, is the essential thing. But the field is crossed by currents. Each of the lectures in the book corresponds to one of these currents, that is, to a certain type of passionate questioning. The book could have been given the same title as the paper I read to the Société de philosophie, "The Questioning of Being."[1] But while this title would no doubt have indicated what is most profound in these investigations, it would also have had the disadvantage of emphasizing what is most abstract. And it is important to see that my inquiries here have to do directly with the concrete situation of man today. This situation is undergoing a change which man surely originates, but which nonetheless alienates man from his usual surroundings.

Here the term "situation" is primary; it is worthwhile explaining in what sense.

For almost twenty years I have consistently rejected the label of "Christian existentialist" which was first applied to me by

1. See chapter 4.

[xxxi]

Sartre and then by countless popularizers. I have taken every opportunity to emphasize the difference between philosophical research which deals with existence and a doctrine which makes existence prior to essence. Indeed, for me "essence" constitutes the locus of a renewed meditation, and I would be wholly against subordinating it in any way to the notion of "existence."

I have often spoken of a philosophy of light since the day the idea struck me that there might be a *light that would be joy at being light.* In this perspective I have asked whether essence might not be considered a modality of enlightenment, or, perhaps, of the enlightening. This interpretation would allow one to resist the continual temptation for thinking to objectify everything. I think Hocking's profound views on this idea in his great work, *The Meaning of God in Human Experience,* oriented me in this direction a very long time ago.

Now that I am an old man, I look back with profound gratitude to this thinker who is practically unknown in France. Even though my first contact with Hocking's work dates from 1913, I was able to meet him only in 1960. In 1927 I dedicated my *Metaphysical Journal* to Hocking and Bergson, and I would dedicate the present volume especially to Hocking. Recalling the discussions we had on two occasions in his cabin in New Hampshire, I would say that Hocking most perfectly embodies the idea of the philosopher as it appears in the following pages. I would add that just before Royce's death Hocking stood alone, or almost so, at the confluence of American pragmatism and Husserlian phenomenology.

I hope you will excuse this parenthesis, but if there is one habit life has continued to nourish and strengthen in me it is that of acknowledging my intellectual debts. And now, at a time when structuralism is appearing on the philosophical scene with a kind of thinking quite alien to mine, it is natural that I should feel a need to reaffirm my bond with the men who long ago planted the seeds that would grow to become my own inquiry. That is why I bring up Hocking, and also Bergson—Bergson whose discreet yet electrifying words I can still hear echoing from the past as I write these lines.

It would perhaps be useful to indicate how I think a philosophy of light can illuminate specific situations. The human situation can be seen as a certain way of being exposed to the light of truth. To take an example, one which I developed in "Truth and

Freedom," [2] at the time of the 1956 uprising the Hungarians re-acted violently because they could no longer bear the lies cir-culated by the official press (the only one tolerated in their country). In other words, they found themselves in a situation where they distinctly *saw* the degraded condition their oppres-sors intended to reduce them to, and on the basis of this aware-ness they revolted.

In this discussion it is important to see that the notion of ex-posure I introduced above cannot be taken in the sense meant, for example, when we describe the condition of a plant which remains relatively inert in relation to the external action of the elements to which it is exposed. Truth, even when understood as a light, cannot be regarded as an agent operating on a relatively passive entity. Truth is truth only if it is *recognized;* and recogni-tion involves a movement of attention in the direction of truth.

In my *Metaphysical Journal,* more than in any work since, I drew attention to the central and even primordial importance of attention. Many of the texts in the present volume could doubtless be reinterpreted in the light of a theory of attention. As numerous philosophers, including Bergson, have seen, the relationship be-tween attention and freedom is very close. This is what seems to escape entirely those philosophers who, with Sartre, interpret freedom as fundamentally a lack or privation. My attention, I would say, is the measure of my freedom. This formula has the advantage of displaying the central fact that freedom can only arbitrarily be dissociated from some kind of reference to the real, that is, from embodiment. I am not sure that the word "freedom" still means anything if we try to apply it to an omniscient and incorporeal being.

Perhaps even some conclusion about the relation between finitude and freedom could be drawn from this. Finitude would be seen as that field—necessarily limited—in which attention is exercised.

Unlike Spinoza and his epigones, I have insisted not on the negative character of determination but on its positive aspect. Moreover, this insistence is wholly consistent with the way in which, throughout my long and complicated philosophical jour-ney, I have tried to approach being. In this regard I would especially draw the reader's attention to the essay "The Ques-

2. See chapter 5.

tioning of Being" which appears in this volume. Here I show that I am poles apart from any philosophy which grounds itself in an intuition or even a preliminary affirmation of being. Being appears always as still veiled, as something which can only be approached. This prudent and discreet position implies that humility is a primordial metaphysical virtue; it is a position quite inimical to Hegel's panlogical *hubris*. Here one sees that suspicion of generalities which has so much marked my research in different areas. In this idea of philosophical humility we have the foundation for a criticism of the idea of totality, a criticism related perhaps quite directly to the one William James developed in his pluralistic period. But this comparison should not be pushed too far. I have always had certain reservations about pluralism because it seems to represent reality as a mere juxtaposition of elements, and is thus overly dependent on a visual metaphor, a viewpoint I have always tried to move beyond.

Coming back now to what I said earlier about the themes of attention and freedom in my work, I would say that both are present in my criticism of the "natural whole" which dates from the time of the first *Metaphysical Journal*. I am alluding here to the reflections on the body-subject and on sensation which were at the origin of my existential thought. The "natural whole" is something one is so habituated to that one no longer pays any attention to it.

Here I would like to mention the connection I have always sensed between the vocation of the philosopher and that of the poet. This relationship will come up in the pages that follow, and I want to make one important clarification with regard to it. While it is true that the philosopher, like the poet, must appeal to those powers of wonder which in most men are blocked by habit and prejudice, he also has a complementary task of his own which consists in vigilantly exercising his faculty of discrimination; for without discrimination the worst confusions are liable to prevail.[3]

IF THERE IS TODAY A NEED to appeal for a tragic wisdom as I have done in this book, it is especially because of the threats felt by a humanity betrayed by its own creations, by the exag-

3. Some topical remarks about the events of May, 1968, in Paris which Marcel added here to his original text have been deleted.— Translator.

gerated development of a global technology which can only lead to emptiness. And this emptiness, as Nietzsche distinctly saw in the moment of his greatest lucidity, is nihilism.

I agree with those who think that the ultimate meaning of man's present condition is to be found much more in the line of Nietzsche's thought than in that of Marx and his followers. It is in the spirit of Nietzsche that the following reflections are offered.

GABRIEL MARCEL

Tragic Wisdom
and Beyond

1 / What Can Be Expected of Philosophy?

I SHALL BEGIN with a remark I think is important. It would be entirely wrong to think that the question "What can be or what should be expected of philosophy?" can be answered in a way that would apply to any philosopher whatever. It would perhaps be possible to get such an answer if one were asking what can be expected of a scientific discipline or, a fortiori, of a technical procedure. But the words "any philosopher whatever" are probably no more meaningful than the words "any artist whatever" or "any poet whatever." And this is because philosophy, like art or poetry, rests on a foundation of personal involvement, or to use a more profoundly meaningful expression, it has its source in a vocation, where the word "vocation" is taken with all its etymological significance. I think that philosophy, regarded in its essential finality, has to be considered as a personal response to a call.

It goes without saying, of course, that like all other human activities, philosophy can be degraded, it can degenerate more or less into a caricature of itself. This happens, for example, when philosophy is treated as something that can be displayed in an examination. In France, where we have an organized program of studies in philosophy and give a baccalaureate degree, this danger is very much present. There is always the unfortunate possibility that the teacher who has the job of getting a student ready for the final comprehensive examinations will follow the lead of his colleagues in history and the natural sciences, simply preparing the initiate to give answers to the written or oral questions he will have to face. The frightful word "cramming" ex-

[3]

presses admirably this sort of intellectual stuffing, which is not only unsympathetic to philosophy but is exactly its contrary. Of course it is possible that those responsible for this cramming job might originally have heard that call which I mentioned above and which I shall try to describe. It is possible that they have heard it, but not certain; and in any case it is certain that very often this increasingly tedious task snuffs out whatever spark of philosophy the professor may have had at the beginning, smothers it as one smothers the last embers of a campfire. Not that this is inevitable. I have known professors who were able to hold onto that special sort of ardor without which philosophy loses its vitality and shrivels to nothing save the mere husks we call words.

But we ought to consider this matter from the point of view of the student or disciple as well. The genuine philosophical relationship, as Plato not only described it but lived it for all time, is that of a flame awakening a flame. In such a relationship anything can happen. For example, it may actually come about that through a relatively dry kind of teaching a young man in whom philosophy exists potentially would, in spite of everything, discover the reality that he longs for and to which I might even say he already belongs in a certain way without knowing it. I can point to my own personal experience here. I had one philosophy professor, a man of great learning, whose teaching was distinguished by remarkable clarity. But now, looking back at his teaching from a distance, objectively, I must admit that it lacked that passion, that inspired warmth without which today I would be tempted to say no philosophical teaching can be alive. Yet my own desire was such that from the very first lesson I was telling my family that I had found my path, that I was going to be a philosopher, and this conviction never flagged.

Under such circumstances, it would obviously be wrong to expect generally valid conclusions following from a broad investigation into the original question of this essay. Indeed it would be wholly consistent with my thinking to say that the very notion of investigation, if it is not closely linked with that of a search, is without a doubt quite foreign to philosophers as such.

At this point an objection something like the following may occur to my readers: "In insisting as you do on the role of personal involvement in philosophical activity, do you not risk depriving philosophy of any objective weight, making it nothing but a game to be played according to individual caprice?" This objection must be faced squarely in order to get rid of a confusion which could lead to the worst misunderstandings.

The confusion I am thinking of has to do with the very idea of subjectivity. Perhaps it will be clearer if we focus our attention on art, which in certain respects is comparable to philosophy. At the origin of a work of art we find—or we assume—the existence of a personal reaction, an original response to the many and often inarticulate calls that things seem to address to the consciousness of the artist. But I think it would be agreed that this subjective reaction has no artistic value by itself. That value appears only with the structures constituted through what we call the creative process, which offer themselves to the appreciation not only of the subject, in this case the artist, but also of other possible viewers or listeners. Of course, it would be foolish to speak here of universality in an extensive sense, for surely these structures will not be appreciated or even recognized by *everyone.* Indeed "everyone" is an empty and inappropriate concept here. I remember very well that before the music of Debussy became widely accepted there were a great many people who claimed it lacked any melody; today this affirmation seems odd to us. In a work such as *Pelléas et Mélisande,* for example, there is continuous melody; but it is precisely because it is present everywhere that inexperienced listeners were not able to make it out. For them a melody was something you whistled or hummed on the way out of the theater or concert hall. Of course, it is not enough that form—in this case the melody—be perceived simply as form or structure. It must also be recognized as meaningful, even though the meaning may be immanent, inexpressible in words. Yet it is only on the basis of structure, whatever it might be, that the intersubjective communion can be established without which it is impossible to speak of value. Of course I can converse with another person about the first movement of Beethoven's Fourteenth Quartet, for example, and we might accomplish considerably more than just making some observations about the tonality or the way the different instruments break in here or there—structural matters which could also be observed by a nonmusical deaf person simply by reading the score. If we are sensitive to this music, then through the poor words we are condemned to use we will become aware of a certain quality made present to us through the structure, a certain sadness, a certain distance which is perhaps best expressed by the English word "remoteness"; and we may agree that perhaps never before has the sense of the infinite been so intimately rendered.

I have spent so much time with these examples because I wanted to show that in art subjectivity tends to pass over into an intersubjectivity which is entirely different from the objectivity science honors so much, but which nonetheless completely surpasses the limits of the individual consciousness taken in isolation.

Now some analogous observations can be made about what I shall call philosophical experience. Surely there is not and there cannot be any philosophy worthy of the name without a special kind of experience, which I shall try to describe by comparison with something that can be observed in the world of music. There can be no authentic music where there is no *ear* for hearing. But let us beware of the unfortunate ambiguity of the word "ear." I do not mean simply to repeat the truism that music presupposes the existence of a particular organ of hearing. The word "ear" in its aesthetic sense means something infinitely more subtle, a certain faculty for appreciating relationships, or perhaps again a certain attitude of consciousness in the presence of what is given for hearing. For a person lacking ear in this sense there is no difference between a noise and a sound, and what we call a melody may seem to be just a succession of noises.

The philosophical attitude is perhaps not altogether different from "ear" understood in this way. Notice I am using the word "attitude" now, whereas above I spoke of experience. But there is really no contradiction in this, for the attitude in question can reveal itself only as a certain way that consciousness reacts to what must be called its fundamental situation. Let us now try to specify more precisely the nature of this reaction. It could be defined, it seems to me, as a wonder which tends to become a disquiet. Perhaps, as is so often true, an appeal to negation will best enable us to give an account of this disposition: it consists above all in not taking reality for granted. But what can be meant by reality here? Certainly not this or that particular phenomenon whose explanation might be in question. No, what is meant here is reality as a whole, and it is this ensemble or this totality which is put in question in the philosophical attitude. We ought perhaps also to take special note here of the mysterious relation between the I who questions and the world I am questioning. What am I, I who question? Am I within this world or outside it? In the presence of any given, the philosophical spirit lives this question with anxious impatience.

Let me use an example here which I think is highly significant. A person with a philosophical mind will not simply accept the fact that reality appears to us in an ordered succession of moments. The order here, which may sometimes also appear as disorder, will undoubtedly awaken in him a kind of cautious suspicion, as if he were on ground that did not offer sure footing. He will perhaps ask himself whether the orderly succession is not really a certain mode of appearance for something which under other circumstances could appear quite otherwise; and this question might in turn lead him to ask whether ultimately a thing could exist in itself, beyond any mode of appearance whatever. It could easily be shown that these questions are related to others pertaining to the self that I am and to whom appearances are given. For example, inasmuch as I am the location of appearances, am I not myself existing in some sense at the level of appearance? Following up such reflections would lead perhaps to a philosophy like Bradley's.

Please understand that I do not mean to say that a philosophical mind *as such* would ask itself questions like this. Remember what I said just above: it is no more legitimate to speak of the philosopher in the abstract—as "any philosopher whatever"—than it is to speak of the artist or poet in that way. Such designations are appropriate only in the domain of pure objectivity, in the experimental sciences, for example. If we mix any particles whatever of given chemical substances (chlorine, sodium, etc.) the inevitable result will be a standard reaction which can be verified by any observer whatever. Here, of course, we have the experience for which Kant claimed to have specified the a priori conditions. But the peculiarly philosophical experience, or the experience of the artist, is of an absolutely different kind. One could even say that it takes place on a completely different level of reality.

Now there is something quite remarkable to notice here, and that is that different philosophical (or artistic) experiences can enter into communication with one another. I would even say that a philosophical experience that is not able to welcome an experience other than itself in order to understand or if necessary go beyond it ought to be regarded as negligible. It is essential that philosophical experience, once it is explicitly worked out, confront other experiences which are themselves fully elaborated and generally formulated in systems. One could go further, and say that this confrontation itself is actually part of the experience in question insofar as that experience comes to be clarified and crystallized in concepts. This is especially clear with a thinker like Heidegger, who seems to be engaged in a perpetual dialogue with the philosophers that preceded him: not with all of them, of course, but with those he feels close to—the great pre-Socratics, Plato and Aristotle, and among the moderns, mainly Kant, Hegel, and Nietzsche.

Let me mention something here about Heidegger which is significant for our discussion. Heidegger came to France for the first time in 1955, and was invited to the Chateau Cerisy-la-Salle where several philosophers and students had gathered to hear him. Everyone hoped that he would give explanations of certain passages in his works which were especially difficult to make sense of. What a surprise when, after an introduction to philosophy in general, he set out to comment not on his own works but on certain texts of Kant and Hegel! He explained, to those who expressed their surprise and disappointment, that his method consisted precisely in clarifying his own thought through the encounter with great philosophers he had studied carefully. Of course it is important to see that such efforts by a man of Heidegger's originality always issue in a creative reinterpretation of the philosopher in question; this is especially true with respect to his encounters with the pre-Socratics and with Kant. Moreover, it should be recognized that there are some general problems concerning the history of philosophy itself which are eminently worthy of reflection. Certain philosophers, especially in France, have seen this. Today more than ever before it is acknowledged how necessary, though at the same time how difficult it is to achieve a philosophy of the history of philosophy.

In any case it seems that philosophical experience, even if it necessarily begins as an instrumental solo, needs to become part of a whole symphony. This is true even where such experience stands opposed to the views of other philosophers, for opposition is one form of dependency. Such was the relationship between Kant and David Hume, for example, or closer to our own time, of Bergson and Spencer. If I may mention myself in this context, I might say that my own thought developed in concerted opposition to contemporary Neo-Hegelians, especially Bradley, and to a certain French Neo-Kantianism.

At this point some of my readers may be inclined to object. "If we understand you correctly," they might say, "you are offering a very strange and misleading answer to the question you raised at the beginning of your inquiry. First you said that philosophy can only exist for someone who has a certain kind of personal experience, or at least has an ear for philosophical thought. Now you say that philosophical experience requires a living communication, a dialogue with other experiences already elaborated, that is, a dialogue with other philosophers. But doesn't this amount to saying that all philosophy happens within a kind of magic circle of privileged initiates, a sanctuary to which the uninitiated can have no access? Those of us who would actually ask the question "What can be expected of philosophy?" are interested in what philosophy can bring to the uninitiated, to outsiders such as ourselves. If it is just a game for a few qualified people, then we are not interested in it, any more than someone who doesn't play chess or know its rules would be interested in watching a chess game."

This objection forces me to make some clarifications. First of all, I think it would simply be wrong to imagine that there is anything like a dividing wall separating the philosopher and the nonphilosopher. There really never has been such a wall, but today it is especially difficult to see any line of demarcation, since literature—what everybody reads or is supposed to be reading—is so full of philosophical thought. This is true not only of the essay and the novel, but also of the theater and the cinema. To take the work of Sartre, for example: precisely where his drama and fiction leave off and his philosophy begins simply cannot be determined. The same is true of my own dramatic and philosophical writings. Or take a writer like Paul Valéry who, even though he claimed to distrust philosophy, was actually so much a philosopher even in his purely poetic creations that a professional philosopher like Alain could see fit to devote an extended and careful commentary to his great collection of poems, *Charmes*. But I would go much further and assert that every thinking person, especially in our time, has at least moments where he enjoys an elementary philosophical experience. This experience appears as a kind of vibration in the presence of those great and mysterious realities which give all human life its concrete structure: love, death, the birth of an infant, and the like. There is no doubt in my mind that every personally felt emotion resulting from contact with such realities is like the embryo of philosophical experience. In the great majority of cases, of course, this embryo not only fails to develop into an articulated experience, but even seems to require no such development. Yet it is also true that almost every human being, in certain privileged moments, has experienced this need to be enlightened, to receive an answer to his own questioning. It must be added that this becomes more and more true to the extent that religion as such declines or at least changes to the point where people are less and less satisfied with the ready-made answers which it seems they once accepted without question.

One other thing seems to me important in this regard, and that is that some scraps of philosophical thought conveyed through newspapers, magazines, and ordinary conversations find their way to one extent or another into all minds. Most of the time these scraps could just as well be burned like household garbage, and it is perhaps one of the more important functions of true philosophical thought to carry out this kind of trash-burning.

Let us now take up a possible objection which is even more troublesome than the one we have just considered. "You acknowledge that a certain relationship may be established between the 'nonphilosopher' and the philosopher. But what philosopher are you talking about? A novice is bewildered and suspicious when he is faced with the great number of existing philosophies, many of which seem to be mutually exclusive. The very fact that he would have to choose among them (leaving aside the question of how and by what criteria the choice might be made) seems irreconcilable with each one's claim to express a truth or truths. Yet on the other hand, doesn't philosophy become a mere game if it gives up such claims to truth? To put the question in another way: How, considering this irreducible plurality, is it possible to speak of philosophy in the singular the way we speak of science in the singular?"

Certainly we cannot avoid such an objection, and the answer to it will have a direct bearing on our original question about what can be expected from philosophy. First of all I think we ought to deal straightforwardly with an image more or less explicitly entertained by those who would raise such an objection. I refer to the image of a shop window or display case where different philosophies would be arranged side by side so that a customer could easily choose among them. One of the surest benefits of a little historical reflection would be the realization that this comparison is absurd, for such an arrangement is possible only for objects, for things, and a philosophy can never be treated as an object or a thing. A philosophy is a kind of experience; it is an adventure taking place within the greater adventure of human thought itself. Or if philosophy is a manifestation of the Spirit and the Word—if it is a theophany—then it is an adventure taking place at the heart of something that transcends human thought.

But from another point of view, anyone who has grasped my remarks at the beginning of this essay will see that a philosophy must always be thought of as a function of a certain inner demand. The history of philosophical doctrines is in large part the history, not yet wholly revealed, of the inner demands of the human spirit. These demands must be effectively related to the general concrete situations that have helped bring them to birth. Indeed, this relationship between situation and inner demand is itself an extremely complex one which philosophical reflection must clearly bring to light. There would be no sense in saying that a situation can by itself *produce* a demand. We are not dealing with a causal relationship here, nor for that matter with the much simpler one prevailing when we say, for example, that a certain kind of soil favors one type of vegetation over another. The verb "favor" here refers to an extremely complex knot of relations.

Thus for the misleading image of a choice among ideal objects on display we must substitute the image of different levels reached by the human spirit according to the type of inner demand it is responding to. In this way a philosophy based on the inner demands of the person, of personality as such, will stand opposed to Marxism, not necessarily because of its method (for surely the Marxist method can be fruitful when applied within well-defined limits), but because it pretends to be a total and ultimate interpretation of life and history; for Marxism cannot provide anything like an adequate response to these fundamental demands—it can only ignore them.

In this last part of this essay I would like to try to point out the special and insistent form in which I think the philosophical demand appears in our time. I do not deny that I am speaking in my own name here, but I would ask you to recall what I said at the beginning about how there is not and cannot be any philosophical thought without personal involvement. Moreover, I am aware that I will be appealing to those who in a more or less articulate way are experiencing the very demand I want to define. As for the others, they will have to acknowledge this demand at least enough to ask themselves whether they are able to ignore it or reject it completely. Thus what I say here can and must be personal, but at the same time it is more than purely subjective in the sense of simply representing some individual and isolated feeling or some arbitrary wish.

I would like to begin my remarks with a general description of the situation of mankind today, or at least of Western man, whom our observations fit best. I shall quote here from some of my earlier writings. They date from 1933, but I would not retract or change one word of them today.

> The characteristic feature of our age seems to me to be what might be called the misplacement of the idea of function, taking function in its current sense which includes both the vital and the social functions.
>
> The individual tends to appear both to himself and to others as an agglomeration of functions. As a result of deep historical causes, which can as yet be understood only in part, he has been led to see himself more and more as a mere assemblage of functions, the hierarchical interrelation of which seems to him questionable or at least subject to conflicting interpretations.
>
> To take the vital functions first. It is hardly necessary to point out the role which historical materialism on the one hand, and Freudian doctrines on the other, have played in restricting the concept of man.
>
> Then there are the social functions—those of the consumer, the producer, the citizen, etc.
>
> Between these two there is, in theory, room for the psychological functions as well; but it is easy to see how these will tend to be interpreted in relation either to the social or the vital functions, so that their independence will be threatened and their specific character put in doubt. In this sense, Comte, served by his total incomprehension of psychical reality, displayed an almost prophetic instinct when he excluded psychology from his classification of sciences.
>
> So far we are still dealing only with abstractions, but nothing is easier than to find concrete illustrations in this field.
>
> Travelling on the Underground, I often wonder with a kind of dread what can be the inward reality of the life of this or that man employed on the railway—the man who opens the doors, for instance, or the one who punches the tickets. Surely everything both within him and outside him conspires to identify this man with his functions—meaning not only with his functions as

worker, as trade union member or as voter, but with his vital functions as well. The rather horrible expression "time table" perfectly describes his life. So many hours for each function. Sleep too is a function which must be discharged so that the other functions may be exercised in their turn. The same with pleasure, with relaxation; it is logical that the weekly allowance of recreation should be determined by an expert on hygiene; recreation is a psycho-organic function which must not be neglected any more than, for instance, the function of sex. We need go no further; this sketch is sufficient to suggest the emergence of a kind of vital schedule; the details will vary with the country, the climate, the profession, etc., but what matters is that there is a schedule.

It is true that certain disorderly elements—sickness, accidents of every sort—will break in on the smooth working of the system. It is therefore natural that the individual should be overhauled at regular intervals like a watch (this is often done in America). The hospital plays the part of the inspection bench or the repair shop. And it is from this same standpoint of function that such essential problems as birth control will be examined.

As for death, it becomes, objectively and functionally, the scrapping of what has ceased to be of use and must be written off as a total loss.[1]

It cannot be denied, I think, that this sobering diagnosis becomes increasingly accurate each day, and as I wrote a little further on:

> Besides the sadness felt by the onlooker, there is the dull, intolerable unease of the actor himself who is reduced to living as though he were in fact submerged by his functions. . . . Life in a world centered on function is liable to despair because in reality this world is *empty*, it rings hollow; and if it resists this temptation it is only to the extent that there come into play from within it and in its favour certain hidden forces which are beyond its power to conceive or to recognise.[2]

Now for the purposes of our present study this last phrase is of the greatest importance, and in its light it will now be possible to formulate a precise response to our original question.

What can be expected of philosophy at this particular moment of history is first of all that it make clear, as I have just

---

1. Gabriel Marcel, "On the Ontological Mystery," trans. Manya Harari, in *The Philosophy of Existentialism* (New York: Citadel Press, 1956), pp. 10–12.
2. *Ibid.*, p. 12.

done in a partial but significant way, the danger of dehumanization which accompanies the intensive development of technology in our world. Philosophy must bring to light the profound but usually unarticulated uneasiness man experiences in this technocratic or bureaucratic milieu where what is deepest in him is not only ignored but continually trampled underfoot. And philosophy can be expected, through extremely delicate and careful probing, to locate those secret powers I mentioned just above. What are these powers? It is very hard to name them, first of all because words are most often too withered, too lifeless for the task. But speaking very generally I would say that these powers are radiations of being, and thus it is being, as all the great philosophers of the past have seen (and as Heidegger, the deepest thinker in Germany and perhaps in all of Western Europe, is reminding us today), it is being, I say, which must engage the reflection of the philosopher.

"But," you may ask me, "when you speak of being, aren't you hiding behind an empty abstraction devoid of all concrete meaning?" I must answer that being is really the very opposite of an abstraction, although at the level of language it does almost inevitably become distorted, even to the point of looking like its own opposite. This is the cardinal problem for a philosophy of being, and this is why in the work I have just quoted, which is central to my thought, I insisted on the importance of what I called "concrete approaches." We cannot, I think, install ourselves in being itself, we cannot capture it or seize it, any more than we can see the source giving off light—all we can see are surfaces illuminated by the light. I think that this comparison between being and light is a fundamental one. And I hardly need mention that at this point I am very close to the Gospel of John where he speaks of the "Light which lighteth every man that cometh into the world." In another book of mine I have spoken of a light which would be joy at being light; to be a human being would be to participate in this light, while failing to do so would mean sinking to the level of the animal or lower still.

Let me anticipate and quickly answer one final objection which might occur to my readers. "If philosophy answers in this way," the objection might run, "is it not offering something very much like a religious answer? It is very difficult to see what distinction you would make between philosophy and religion." This question is very important, and my answer would be the following: I am deeply convinced that there is and there must be a hidden cooperation between philosophy and religion, but I also believe that the means employed by each is different. Religion can finally depend only on faith. The instrument of philosophy, on the contrary, is reflection, and I must say that I will always regard with suspicion any philosophical doctrine that claims to rest on intuition. But I have tried elsewhere to show that there are two different but complementary forms of reflection. One of them is purely analytical and reductive—primary reflection—and the other is reconstructive or synthetic. It is this second reflection which dwells on being, depending not on an intuition but on an assurance identical with what we call our soul.

2 / The Responsibility of the Philosopher in Today's World

THE IDEA OF COMMITTED THOUGHT has been discussed ever since the end of the Second World War; this discussion should not be considered closed. It may even be that today this discussion demands especially close attention, particularly in France at a moment when one is tempted to ask oneself whether the very existence of philosophy is not in question. What I hope to be able to show in this essay is that the existence of philosophy can be supported only if it is established that it involves an actual responsibility in the face of the unprecedented crisis confronting man in these last twenty-five years.

The problem to which I shall direct my reflection appears the moment I venture to ask myself the following questions: Can I be sure that my readers or listeners give the same meaning as I do to the word "philosophy"? More profoundly still, can I affirm that in my own thought, for myself, this word is wholly without ambiguity?

Let us begin by considering the first of these questions. Experience shows us undeniably that in most of the Anglo-Saxon world the word "philosophy" is taken in an absolutely different sense than it is where phenomenology, proceeding from Husserl and Scheler, has progressively exerted its influence.

It would obviously be very easy to turn to the past and find oppositions that are in some ways comparable. At the end of the last century, for example, a Neo-Hegelian from England wasn't speaking the same language as his empiricist colleague formed in the doctrines of Spencer and the associationists. This is incontestable, although it might well be observed that the element of truth contained in associationism could after all be integrated in a synthesis like that of Bradley. But to give another example, when I was at the Lima Convention in 1951 I spoke with A. J. Ayer about a "philosophy of reflection"; these words, which in France designated an incontestably venerable tradition, were meaningless for him. Much more recently, talking with students at Harvard, I found that many of their philosophy professors were discouraging them from looking for a relation between the almost exclusively analytic thought in which they were being trained and life—the problems that life poses to each one of us but which seemed in the professors' eyes to be merely matters for personal discretion.

Here again, of course, precedents could be cited. But what gives the present situation its peculiar character is the fact that disciplines which were considered up until the beginning of this century to be an integral part of philosophy—sociology and psychology, of course, but also logic—now claim not only autonomy, but radical independence. In these conditions, philosophy itself unfortunately may appear as a remainder, even a leftover, whose continuing presence is merely tolerated out of respect for traditions which are themselves less and less respected.

Quite often, too, with men who are well set up in life but who think back somewhat sentimentally to their student days, one finds the notion that philosophy is a kind of intellectual game, a limbering-up exercise for the mind, worth practicing for awhile so long as one has no illusion that it might have real importance. I would answer that if philosophy were reduced to that level, then its disappearance would be desirable. If it is only a game, it is not enough to say that it stands outside any life really and seriously lived: it may also appear as an imposture, for it has always involved claims which can greatly influence young minds, and in the game hypothesis these would have to be regarded as deceptions. For my part, I would not hesitate to say that philosophy has no weight and no interest whatever unless it sounds an echo in our life, a life which is today so threatened at every level. Furthermore, it must be said that this echo itself depends on the way in which philosophy is situated in relation to truth.

Yet a few years ago a professional philosopher—a professor at the Sorbonne whose authority is indisputable—declared in a televised talk directed to young teachers that the term "truth" had no definite meaning except in the sciences. To say this is simply to proclaim the surrender of philosophy. We might mention at once that among the great philosophers of the past there is probably not a single one who would have refused to give truth undisputed reign in his thought. Even an irrationalist like Schopenhauer no doubt judged that he had discovered the truth at the basis of things. The only exception, probably more apparent than real, would be Nietzsche, to the extent that his thought appears in a certain way to be situated not only beyond good and evil but beyond the true and the false as well. Yet even Nietzsche's thought can only be judged consistent if in spite of everything it recognizes that a certain type of truth, for example, scientific truth, must be transcended. But does not this movement of going beyond inevitably end up with the founding of a superior truth, itself irreducible to what is ordinarily designated by this term? If one imagines that he can escape this necessity, is he not inevitably setting off on a road which leads to delirium? From this point of view it is legitimate to think of Nietzsche's madness that it is not just a fact for medical observation, but that it holds a further meaning, that it may indicate the violation of a fundamental prohibition.

It would be well to anticipate here a possible objection regarding my use of the word "philosopher." "When you speak of the philosopher," someone may ask, "do you mean the philosopher in general or rather some particular philosopher with whom you feel some affinity? If you hold to the second interpretation, how can you escape being arbitrary? On the other hand, is there really any meaning in speaking of the philosopher in general?" It must be admitted at once that the question is pertinent and cannot be left without response. First of all, I mean the philosopher *today*, that is, in a certain context which cannot be left out of consideration. Still, this indication is quite obviously insufficient. One important question that must be answered is whether when I speak of the philosopher I mean what might be called the *professional* philosopher. And here we are immediately in difficulty, for we must ask whether the professionalization of philosophy is itself possible without contradiction.

When one speaks of the professional philosopher, one thinks of the man who has a degree and who thus may have a job teaching in a university or college. But after the least bit of reflection it is hard to avoid feeling uneasy with the idea of a degree in philosophy and the conditions in which it can be awarded. This uneasiness is tied to the awareness, perhaps quite confused at first, of a contradiction which must be clarified at the level of distinct thought. Does not the word "philosophy" evoke the idea of an essentially free investigation? Is it not contradictory to imagine a stamp of approval which would be conferred from outside on the person who intends to devote himself to this investigation, a stamp which would in effect proclaim in advance the validity of the work? And is the notion of validity applicable here? Validity in the name of what, and based on what? But we must go further and ask what could be the nature of the authority by which people deliver such certificates. For all evidence points to a difference between philosophy and the specialized branches of knowledge, where the above questions do not arise. A candidate for a chair of mathematics or history can without contradiction be regarded as having satisfied certain tests instituted by mathematicians or historians in such a way that qualified persons can legitimately acknowledge and finally proclaim that this candidate is now effectively in a position to transmit to others the knowledge he has.

But reflection shows that the situation is quite otherwise when it comes to legitimizing the teaching of philosophy. It is true that one could try to introduce a distinction here between the philosopher properly so-called—the philosopher as seeker—and the philosopher as teacher, and say that the tests, successful completion of which results in a stamp of approval, are meant simply to show whether the candidate possesses a certain intellectual stock in trade and is able to pass it on to others. This might be acceptable, but only if it is observed immediately that the notion of stock in trade is quite equivocal here, and that philosophical teaching which is reduced to passing on this stock actually does not at all respond to the demand it is supposed to satisfy. In philosophy one must be less a teacher than an awakener. And experience shows indubitably that officially established tests are only rarely and imperfectly adequate for finding out whether the candidate has this essential quality.

Thus it must be seen that there is something essentially ambiguous in the very notion of the professor of philosophy. It can even be asked in all seriousness whether the act which translates the words "make a profession of" is not in a certain way incompatible with what is most intimate in the philosophical vocation. We have to stress the term "vocation" when we speak of the philosopher. And yet it must certainly be granted that the precise sense of this vocation is not easy to define if we distinguish it, as we must, from the vocation of professor in general.

I am leaving aside, moreover, the difficult problem of knowing whether the vocation of professor as such really deserves this name, and whether it is as distinct as the vocation of doctor, for example, or priest, or even engineer.

What must be seen, I think, is that one does not set about doing philosophy exclusively for himself, that is, in order to pass from a state of perplexity or turmoil into a self-satisfying equilibrium. Rather everything proceeds as if one means to take in charge the doubts and anxieties of other persons whom he does not know individually, but whom he feels bound to by a fraternal tie.

It is certainly embarrassing, but perhaps inevitable, to speak of oneself in such a context. I would hardly hesitate to say that my own philosophical vocation was born one day when I was about eight years old. I was in the Parc Monceau in Paris, and having learned in response to my questions that it was not known with certitude whether human beings survived their death or were destined to absolute extinction, I cried out to myself, "Later on I shall try to see that clearly." I think it would be a grave mistake to take that as nothing but a child's mock seriousness. It is absolutely certain that in my case, as in that of Unamuno, this concern with the problem of immortality, I might even say this obsession with it, has appeared as a thread in everything I have written, especially in my dramatic work. But it is obvious too that I expected, quite naïvely I admit, to some day see more clearly not only for myself but for all those whom I imagined suffering from the same anguish as mine.

I am not sure this could be absolutely generalized. It is doubtful that with all philosophers one could go back to the existence of a particular problem which imposed itself early on the questioning and anxious attention of the future seeker. On the other hand, it can undoubtedly be affirmed that at the origin of any philosophical quest there is always a kind of wonder, a certain way of not taking for granted, not finding wholly natural the data that the future philosopher finds before him. This is probably too obvious to have to insist on. But what is no less clear—and thus I return to what I said above—is that this questioning invariably appears as tending toward a truth to be discovered. The words "a truth" are not exactly appropriate, however. Fragmentary truths, which can be isolated from one another, are the province of the sciences and not of philosophy. Philosophy is always interested in *truth*. As soon as reflection has reached a certain level, questioning is brought to bear on truth itself, by which I mean that one is led to ask what this word signifies, and what are the conditions and the limits in which the aspiration for truth can be satisfied.

I would now like to take up and answer with the greatest possible precision this perplexing question: When I speak of the responsibility of the philosopher, is it myself, my responsibility which is in question? It seems that I must choose one of two answers. Either yes, I am actually talking about myself and in that case the kind of disguise I am decked out in is ridiculous. Or, on the contrary, I acknowledge that it is not me, in which case it is very hard to see how I am related to that philosopher I am aware of *not* being. It seems that this is a dilemma I cannot escape. Yet in spite of everything I think I must adopt the second position. I am not referring to myself. I have to admit that I am required to transcend in thought what I have individually been able to or can still accomplish. In short, I have to hold on to the thought of many diverse philosophers among whom I must somehow situate myself, yet without pretending to equal them. One of the difficulties I have to face is the fact that it would be vain to hope to find a common denominator for these philosophers. Or at least this denominator would have to be reduced to something purely formal, unless it would be a personal commitment to truth, or more exactly, to a search centered on truth.

But I must now apply these reflections to the subject I have set out to treat in this essay. When I speak of the responsibility of the philosopher, am I thinking of myself and my own philosophy? I am afraid this would have to be answered at once yes and no. Insofar as I am a philosopher myself, I can in no way exclude myself from what I would have to say. But at the same time, insofar as I am conscious of my inadequacy and my probably unavoidable infidelity to a calling which exceeds my own possibilities, I may be led to make affirmations which I know are merely in the spirit of a vocation which unfortunately I myself cannot wholly fulfill. There is a gap here which probably cannot be entirely closed. And to recognize this gap is at the same time, at the same stroke, to recognize how strictly a kind of pride or arrogance is by definition forbidden to me.

Perhaps one thing more must be added in anticipation of what I shall be saying further on. It is quite possible that I am structurally incapable of establishing a completely rigorous distinction between what I think as philosopher and what I say as nonphilosopher, although certainly I am bound to do my utmost to become more distinctly aware, more strictly demanding on this point.

This long preamble was necessary, it seems to me, in order to mark out the conditions in which the problem of the responsibility of the philosopher has to be dealt with. It is an abstruse problem, to be sure, but I think it must also be admitted that its data have been wantonly jumbled, as it were, by a certain brand of existentialism. We shall have occasion to see this later on.

The first question that inevitably arises, then, is this: To *whom* is the philosopher responsible? If this question cannot be answered, then it is doubtful whether the word "responsibility" will retain any specific meaning. We shall begin with an extreme example, that of a totalitarian state such as Nazi Germany or Soviet Russia. Here the answer to the question is really quite clear. The philosopher is responsible to society. Or more precisely, the philosopher is responsible to the party or to those who represent the party and plume themselves on having the truth all formulated in a new Koran called *Das Kapital* or *Mein Kampf*.

But we must remark immediately that the "philosopher" who in this way puts himself in the service of what might be called the sovereign, by that stroke surrenders a condition of philosophical inquiry which must be held as essential, and that condition is autonomy. Certainly the philosopher who subjects himself to a pseudo-truth someone else declares to be unconditional can, without hesitation, be accused of apostasy. What we are faced with here is a new manifestation of the same spirit which animated the theological dogmatism of earlier centuries. But this spirit is considerably less acceptable in its new form, because the new dogmatism cannot claim to be founded on anything like a revelation. Yet in emphasizing autonomy as the peculiar mark of philosophical research, do we not at the same time release the philosopher from everything which could appear as a responsibility? Are we not in danger of confusing the situation of the philosopher with that of the artist? After all it does seem difficult to assign any actual responsibility to a painter or a composer as such.

Here another objection naturally arises. Society is not necessarily a totalitarian state. Can we not envisage a responsibility of the philosopher to the society of men, this term being taken in a very broad sense which is compatible with the freedom that any reflection worthy of the name presupposes? But the answer must be that the word "society" is in itself extremely vague. Society in general does not exist. What society are we talking about? Certainly we can only mean a definite society to which the philosopher happens to belong, a state, for example, or a church. Let us take an example. Is the philosopher responsible to the national community? If we try see what lies beneath these apparently clear words, we will not be long in discovering that they mask a profound confusion. This can be shown by considering the concrete decision that not long ago faced us all as a result of very painful events: Should the philosopher abstain from denouncing the widespread use of torture by the French army in the Algerian war? It is impossible, in my view, to agree to this. Let us suppose, though this is certainly not purely and simply true, that the leaders of the French army had judged such practices indispensable for winning the war. I would then ask whether these leaders ought to be considered qualified representatives of the national community. This would be a very difficult judgment to make. To disown them publicly would seem in fact to serve the enemy, and in a way to become guilty of treason. What an agonizing decision to face! Yet it seems to me that there can be no hesitation in saying that a philosopher worthy of the name ought to judge that a France served by such means in some way ceases to be France, ceases to be faithful to a certain vocation which the best minds have always regarded as belonging to the French people. Could it not be said that in these circumstances the philosopher's responsibility was to this idea of a vocation, rather than to an actual authority which in this case betrayed the idea?

We must, however, be aware of the difficulties involved in this way of thinking. As for me, while I came out publicly against the use of torture, I also came out against a manifesto signed by numerous intellectuals at that time which appeared to me equivalent to a call for desertion. Certainly in such cases we walk a narrow ridge, and it is very difficult to determine exactly how to place our feet so that we follow the true line of responsibility. I am convinced, however, that it would be wrong to say that anyone who conceives his responsibility as I have described it is refusing an indefeasible duty, that of respecting the laws of the country, in favor of a completely subjective whim, a simple personal preference. The reader will of course notice that here we meet in a new form the central problem of the Platonic ethic, the same opposition which in the *Gorgias*, for example, marks the confrontation between the philosopher and the Sophist.

Several years ago I tried to show that a permanent solidarity exists between truth and justice, so that to sin against truth is to sin against justice, and inversely. To illustrate this there is no more striking example than that of the men who, in the perilous conditions of 1898, took a position in favor of Dreyfus against an official truth which would later be revealed as a lie. It is true that these men were not professional philosophers. But what is important here is that they adopted precisely the philosophical attitude with regard to the Dreyfus affair. Only the sophist could condemn their position.

It was reflection on the Dreyfus incident which led Charles Péguy to formulate, in *Notre jeunesse,* the distinction between *politique* and *mystique* which later became famous. In its deepest meaning this distinction certainly remains valid, but I am not sure that the terminology itself ought to be retained. I recall the famous sentence: "Republican mysticism meant dying for the Republic; Republican politics at present mean living on it." [1] No doubt Péguy was right in denouncing the political exploitation that occurred in the wake of the Dreyfus affair by those who tried to use it as a platform for their partisan ambitions. But I am not happy with the use of the word *mystique* in this context. It seems to me that this distinction might better have been formulated in terms of the opposition Blondel establishes between *pensée pensante* and *pensée pensée.* But from the moment ideas are objectified, reduced to formulas, and made into propaganda thought is perverted and becomes demagogic.

Now I would hold—and here I return to the main line of my argument—that generosity must be the hallmark, as it were, of any philosophical thinking worthy of the name. This truth is not easy to see so long as we take generosity to be the kind of verbal and sentimental effervescence characteristic of the ideologist. But the difference between the philosopher and the ideologist must be safeguarded at all cost. The typical failing of the ideologist is to stray from the rigors of the regulative and critical thinking whose demands the philosopher as such must scrupulously meet. This means that philosophical generosity has to

1. Charles Péguy, "Politics and Mysticism," in *Basic Verities,* trans. Ann and Julian Green (New York: Pantheon, 1943), p. 109.

remain tied to a certain prudence—which, like courage, is a virtue in the literature of moral theology.

Hence, with the small reservation I made above it can be said that even today, in 1968, Péguy was right when he wrote in 1910:

> This value in the Dreyfus affair, this worth, still appears constantly, whatever you think of it, whatever you make of it . . . from the good point of view, the point of view of *mystique*, it has an unbelievable power for virtue, a quality of unbelievable virtue. And from the bad point of view, the point of view of *politique*, it has a power, a quality, of unbelievable vice.[2]

But can the lessons of the Dreyfus situation in any way be applied to what I have called today's world? Here I think a carefully nuanced answer is necessary. At first, the conditions in which the Dreyfus affair developed might seem no longer to exist, or at the very least to have considerably altered in Western democracies. After all, they involved the existence of a certain military caste which is today no longer prominent. But I wonder if this is not a rather superficial way of judging the matter. First of all, what we see happening in many countries shows that in the event of a conflict, or even a threat, this caste can rise to prominence again. But above all it would be a serious mistake to think that such a caste is the only one which can seriously threaten those values of justice and truth to which the philosopher must remain fundamentally committed. It is enough to recall what happened in the Eastern countries in the Stalinist era, and even, to a lesser degree, since then in order to comprehend the danger which lies in the triumph of any party whatever when it achieves absolute hegemony.

I wrote recently, in another context, that democracy should doubtless be recognized as the only possible mode of existence for societies today. The alternatives are adventures which can only turn out badly. We seem here to be faced with a certain irreversibility very much like that which pertains to the control exercised over human existence by science or by the technology which issues from science. This is a simple statement of fact, and not at all a value judgment. For everything we have lived

2. My translation.

through and everything which we are no doubt still called on to live through in our different countries shows how precarious equilibrium is under a democratic regime. There are several reasons for this, but I shall limit myself to indicating one that is in my eyes particularly threatening. I refer to the corrupting influence of money which Péguy—again Péguy—denounced with such vehemence. But it will always be hard for plutocracy to admit its own nature; it will inevitably have recourse to alibis which are not always brought into the light of day as they should be. These brief remarks are only meant to show how closely attuned to events the philosopher must be, never giving way, however, to the temptation of partisanship. It is enough to say that he is obliged to make his way along a narrow ridge, as I said above, and that he is doomed to a certain solitude. I don't think this solitude is anything to be proud of. Indeed, such pride is actually one more temptation he has to resist.

But these remarks do not seem to me adequate for answering the central question I posed in speaking of the responsibilities of the philosopher in the world today.

I think I see on the one hand, as I indicated when I began, that this world is less and less disposed to accept, even in principle, the advice or the recommendations of the philosopher; and yet this suspicious and basically contemptuous attitude conceals a fundamental illusion, which the philosopher, and he alone, has the duty to expose. Perhaps his essential responsibility lies in this obligation. What is the illusion? It comes down to thinking that this world bears its own justification in itself.

The idea and the term "situation" have already appeared in the course of this exposition, but now let us return to consider it more fully. I doubt whether there would be any sense in asking about the responsibility of the philosopher *urbi et orbi,* by which I mean in an atemporal or detemporalized perspective. An analysis of responsibility in general would show that it can only be exercised in duration, or more exactly, in a temporal context. Thus, it must be repeated, it is in the context of a particular present situation that we have to consider the responsibility of the philosopher. What is this situation?

It seems to me that this situation is what follows from man's seizure of power. Let us be more precise. It is the crisis intervening in history as a result of this capture of power which dates from the first technological conquests. This present situation is from all evidence without precedent, for it involves the possibility that man could destroy his earthly habitat by means of the techniques he has perfected—in short, commit suicide on a species-wide scale. It seems to me that it is in the sombre light of the idea of suicide that the frightening possibilities that have taken shape under our eyes since 1945 are properly to be interpreted.

Moreover it would be a grievous mistake to consider this situation exclusively from the point of view of science fiction. As Heidegger seems to have seen very clearly, this development is related to a much more general evolution affecting consciousness or subjectivity itself, one which culminated in Nietzsche's "God is dead." I would introduce another reference here—the famous phrase that Dostoevski placed in the mouth of one of his characters: "If God does not exist, everything is lawful." Anyone who would unleash the machinery of an atomic war, whatever the reasons by which he might try to justify an initiative of this kind, would be guilty of an outrage greater than any crime committed in the course of history. Such a man would demonstrate *ipso facto* that he no longer respected anything that mankind has always held to be sacred.

But I am afraid we must push on even further. We can ask whether all those who, at their respective levels, contribute to making such an initiative possible do not by anticipation actually make themselves accomplices, regardless of what arguments they might offer to justify themselves. Perhaps we are here in an order where, ethically speaking, the unconditional refusal is the only acceptable one. I am inclined to believe that the mission proper to the philosopher, in the presence of this tragic situation which controls the destiny of all of humanity, might well be precisely to articulate this unconditional condemnation. Perhaps the voluminous work of Jaspers on this formidable problem is just the sort of thing needed. Accomplice or not accomplice: I ask myself, not without anguish, if this is not precisely the dilemma the philosopher faces. And does he not fail in his mission if he remains silent or gives in to the temptation of opportunism?

In all honesty, however, I feel I must introduce a reservation here, or more exactly a question mark. Is it not a bit too easy simply to make such a condemnation? Does this not come down to granting ourselves a certificate of purity at very little cost? Is this not to dismiss very lightly some real historical conditions in which the so-called free world finds itself today? Is this not to forget, inexcusably, that if America, since the end of the war, had not possessed nuclear weapons, Western Europe would probably have been swept up in the Soviet tide?

It seems to me, then, that the responsibility of the philosopher involves *two* factors which are difficult to reconcile. On the one hand, it is certainly necessary that he enunciate untiringly certain principles which cannot be compromised, and that he apply them rigorously without ever giving in to the temptation to judge differently according to some partisan interest. For example, whatever his nationality, he will have to declare that the bombing of Dresden was a war crime, an unforgivable collective atrocity. But, on the other hand, he must understand that his affirmations, in order to merit consideration, ought to have historical weight. They should have relevance to a historical context, for if they do not, they fall into the void. For the philosopher, as I said at Frankfurt in my lecture "Le Philosophe et la paix" in 1964, this means sustaining a contradiction which is painful and humbling.[3] But perhaps after all the philosopher should feel humbled. For doubtless this is his only means of being immunized against the sin of pride.

I think these general remarks are sound, and they need not be taken as an attempt at evasion. It is certainly true that any responsibility worthy of the name must pass into action. But in this particular and agonizing case, what form could such action take? I do not think that the philosopher has the duty, or perhaps even the right, to participate in showy demonstrations like those in which Russell has participated in England. Neither, I think, is there much point in his prostituting his signature at the bottom of petitions published in the newspapers. I do think, on the other hand, that the philosopher is bound to keep in touch with scientists, especially physicists and biologists, and that he must also try—this is surely much more difficult—to make himself heard by the men who have the formidable task of directing public affairs. It is only at this level, in this middle position, that he can, it seems to me, usefully have a say, and then always in small groups, not in front of great crowds assembled in immense halls where passions are electrically discharged.

3. See Gabriel Marcel, *Paix sur la terre* (Paris: Aubier-Montaigne, 1965), pp. 41 ff.

As I also said in my Frankfurt speech, it is necessary to take account of time, of an evolution which certainly is operating, e.g., in the Eastern countries.[4]

Everything sudden is deeply suspect and dangerous. The philosopher careful of his responsibilities must be attuned to and collaborate with the gradual but profound forces of life, and he must do so with a perpetual awareness of his own inadequacy, his weakness. Let him never take himself for an oracle: in this domain the oracular inevitably falls into charlatanism, and what is more contemptible and ridiculous than a charlatan who doesn't know that he is one?

Realizing now that the stakes we are playing for are nothing less than the life or survival of humanity, we must push our inquiry further. Only here it is necessary to be more precise, for it is not simply a question of physical survival. There are many ways for man to destroy himself or, more exactly, to dehumanize himself. Here again an untiring vigilance is required of the philosopher. But it is clearly not enough that he post a guard, so to speak, as one might do to protect a public building. Above all it is incumbent on him, and on him alone, to bring forth a conscious awareness of what man is as such. What I especially have in mind here is a philosophical anthropology like Martin Buber's, though certainly precedents for his thought can be found in many other thinkers. But today it has become astonishingly clear that man must be considered as *vocation* and not, as was still perhaps appropriate until relatively recently, as *nature*. In very general terms it could be said that the merit of existentialist thought has been to bring this to light. Unfortunately, in certain cases which have received a kind of publicity quite inappropriate to the dignity of true philosophy, existentialism has displayed the most distressing confusion, avoiding radical anarchism only to tumble back into a dogmatism improperly linked to Marxist thought. These are indeed the two reefs through which existentialist thought has to steer its way in today's precarious and even dangerous circumstances. Thus I believe that the task of the philosopher is much more difficult today than it has ever been—

4. On the one hand, the events which took place in Czechoslovakia in the spring seem to bring a valuable confirmation of the remarks formulated above; but on the other hand, the Soviet intervention of last summer [1968] shows, alas, that in Moscow things have not changed in their essentials.

and with that of course I rejoin the observations presented at the beginning of this study.

Something of this difficulty can be illustrated by considering an objection which might well arise with reference to the remarks I have made above, as follows: "When you denounce the process of dehumanization which you claim is underway in the world today, there is behind your denunciation a certain idea of man which you hold (and which of course needs to be made explicit). But with what right can you claim that the philosopher (in general) is bound to accept your idea and, on the basis of it, criticize the new values which are or will be discovered by new generations and which will rightly deviate from your (now 'traditional') idea?"

This question is of the greatest importance and it must not be evaded. I would even say that the philosopher is bound to embrace this objection, at least methodologically; I mean that his thought can remain alive only if it welcomes and even nurtures an eristic whose core is this objection. In this case my answer to the objection will recall in a very general way the position I adopted with regard to the problem of atomic weapons.

To begin with, the philosopher must rid himself of the spirit of facility. Thus he must ask himself whether the idea of man and of human values he holds is not tainted with pure subjectivity. But he will have to answer to himself that what are truly important here, what can alone verify any judgment in this matter, are certain exemplary witnesses recorded in history— witnesses which indeed are not only writings, but also and perhaps especially men's lives. These witnesses all converge toward a universalism which can be considered from a rational point of view or from a Christian point of view, or quite often from both. Indeed this word "universalism" is much too abstract, but I mean by it that spirit that tends to promote among men mutual comprehension and respect for each other, without of course involving the sort of egalitarianism which critical thought, especially since Nietzsche and Scheler, has shown to be the foundation of confusion and resentment. Is there really any sense whatever in saying that this universalism corresponds only to a subjective demand? This could be claimed only by playing with words. Besides, the history of the notion of subjectivity shows with what care this concept itself must be handled.

Finally, it is the task of the philosopher to delimit the area in which innovation is possible and the will for innovation legitimate. A long time ago I tried to show that the will for innovation in art, for example, is always suspect and reprehensible. Innovation in art is something which *is met*, and which probably ought not to be *sought*. It is quite otherwise in the order of technology, where it is a question of innovating in order to increase efficiency. But in the ethical domain, as in art, innovation undoubtedly has no place.

I will take an example that I think is revealing. There has probably been no greater innovator in the history of the sciences than Einstein. But when a question of conscience was put to him —that of deciding whether he might have been culpable in giving men means, weapons they might use in a criminal way—it was put in terms which must be called transhistorical. If an answer to this question is possible, it will be affected not at all by the undeniable novelty of the theories that have resulted in the awful consequences we are all familiar with.

Here I come to the conclusion of my admittedly circuitous development. I would say that the task or vocation proper to the philosopher consists in preserving in himself a paradoxical equilibrium between the spirit of universality on the one hand, inasmuch as this is embodied in values which must be recognized as unalterable, and on the other hand his personal experience, which he neither can nor should ignore, for it will be the source of whatever individual contribution he might make. Admittedly the nature of this contribution is difficult to specify, but one thing is certain: it is surely inseparable from the responsibility belonging to the philosopher.

The word "contribution" is not very satisfying because it seems to designate a thing, whereas what I have in mind is rather a shedding of light. The responsibility of the philosopher is much less to prove than to *show*. But we must be very careful, for here we are not in the order of things, where to show is to point out what is already there. Rather we are in what can very generally be called the spiritual domain, where to show is to make ripen and thus to promote and transform.

In a completely different context, I recently tried to make clear what I called an existential maturity. And here it could be said that the essential task of the philosopher is not only to develop this maturity himself, but above all to determine its general conditions. For that he must first of all distinguish very carefully between what is mature and what is on the way to decomposition. Notice that we are thus approaching the traditional idea of perfection, but approaching it in connection with the idea of life. Perfection separated from life is merely an eidolon that the philosopher must find suspect.

Finally, I would say that perhaps it is in the light of this idea of existential maturity that one can best grasp the meaning of responsibility. I would say that the philosopher's responsibility toward himself can only by abstraction be dissociated from his responsibility toward other men. Under no circumstances can he break away from them and grant himself some privileged status. In my view a philosopher worthy of the name can develop and be properly defined only under the sign of fraternity.

3 / Authentic Humanism and Its Existential Presuppositions

WHEN THIS PAPER was first presented in Austria, its German title was "Die existentiellen Urgewissheiten des wahren Menschseins." But the word *Urgewissheiten* [primitive certainties] can be misleading. The prefix *Ur-* must not be taken in a chronological sense. Nothing would be more hazardous than an attempt to determine the certitudes of primitive man, especially since the very notion of primitive man is not altogether clear. We need only think of the kind of certitudes a child holds to see that *Ur-* could not possibly be meant here in the chronological sense. What I do have in mind is something analogous to what Max Picard calls *"das Vorgegebene"* [something given in advance].

I mean also to emphasize the adjective "existential," and I would add that I strongly prefer the term "assurance" to the term "certitude." Certitudes arise in the domain of objectivity. I think, just as I thought long ago when I was writing the last part of my *Metaphysical Journal* and the article "Existence and Objectivity," that these terms must be distinguished. However, this distinction does not at all coincide with the traditional distinction between subject and object. Insisting on this point can forestall a needless misunderstanding.

Certitude must be conceived not only as immune to doubt but also as unshakable. Certitude is generally expressed by an impersonal verb, such as *constat* in Latin or *es steht fest* in German. For example, someone might say it is certain that water boils at 212° Fahrenheit, or that the sum of the angels of a triangle is equal to two right angles. It is impossible to think of an objective structure without at the same time thinking more or less explicitly of the certitudes related to it.

If we now consider human beings objectively, that is, insofar as they belong to a certain species, have a detailed anatomical structure, and so on, it is clear that we can make judgments about them which are certain but which would not be called existential.

But the words *das wahre Menschsein* figure in the expression of the judgment. Clearly, the reference here is not to the order of the natural sciences. Actually, this word "truth" must be taken here in a somewhat normative sense. We could even replace the word "true" with the word "authentic." But we need to make the meaning of the verb "being" in *Menschsein* more precise. We might at first be tempted to substitute a verb like "to behave." The problem then would bear on the existential assurances that are at the basis of authentic human behavior. But it seems rather dangerous to use an expression that could imply a narrow behaviorism. I think we have to resist the common temptation today to define man in terms of some specific behavior. Such a procedure amounts to forgetting that what defines man are *exigences*, like those embodied in the idea of truth, which go beyond all behavior.

In this perspective it could be said that what properly characterizes man is giving witness. But the nature of this witness, or of the reality testified to, must not be prejudiced.

These indications, however indeterminate and insufficient they may be, allow us to clarify the distinction I made earlier between the objective and the existential.

Roughly speaking, what is objective is what does not concern us. However, this can seem equivocal. Can I say that the objective laws that govern the functioning of my organism do not concern me? In a sense this would be absolutely false. In some way my being *depends* on these laws; how can I say that these laws do not concern me? What I mean is that these laws do not take me into account. But this phrase here is too indeterminate. A more precise notion ought to be substituted, for example, the notion of my purpose or my fundamental project. This is what is expressed by all the thinkers and principally the poets who have stressed the fundamental indifference of nature. I am thinking, for example, of Victor Hugo's famous lines in "La Tristesse d'Olympio:"

Nature, with your untroubled brow, how you forget!
How little time is needed to change all things
And how you shatter with your metamorphoses
The mysterious bonds to which our hearts are tied!" [1]

The question here does not concern our objective structure, but rather the many physical changes operative in the world of things. These changes are of such a nature that the poet who comes back after very many years to a garden where he had lived as a child no longer finds anything of what he remembers.

But existential categories cannot intervene until the gap that separates the subject from the object is, if not filled in, at least bridged. An opposition is established then between a domain of separation and a domain, not, perhaps, of unity, but of connection—I would even prefer to say of participation. Participation seems to be implied in the very notion of witness. A being radically isolated from other beings, closed in on itself, and capable only of considering a particular exterior spectacle cannot be a witness without the word "witness" being emptied of its concrete and positive meaning.

From the moment we enter the domain of the existential we come on commitment. It is now appropriate to clarify why the problem of authentic humanism is posed in our time with such tragic sharpness.

No one can deny that in the course of the last half century the worst examples of inhumanity have proliferated. I am thinking particularly of the concentration camps and their nameless horrors. But I am thinking also of those massive deportations in Eastern Europe, in Asia, and elsewhere. I think we would agree, at least on this side of the Iron Curtain, that such practices were not possible without a radical misunderstanding of the conditions which being authentically human implies. But it is important to try to conceive the state of mind of those in the East who would revolt against such a judgment. For example, we know that these people have energetically defended the thesis that in their country there were correction camps only and no concentration camps. Decrying the unbelievable hypocrisy involved here is inadequate; I think it is more interesting to try to discern the

1. My translation.

assumption behind similar attempts at justification. These assumptions seem to be connected with the idea that being truly human is still a possibility in the future, that we have arrived at the critical and decisive moment of history where the awakening of human consciousness is taking place on a large scale; that this consciousness must be institutionalized on the ruins of a fallen world. In this perspective every means may seem legitimate to facilitate the coming of this new kind of humanity.

But—and this would be the first concrete illustration of the general theme in my paper—this kind of thinking must be categorically rejected in the name of what might be called a primordial existential assurance.

I would note in passing that the move here is similar to defining dogma in relation to already defined heresies. Doubtless one of the most baneful heresies is this belief in a future man to be brought into the world by a pseudo-elite regardless of the sufferings of those sacrificed without scruple to the idol. Actually this idea of a future man is merely the schematic expression of a wish that is rooted not only in man's ongoing historical experience but also in abstract understanding. But the words "rooted in" are out of place. A living being, a plant for example, cannot take root in cement or in asphalt. Yet abstract understanding really must be compared with these lifeless materials. In the last analysis this man of the future can only be compared to the diagram of a machine which someone comes up with before he is able to imagine the machine concretely. But a machine must be in the service of man, although tragic experiences have taught us that this relationship can be perverted so that that man is put to the service of his own machines. In comparing himself to machines, as Gunther Anders has admirably shown in his recent book *Die Antiquiertheit des Menschen,* man comes to depreciate himself.

The appropriateness of this comparison can be disputed, of course. The man of the future, someone might say, will be distinguished from the man of the present by his liberation from all the servitudes that still burden him today. But what is abstract and chimerical is precisely this idea of absolute liberation. It is probably just as absurd to believe in the possibility of absolute liberation as it is to imagine human beings liberated from such laws as gravitation. The connection here between man and machine is based exclusively on the fact that a machine is a product of abstraction whereas an organism cannot be isolated from the cosmos in which it is born nor from a line which plunges into the unfathomable.

These reflections enable us to be more aware of what I spoke about earlier, the existential assurance required by every authentic humanism.

But a difficulty may still arise here. It might be objected that the heresy I alluded to must be rejected in the name of an assumption about the essential dignity of man, which could easily be related to the postulates Kant elucidated in the *Critique of Practical Reason*. But how could the Kantian postulates be taken as existential assurances? This seems completely impossible. The Kantian postulates are not implications of the moral law but of the relationship between the moral law and perceiving selves. But an implication could not be existential. Perhaps we are touching here on one of the limits of Kantian thought.

I think we must dispute this assimilation of existential assurance to Kantian postulates. To make this clear let us take up again the concrete examples I began with, particularly the problem posed by the deportations. When I say that these deportations were accompanied by contempt for something which is intimately involved in being truly human, am I restricting myself to saying that they go against a certain spiritual *exigence*? Surely not, because it is a matter here of an embodied *exigence;* the embodiment is what is important. I mean that when we condemn these deportations we have in mind—and this is the very basis of our judgment—the existence of innumerable human beings who were able to fulfill themselves in their vocation only because it was their lot to live for generations in a particular land they were united to by a loving bond. The idea of the mutual belongingness of man and of the particular space he dwells in seems fundamental. Of course this idea must not be understood in an absolutely rigid way, as a much too narrow and dogmatic traditionalism would like to understand it. Very often in the past the idea was formulated in a way we can no longer accept today; for today we recognize fully the individual's right to emancipate himself from this relationship to the land wherever he experiences it as demeaning. But the emancipation must be voluntary. This qualification has nothing in common with the abstract planning legislated by a totalitarian state or its satellites to transplant a population.

In writing these lines I am thinking of a great German writer who, after many years of relative oblivion, has once again been given the place he deserves: Jeremias Gotthelf. No one has had a more immediate and more profound sense of this mutual belongingness. Perhaps it is partly because this mutual belongingness is so tragically misunderstood and violated that Gotthelf's work seems such an indispensable reminder of the existential givens of a true humanism. By evoking this work I think I am sufficiently clarifying what I meant when I spoke of an embodied *exigence*.

Another more recent illustration could be found in Péguy's work or in parts of Claudel's work. These references show how far we are from the postulates of practical reason or anything like them. I think we must stress the fact that these very great poets, who knew little of philosophy and nothing of Kierkegaard and the doctrines of his disciples, have expressed much more distinctly than the metaphysicians the existential assurances I am trying to make intelligible here. But we have to clarify the basic difficulty in such an enterprise. In trying to render this existential aspect intelligible, we run the risk of losing sight of it altogether. For, generally speaking, to make something intelligible is to conceptualize it. But here conceptualization subtly betrays what is being conceptualized. This is what happens to what I have called the mutual belongingness of man and his *Umwelt*. Must this mutual belongingness be evoked by means more akin to poetry and even to music than to abstract thought? The function of abstract thought is above all the recognition of its own insufficiency and thereby the preparation of new modalities of thought which transcend abstract thinking without repudiating it.

At the end of this long analysis we can say then that the fundamental existential assurance required by an authentic humanism is the affirmation of a primordial bond, a kind of umbilical cord, which unites the human being to a particular, determined, and concrete environment.

But we have noticed that the human being characteristically takes a position with respect to this primordial unity, and as a result is eventually able to break with it. There can be no freedom without the possibility of position: no freedom and no thought either. The conditions of both thinking and freedom are, in a very profound sense, identical.

When freedom is conceived in this way, however, it can seem to be a kind of capacity for tearing oneself from existence, even for destroying oneself. This reflection provides a way of reconstructing the history of some philosophers who made an abstraction of existence, as one sees, for example, in certain forms of a particularly bloodless idealism.

But defining freedom in terms of this capacity is dangerous and inaccurate. Freedom does include this possibility, which at the limit is actualized in suicide; but it also includes the opposite possibility, that is, the possibility of resisting this temptation which in times like our own and in quite specific social conditions can become almost insurmountable.

If we are to say anything about an existential assurance in relation to freedom, we must restore the central and often overlooked relation between freedom and embodiment. This is what will emerge more clearly in the following reflections on intersubjectivity.

Earlier, we tried to clarify how to exist is in some way to belong to an ambient reality from which we are never able to separate ourselves without danger, even though this separation can become necessary. Now we must recognize that growth requires opening ourselves to others and the capacity to welcome them without being effaced by them. This is what I have called intersubjectivity. However, intersubjectivity cannot be regarded as a simple fact; or, more exactly, it takes on value only when it is more than a fact, when it appears as a progressive conquest of everything that threatens us with self-centeredness. Briefly, intersubjectivity does not exist and cannot exist without freedom. And this is clearest where intersubjectivity appears as a positive power, the polar opposite of the negative charge it assumes when it is detached from the existential.

But there is no question here of a simple practical postulate or desideratum. Existential assurance relates to the structural conditions that allow an individual to open himself to others. Just because this assurance is fundamental does not mean that it can be easily discerned. Whenever we try to translate it into a general proposition we greatly risk distorting it. To speak of structural conditions, as I have just done, seems to involve a commitment to a formalism. But an existential assurance is opposed to any formalism whatever. To attain such an assurance we must again turn to poetry, to poetic experience. For example, I have in mind the basic experience behind Walt Whitman's poems.

> My spirit has pass'd in compassion and determination
> around the whole earth,

I have look'd for equals and lovers and found them ready
   for me in all lands,
I think some divine rapport has equalised me with them.[2]

An apparently serious objection must be anticipated here. "Whitman's work," someone might say, "derives from a certain *Stimmung* [frame of mind] which is, despite everything, a subjective disposition only; hence it seems completely arbitrary to speak of an existential assurance here."

This important objection presupposes, I think, a particular opposition we are trying to overcome, the opposition between a simple fact of individual psychology and something valid for everyone, valid for consciousness in general. Existential thinking tries to establish itself on the other side of this distinction, which is of epistemological value only. Perhaps mention should be made of that prophetic element without which there is probably no great poetry. Of course I am not taking the word "prophetic" here in its usual temporal sense. A prophetic word is a word offered for or in the name of another, here an infinity of others. Whitman certainly is a prophet in this sense. He spoke for innumerable beings incapable of expressing themselves. He was their voice. If American democracy considered in its purest and most universally human intention has found an organ for expressing itself, that is, for existing, then this organ, I think, is Whitman's poetry. Of course, this poetry has gone beyond the limits of the American continent and has contributed to awakening an entirely new poetry in Europe and particularly in France. But this has been possible only because at the very heart of this poetry lies a certain basic experience: the experience of man's openness to man. "Basic experience" here means something far beyond the restricted sphere of a purely individual *Stimmung*. Different but converging examples could be taken from the domain of music. The greatest musicians were also prophets or representatives.

"But," someone might ask, "is it not completely arbitrary to choose examples like these and to neglect certain fundamental experiences like those of solitude and despair?"

My answer is twofold. I would not think of neglecting or rejecting these painful and bruising experiences, any more than anyone else would. To me they are essential. But can these ex-

2. "Salut au Monde," *Complete Poetry and Selected Prose*, ed. J. E. Miller, Jr. (Boston: Houghton Mifflin, 1959), p. 107.

periences be defined or understood as a negation of the universal communion Whitman expresses or, let us say, Beethoven expresses in his "Hymn to Joy"? Doubtless, each of us is exposed to many threats, to solitude, and to despair. But nothing about these threats weakens or calls into question the primordial value of the experiences of communion, even though one of the most important reflective tasks may be discovering just how these threats are possible and how they take shape.

My task has been to discern the existential assurances which the constitution of an authentic existential humanism requires. In this perspective—and notice within that of religion properly speaking—this experience of communion and of men's openness to one another assumes a particular importance; by the same token, everything that contributes to diminishing this experience in human consciousness becomes an obstacle to an authentic humanism. Here I have in mind prejudices of race and class, as well as a certain kind of nationalism which today is rather out of date.

But we would have to make these observations more precise, because formulating them in a general way may invite serious errors. I am thinking of those errors emanating from that abstract humanism and vague pacifism which not very long ago were allied with the most terrible powers of oppression. In other words, it is an extremely difficult and complex problem to know *how*, that is, in what concrete conditions, the spirit of universality can weaken human relationships. But this is not my topic here. These qualifications need to be introduced to avoid troublesome confusions.

But in connection with these positive assurances relating to embodiment and intersubjectivity, we have yet to allow for another existential assurance which bears on my radical finitude, my mortality. I am referring to Heidegger's remarkable analysis in *Being and Time* on *zum Tode Sein*.[3]

As I pointed out some years ago in Berlin, Heidegger's phrase is dangerously ambiguous. This is partly indicated by the fact that his expression cannot be correctly translated into French. Heidegger's most recent French commentators have wanted to introduce the expression *être vers la mort* [being-toward-death] to avoid using the preposition *pour*, which could seem to involve the idea of finality or of a destination.

3. See *infra,* chapter 8.

I don't intend to discuss this in detail here, but to merely give the position formulated in the paper I contributed twenty years ago to the International Philosophy Convention at Paris.

When I try to become aware of my situation as an individual being, and when I consider this situation in relation to what I call my future, I notice that the only indubitable proposition seems to be *I will die*. But I am completely unable to determine the spatial and temporal conditions of my death. In this perspective my situation resembles the situation of a condemned criminal who is locked away in a prison with movable walls that are closing in minute by minute. There is nothing in my actual existence that cannot be, so to speak, dried out or devitalized, that is, deprived of all interest by this imminent presence of my death at the horizon. This sinister possibility of letting my death preoccupy me to such an extent that I consider all my concerns and those of others stupid is inscribed in my structure as a finite entity. Here we are faced with an anticipation of suicide at the very heart of life. It would be useless and inept to reply that such an attitude is pathological, because a derogatory label would change absolutely nothing in the situation.

All of this is, in my eyes, indisputable. I am speaking, of course, of the possibility that my situation can be regarded in this way and that consequently I am exposed to the temptation to a despair which seems at first glance without recourse.

Is there a primordial existential assurance there? Nothing seems more doubtful. Everything seems to happen as if the certainty of my future death would come to attach itself like a foreign body to the fundamental assurance of *being* or, when this assurance becomes reflective, of participating in being eternally. Of course this ties in with Spinoza's *experimur nos aeternos esse* [we find ourselves to be immortal] (this does not, however, imply a commitment to Spinoza's metaphysics). The central deficiency in existentialist philosophies of anxiety, I think, is the completely arbitrary overlooking of a fundamental experience I like to call the *gaudium essendi*, the joy of existing. A certain threat does in fact menace this *gaudium essendi*, a serious shadow is projected upon it. And there is the tragic aspect of our situation. But if this primordial fact of the *gaudium essendi* is overlooked, then we will have only a mutilated and deformed idea of our situation.

Moreover, when I reflect on the fact that the idea of my future death tends to paralyze my activity, I come to recognize that this is possible only with the cooperation of my freedom. My death can do nothing to me without the collusion of a freedom that betrays itself by conferring on death this apparent reality whose power to fascinate I have already verified. In the last analysis only this freedom really has the power to conceal from my view both the richness of the universe and everything which in the life and values of others would not be affected at all by my death. The fact of sacrifice is an existential refutation of this despair, which is itself equivalent to a practical solipsism. Yet an argumentative kind of thinking can claim that sacrifice is absurd, that sacrifice is a kind of optical illusion which is only too easy to expose. But it is the greatness and the dignity of man to be able to reject arguments of this kind in the name of an experience which itself cannot be rejected.

Here again we find a primordial existential assurance, which is finally perhaps nothing other than a very mysterious radiation of the *gaudium essendi*. And this radiation is hope.

I will not repeat here the analysis in *Homo Viator*. I tried to show there the radical difference, often overlooked by philosophers (especially Spinoza), between desire and hope. What can be called the ontological status of each of these terms is completely different. Desire is centered on the "self," whereas hope is inseparable from love, from what I have called intersubjectivity.

But if in the course of these reflections we have been able to rediscover the roots of two of the theological virtues, perhaps we can go on to discover the roots of the third, which is faith.

The difficulties here are even more serious than the previous ones. To subscribe purely and simply to the idea of a natural religion which would be the primitive lot of human beings is dangerous. I do not claim that this idea is false; but it could be accepted only after an extensive inquiry, the conclusions of which would always remain somewhat hazardous. There is a risk here too of contradicting what I formulated at the beginning of this paper in remarking that the word "primordial" must not be taken in a chronological sense.

There is a line of thinking that ought to be pursued on the basis of a meditation on what man is becoming in a world where the death of God is proclaimed.

Here too we can employ heresy as a means to understanding, where "understanding" means the full recognition of the conditions for being authentically human. But we need to distinguish precisely between a *professed* atheism and a *lived* atheism. Where it is at the basis of revolt, professed atheism sometimes can be characterized by an *exigence* which in the last analysis is not at all alien to any genuine religion. But lived atheism, where it is at the basis of a satisfied and sated world more and more delivered up to the technological which ends by functioning for itself alone (no longer dependent on a higher will which uses it for an authentically spiritual end), lived atheism, I am saying, can only open the way to that despair I spoke of earlier. This comes down to saying that lived atheism can only be a path to death.

At the present moment, for a philosopher who is conscious of his responsibilities and at the same time of the dangers which menace our planet, there is probably no more pressing task than finding fundamental existential assurances which are constitutive of being truly human in the image of God.

4 / The Questioning of Being

IT IS QUITE OBVIOUS that the inspiration for this meditation lies in my reading of Heidegger's later writings, but I have no intention whatever of engaging in a direct critique of Heidegger's thought.

I might say that reflecting on being has been at the heart of all my thinking from the very beginning, especially in my distinction between problem and mystery. Now I have no reason to reject this distinction, but in my eyes it is of value only if it remains an instrument of thought, or to use a more precise metaphor, if it serves as an open channel for a kind of intellectual or spiritual navigation. But in fact experience shows that this distinction is in constant danger of running aground in verbalism. This being true, I shall refrain from introducing the term "mystery" in what follows, for, as is well known, I have always been on guard against the decay of philosophical language. I am convinced that philosophical language must be constantly revitalized, and the revitalization can take place only through vigilant reflection which remains perpetually in touch with experience. It seems to me, then, that we ought to start our questioning from point zero.

Some twenty years ago I had a discussion with a disciple of Jacques Maritain regarding what he called "the intuition of being." I felt I had to keep asking the same question: "If this intuition of being exists, how is it that so many minds are completely unaware of it?" I myself must admit that when someone speaks of an intuition of being, the words signify nothing whatever for me, strictly speaking. At most I might acknowledge today, as I have explicitly done in *Being and Having*, a blinded or

[45]

blocked intuition. But I think it is debatable whether intuition is even the right word to use for that.

One might wonder whether this idea of an intuition blinded by the play of discursive thought, especially technological thought, has any relation to the Heideggerian notion of the forgetfulness of being, the *Vergessenheit des Seins*. But what sort of thing actually lends itself to being forgotten? Does being? I must say that Heidegger's expression seems to me annoyingly imprecise. The words "lost from view" would doubtless be preferable to the word "forgotten."

In any case it seems to me that we are forced to question being. I think we should have to do so even if we were privy to this famous intuition which I don't believe in. But our reflection must bear on the nature of this questioning and on the conditions in which it is undertaken. That means that we must finally question the subject of a question—and at once we see the difficulties pile up before us.

Can we use the expression "to question" without asking ourselves immediately *who* is questioning and *who* is being questioned? It would certainly be legitimate to answer that it is "I" who questions. But it must be well understood that we do not have the right to say "me" instead of "I." Now beyond making that reservation we shall not get tangled up in the problems that immediately appear when we try to make explicit what the "I" is. In fact it seems to me that such an explication is forbidden, as it were, since no doubt it is precisely characteristic of the "I" not to lend itself to explication. But the other related question remains: "Who is questioned?" The answer that immediately comes to mind is: "I am questioning myself." But although we use this verb in its reflexive form so easily, so spontaneously, without suspecting any difficulties, may it not hold a few surprises for us?

Let us look at everyday experience for a case where we could unhesitatingly say "I question myself," and try to analyze it. Let us take a case where I question myself about what I am thinking. Of course it is not self-evident that my thinking ultimately needs to be questioned. If the classical notion of self-consciousness which held sway for so long were correct, I ought to know directly what I am thinking, and thus should have no need to ask myself about it. But in fact we know today that this transparency to oneself is exceptional; it is a limiting case and nothing more. Thus let us turn to our example.

I question myself, let us say, about someone I have seen. Or more precisely, I question myself about someone who has come to ask me to render him a service. And when I say "I question myself about this person," I mean "I ask myself what I really think of this person." Here the "What do I think?" is imperceptibly transformed into "What should I think of him?" Yet I am still supposed to be addressing this question to myself, not at all to someone better informed who would be in a position to advise me. Thus it seems we are quite in the dark. Everything happens as if, under conditions difficult to determine, I were coming to a kind of inner adjustment, to what could almost be called a "socialization of . . ." But of what? It seems that words fail here, for we are not dealing with definite knowledge so much as with a situation which aspires to be transformed into knowledge. This situation is not, however, to be confused with a simple feeling,[1] for it involves aspects under which it can be regarded as a mode of knowing. The man I am questioning myself about behaves in a certain way. He has also spoken certain words, which I remember and which might seem appropriate, let us say, to giving a favorable impression. But something in me—and I note in passing how obscure the words "in me" are—tends to reject this impression: something like a reverberation of his behavior, or perhaps of the expression on his face or the ring of his voice. And this something becomes interlocutor, or rather sets itself up as interlocutor. Here, then, the use of the reflexive verb form is subject to caution; for is it not this something that the "I" is dealing with here, rather than with itself strictly speaking?

Although this illustration may at first seem quite removed from our subject, it has in my opinion the great merit of bringing out the obscurity, the fundamental inexpressibility in the act by which *I question myself about*. This is especially true for the act by which I question myself about being. For here these newly created interlocutors are indefinitely numerous, so that one would be reduced to saying that to question myself about being is really just a sure way to recognize my own inability to know who or what I am questioning.

But can the questioning of being even be formulated distinctly? The troublesome ambiguity which characterizes our language appears at once. One might wish to begin by asking the question "Does being exist?" [*L'être est-il?*]. But the meaning of

1. Marcel uses the English word "feeling."—Translator.

this question turns out to be obscure, for it is not obvious that it means "Is there being?" [Y *a-t-il de l'être*?] nor is it certain that even the question "Is there being?" is meaningful. Thus I am forced to carry reflection to a higher level. Before asking myself whether being exists or whether there is being, I must be sure of what I mean when I say "being." And now the ambiguity is forced into the open, for in French "being" [*l'être*] can mean the substantive, as when one speaks of a being or beings, or it can mean the fact or act of being. It is unfortunate that we cannot simply use the substantive infinitive, as in German or Greek; that we must introduce extra words like "fact" and "act."

If I stick to the first meaning, where "being" is taken substantively, I see immediately that a formulation such as "What is being?" is absolutely false. It would be necessary to complete this by saying, for example, "What is being in relation to appearances?" But even corrected in this way, the formulation is imprecise and calls for a complement. It seems to require that we ask "What is being as being?" But this question leads subtly to still another, namely, "What is it to be?," which may well turn out to mean precisely "What is the fact of being?" or "What is the act of being?"

I must go on in this direction, however, asking myself whether I am really sure that this last question is meaningful. I shall have to begin considering questions like "What is it to act?" and "What is it to be passive?" But here at once I note that inevitably these questions bear reference to a certain active or passive subject. (The use of the word "subject" here is still obviously very troublesome. We notice once again the regrettable ambiguity of our language.) Thus the precise form of my question ought to be "What is it for this υποκείμενον (I much prefer the Greek word) to act or to be passive?"

Yet we are still constrained to ask ourselves how far this is applicable to the question "What is it to be?" In other words, is it certain that there is any sense in first positing a being [*étant*] and then asking "What is it for this being to be?" It seems to me— and here I am radically opposed to Heidegger—that really this question "What is it for a being to be?" cancels itself out. Recall that when I was questioning myself about what it was for an acting subject to act, my question bore on what appeared to me as a specifying modality. Correctly or not, I was thinking of the subject as somehow being before it was specified in acting. Not that this priority should necessarily be chronological, of course, but nonetheless the fact or act of being comes first relative to any possible specification. From this point of view it seems to make no sense to ask what it is for a being to be. I tend to think this is a pseudo-question, a little like asking, again with Heidegger, how it happens that there is something rather than nothing. Indeed every question arises out of an underlying foundation which can only be being itself. We must therefore end up saying, I think, that strictly speaking one cannot question being since every question presupposes being as a base. And it should be added that it is perhaps impossible to determine the nature of this base or foundation [*soubassement*], so that perhaps any question about it is without meaning. Indeed to introduce here the idea of a nature and a determination of this nature is to forget what we are dealing with, or are supposed to be dealing with, for it is to introduce surreptitiously the idea of specific character into what is by definition beyond any possible specification.

But if that is so, then as I have suspected from the start it is impossible to have anything resembling evidence for being. If I reflect on evidence, if I try to become aware of what can be evident, I will always be led to point to certain kinds of relations; I fail to see what evidence could be apart from certain relations considered to be fundamental. And although it would have to be admitted that evidence itself can almost always be contested by reference to previous evidence, I do not see that this previous evidence could ever be evidence of being either.

However, does not denying that there is evidence of being inevitably come down to admitting that perhaps being is not? (I do not say admitting the contingency of being, for that might well be contradictory.) Here let us watch out for the snares of language. Can we reassure ourselves, like the Eleatics, by declaring that it is perfectly absurd to deny that being is? Here there is a danger of being too easily intimidated by a verbal contradiction; in order to avoid the intimidation perhaps it is enough to make a verbal restatement of the matter. Instead of saying "Being is not," let us say: "The affirmation bearing on being perhaps bears on nothing"; in other words it is possible to say, like the nihilist of Claudel's *The City*:

Nothing is.
. . . .
I have seen and I have touched
The horror of uselessness, in what does not exist,
adding the proof of my hands.

> Nothingness does not lack the power to proclaim
> itself through a mouth that can say, "I am."
> This is my spoil and such is my sole discovery.[2]

Obviously one could call on refutations of the classical type here, and argue that this nothingness which says "I am" admits in saying so that it is not nothing. But what is remarkable is that in spite of the somehow undeniable validity of such claims or refutations they seem to bring with them a certain sense of what I would call inanity. It is a fact that arguments of this kind will never convince a nihilist; it is as if they slide off a surface where they can find no handhold.

In order to avoid remaining a prisoner of words, it seems to me that we must bring in the idea of an *exigence* which is, or is not, or cannot be satisfied. Again of course a logical or verbal refuge may immediately offer itself to us, since it could be said: "Surely that which satisfies or does not satisfy the *exigence* in question, whatever it may be, cannot not be." But a response of this kind is clearly foreign to the sphere where thought questions being in the second sense, which I believe to be the fundamental sense; that is, where being is taken as a verb rather than a noun, where being [*l'être*] is the infinitive taken substantively. From this point of view may I not reject the nihilist claims, which seem to be bound to the obscure notion of a substantive being? Thus everything seems to bring us back to something which does not satisfy me and which I believe can in no way be satisfying. It is an assurance which is unable to commute itself into evidence, which perhaps would finally have to be compared to a prohibition or deprivation, since it is essentially the assurance of an impossibility. Let us attempt, even though it is hardly feasible, to describe this impossibility.

It seems that it is the impossibility of any confining-within. Perhaps it would be better to say the impossibility of any "reducing to something else"; or more simply and truly, "to something," for what cannot be "other than" cannot be "this or that" either. Thus we are well into the nonqualifiable.

All this seems obscure so long as thought continues to slip from the infinitive form of the verb "to be" to its substantive form. However, it all should become clear enough if one holds firmly to the meaning in question, namely being in its infinitive form. It

2. *The City*, trans. J. S. Newberry (New Haven, Conn.: Yale University Press, 1920), pp. 39–40 (translation modified).

might help to remark that what we are dealing with is what in the presence of a thing would be its designation, the act of designating it a "this." But since we are at a level beneath the world of things, the world of "such and such," we are also beneath any determinate "thisness." We are at the level of what might be called thisness in general, or the level of that foundation grounding any "this."

But it seems that we may have to go further in this direction. Being, evoked in this way (I say "evoked" and not "defined," which would be contradictory), is at a level beneath all objectivity. But one would be guilty of serious confusion if he therefore concluded that being is *on the side of the subject,* for that would be just another way, completely fallacious, of localizing being in a separate region of the world of objects.

Here of course I come back to what I have said on previous occasions about the problematic; for there can be objectivity, localization, designation, only where one is dealing with problems, whatever the chances might be of actually solving the problems. But today I would hesitate to speak of the *meta*problematic. This is probably the only point I would change in the position I set forth at the International Philosophy Convention in 1937. No doubt it would be better to introduce the word "*hypo*-problematic," which much better indicates that here we are *beneath* the level where problems have their place.

But the following objection may arise. Can we be sure, inasmuch as we are beneath the level of the qualifiable, that the words we use here are anything but a pure *flatus vocis*? It seems to me that we can be sure, and our affirmation here, as poor as it may seem, ought to be enough to show definitively that the radical nihilism enunciated by Claudel's character is impossible. After all, what is a nihilism like that if not a philosophy of absolute dissipation, self-destructive to boot? But being, grasped beneath the level of all objectification, is the fundamental and indissoluble bond.

We certainly are not at a point here where we could begin to speak of being as it is understood in traditional ontologies. But I evoked just above an *exigence* which seemed able to appear to itself as disappointed or stifled by what might be called the spectacle of the world. Very generally one could say that it is an *exigence* for cohesion and plenitude. It must be added at once that this *exigence* only takes on its meaning, its value as aspiration, in relation to a being who is torn apart and suffering; or again, in relation to a being who is exiled and is more and more painfully aware of this exile. Under such conditions the spectacle which would hope to satisfy is tried and found wanting. From this point of view we might consider Leibniz, for example. His optimism does not seem to carry us beyond the level of a spectacle offered to the intelligence; and our reaction will inevitably be: "What a spectacle! . . . but only a spectacle." I would also be tempted to say that the most profound discovery of Schopenhauer, the one which in a certain way makes him a forerunner of existential philosophy in spite of his persistent Platonism, is the discovery of the intrinsic insufficiency of any representation or spectacle whatever.

But we should note that here we are being led or, more exactly, drawn beyond the world of objects, which is by nature something represented and which even tends to identify itself with its representation. For the moment we can leave aside the question of knowing whether what lies beyond representation is the reality or only the mirage of a promised land. But I do want to observe at this stage of my reflection that the hypoproblematic being I spoke of above at first appears indifferent or neutral with regard to the aspiration toward a being which would be absolute super-being [*plus-être*] or pleroma. Thus it would seem that a duality could be posited between hypoproblematic and hyperproblematic being.

Here I must say everything gets much hazier, and I am far from underestimating the difficulties involved in what I am going to say now.

I do not think that the duality between the hypo- and the hyperproblematic can be taken as ultimate. We cannot accept it as final or give it a permanent place in our thinking except through a misunderstanding, and this misunderstanding is always fundamentally the same: it consists in illegitimately reifying the hypoproblematic. We must remember that the hypoproblematic, far from lending itself in any way to being thought of as a thing, is rather a fundamental situation governing every particular concrete situation. Perhaps it could be called a springboard situation. I like this expression, for it seems to indicate that the situation is inseparable from a nisus, a force or impetus without which I who am questioning, and who recognize the limits of my interrogation, am not; without which, indeed, nothing is.

Almost inevitably I tend to speak of this situation in the language of belonging or participation. But at the same time I am ready to admit the inadequacy of such a usage, to perform a kind of calling into question, almost an indictment, of my own deficient mode of apprehension.

Here the idealist type of philosopher will be gripped by the almost irresistible temptation to hypostasize and glorify that radical subjectivity which has the power of so radical a calling into question, or which *is* this power. But here there is actually an essential choice of direction to be made, and the path I shall personally follow leads by way of the later thought of Schelling rather than that of Fichte. It seems to me that this subjectivity cannot legitimately ratify the act by which the mind would tend to hypostasize it, or, if you wish, by which it would itself tend to present itself or palm itself off as absolute. My path actually amounts to a way, still not fully specified, in which subjectivity recognizes itself as finite.

I admit however that the word "finite" may provoke some misunderstandings. The difficulty seems to lie in the fact that here finitude must not be thought of as it is in philosophies of the object such as Spinozism as it is usually interpreted. Whether or not this customary interpretation is correct is of course another question. The finitude I have in mind can without a doubt only be conceived from the point of view of an itinerant, a wayfarer, a creature who grasps himself as present to himself, but in a presence which cannot be separated concretely from presence to others. It is a precarious and continually threatened presence, but it is not without the aspiration toward plenitude, toward the pleroma. And that plenitude is still being, it is even most genuinely being, but being insofar as it can in no way be given.

A dangerous ambiguity still threatens us here. Shall we say that being, evoked in this way, is a simple ideal? I do not believe this word is suitable. And here I admit I am coming to what is most obscure in my exposition. For I want to speak of the mysterious connection which exists between being-as-foundation [*l'être-soubassement*], the *Grund,* and that anticipated plenitude which is foretasted and *hoped for,* though of course not in the sense where "hoped for" simply means "desired." Here I respectfully refer the reader to all that I have formerly written on the theme of hope.

It remains to be seen whether this connection must not inevitably remain the object of faith, whether we are not here beyond what reflection left to its own devices can accomplish. Up to a certain point this can be clarified by focusing attention on a fundamental question which I have skirted until now: "What is a being?" What are the repercussions of what I have said above on the response to this question? More precisely, are we here again faced with the ambiguity I have insisted on from the beginning?

The main difficulty is obvious. If I say "a being," it seems that I must have recourse to a substantive, that I am prevented from considering being in the sense expressed by a verb. And yet would not the truth rather be that when I speak of a being, which always means "such-and-such a being," though not necessarily "such-and-such a thing," I introduce at the same stroke, if not a contradiction, then certainly a tension which at its limit is very close to becoming a contradiction? I must say that this is one of the points on which I would most like to see some discussion.

The use of the indefinite article here is tied to the fact that I am dealing with a particular, for the sake of simplicity let us say a thing, which can be juxtaposed to other things and with them make up a denumerable group. But when I say the word "being" I have in mind more or less explicitly something that is absolutely irreducible to such a representation, for it makes no sense to speak of beings added on to one another. I would suggest, simply as a hypothesis of course, that perhaps that is indirectly why in German the word *Sein* is not used in the plural. Drawing out certain thoughts of Royce, I would be tempted to say that a being (the fact of saying "a being") witnesses to a certain special preferential recognition. But let us add immediately that this is not enough to say, for it is not merely a matter of preference. One can very well prefer one *thing* to another. What we mean by this special recognition is really an act by which a value, an absolute value, is conferred on something that could never be reduced to a thing.

But this is still inadequate, to the extent that in expressing myself as I have I seem to offer a subjective, or rather "subjectivizing" interpretation of what cannot be subjective unless love lose all reality. Actually a being is given, not at all in the banal and moreover uncertain sense in which philosophers customarily use this word, but rather insofar as it is truly a *gift*. Let us carefully refrain here from considering the gift as a thing. On the contrary, it is an act. Thus it seems that we have been led by this roundabout way to rediscover the act of being.

Of course it is indisputable that the contemplation of this act is continually covered up by a degraded and "thingish" thinking.

But possibly this paradox which announces its presence at the heart of what we call a being presents a kind of token value. It seems to lure us upward in a movement which can be consummated only in the perfect κοινωνία. But here we are leaving the field of questioning thought far behind us, and perhaps in the last analysis it does belong only to faith to bring about the decisive release.

Discussion

MR. GASTON BERGER: Let me first thank Gabriel Marcel for his very fine paper.

In planning this session, the selection committee of our society deliberated just what sort of communication we ought to have for the meeting. We all wanted, of course, to hear some original thought. One of our members put it this way: "We would like to hear a philosopher, preferably a French philosopher, who would come and give us the benefit of his personal thought on the fundamental problems of philosophy." I think that this wish has been amply fulfilled here this evening. Mr. Marcel, your wish was to draw us into your meditations. All your listeners are highly grateful to you for that, and I think that they will show their interest in what you have said by the liveliness of their questions.

MR. BÉNÉZÉ: I am almost entirely in agreement with Mr. Marcel. Any reservations I could have would be minor. Perhaps I would use another language, but in the end we would be in accord on the essentials.

The word "being" is obscure because it has several meanings. You have carefully distinguished these meanings, or at least two of them: "What is it to be?" and "What is being?" You have seen very well, if I may say so, that the second formula, "What is being?," leads us directly to one singular being, the being par excellence, so that, as you say, at its limit the question of being links up with the question of God. There is no denying that. I would only have one slight reservation: there is no need to go to the limits of the question to encounter this connection. It presents itself well within the limits.

The other formula, however, "What is it to be?," suggests a different idea, something capable of repetition—this being here, that being there, and so on. The word evokes a plurality, a plural.

Consequently, and I beg your pardon if I am going beyond your thought, this formula has to do with the spatio-temporal, the phenomenal.

Now of these two meanings, you have retained the only one which is appropriate to being par excellence. Let us return to this, but avoid the word "God," which is too laden with useless complications.

If I understand you correctly, idealism is surpassed, the "I think" is overcome, so to speak, since not only must we give up the "I" (as in the case of the duality of questioner and questioned you spoke about)—there is no pure "self"—but also the "think," which we had come to rely on so much. What is "being" then? We are forced to speak of it in metaphors, for it is apparently unknowable; and the metaphors themselves are directed by a dialectic founded solely on the necessity to pursue, without contradiction and to their very limit, questions which can be posed about being.

I wonder if we could not change the terminology, and without giving up the other meanings of the word "being" (meanings which need not concern us here), retain the ideas of the absolute and the relative. The absolute would be the synonym for "being" in your second formula, "What is being?" The relative would express what is meant in your first formula, "What is it to be?" The advantage of this would consist first of all in the fact that the absolute would better retain its privileged status, for it would not be difficult to show that behind any relative will always stand the absolute, and consequently there would no longer be the confusion of identifying the two meanings of the word "being," an identification which must be rejected, as I believe you have done.

Another advantage, an important one, I think, is that it would be clearer that there is no symmetry between the absolute and the relative. The absolute is, in effect, the foundation, the "within" of every problem. It is not only unqualifiable, but also and above all "unsubstantifiable," so to speak. To speak of substance is in effect to speak, not of a phenomenon, but of something linked to the phenomenon, to qualities. Substance is the absolute already decked out as the relative. But the absolute as such is independent of all that could be "grasped" by perception or imagination. That, I think, is your meaning of the word "being," stripped of any compromise.

By this change in terminology, there would also be a better

understanding of one aspect of the relationship between the absolute and relative things. In any relative thing, I always discover the absolute. There is nothing surprising about this, for an absolute that is not everywhere, if I dare say so, would not be absolute. Thus, a characteristic dialectic develops here. What dialectic? We have a choice. If we refer to the notion of cause, of production, we immediately encounter the in-itself or the through-itself, which makes no sense to speak of in connection with the relative. If we speak of ends we are also unsuccessful at the other extreme. No matter how I name the phenomenon, so long as I use the word "relative," the word "absolute" at once appears.

Here, then, is the dissymmetry I spoke of earlier, which would not be so apparent if we kept the word "being." The relative implies the absolute, but the absolute has no need of the relative; or rather, as the two always go together, in any reflection comparing them I can pass from the relative to the absolute very logically and without contradiction, but this is not true if I try to go the other way.

For example, let us take the Cartesian dialectic of the *cogito*. Let us grant that the *cogito* would be the last possible term of this dialectic. I say let us grant this, for there is nothing to prevent us from pushing further to the "divine thought" of Malebranche, or even to Spinoza's "substance" (you yourself mentioned Spinoza), but without its attributes of course, for both thought and extension will disappear. But let us stop at the Cartesian *cogito*. It was reached by impeccable reasoning before being was even considered, for that consideration would obscure the doctrine. It is irrefutable reasoning, which brings us into contact, so to speak, with what you call the foundation of all determination, not only of knowledge, but also of feeling and action. Thus, there is no contradiction in the passage from the relative to the absolute: transposition, if you wish, transcendence, but all logically acceptable.

But when I am perched on this absolute (if you will allow me the metaphor) and I want to descend again toward the relative, I cannot do it without violating the principle of contradiction. Why? Because the relative is multiple, while the absolute implies unicity, and I cannot logically deduce the multiple from unicity.

The absolute is one, that is, it is indivisible. It is different from the "one" of Parmenides, for the "one" of Parmenides is immobile, and the notion of immobility belongs to the phenomenon. Applied to the "one," it can only be a metaphor, and a dialectic which seeks to bring about understanding must do away with all metaphor, render it inoffensive in some way; whether it be metaphor of movement or of rest, of tendency, of foundation, of aspiration, of ascent or of descent—anything one could think of, in fact, which would derive its meaning originally from the phenomenon. Now, just as absolute unicity cannot give us the multiple without some help which would have to be of a non-logical kind, so the "one," unity, cannot give us the divisible. Here, then, is where the asymmetry appears. Borrowing a vivid expression from Jean Wahl, I would say that *transascendance* is intelligible (logically comprehensible), whereas *transdescendance* is not. And that can be better understood using the words "absolute" and "relative" than the single word "being."

MR. GABRIEL MARCEL: I think that perhaps we are almost in agreement. I do feel a certain repugnance at this change of terminology, however. This is not to say that I am altogether happy with my own, to be sure. But I must tell you that I am very hesitant to bring in the notion of the absolute here, first of all because it is a notion so laden with historical associations . . .

MR. BÉNÉZÉ: So is being . . .

MR. GABRIEL MARCEL: Yes, of course. But I feel that if I use the word "absolute" to characterize what I have called this foundation, I would perhaps be bringing in something which, if I may say so, carries with it certain implications I am not so sure about. I want to return here to what I said above, because it is very difficult, and I think it is indispensable that we refer to it continually. First of all, I am not sure that Mr. Bénézé has wholly understood my thought.

I spoke of the "fact" or "act" of being, because I do not know which expression it would be better to use. Let me say again that really what we have is, on the one hand, "beings," and on the other the act or the fact of being. So, if I say "the absolute," it seems to me, I imply precisely that substantification which you find no more acceptable than I do.

In other words, I am afraid of landing at once in a contradiction, because nothing can prevent the word "absolute" from having just that unwanted "thingish" sound for us.

MR. BÉNÉZÉ: That could be taken care of by simply declaring that in fact the absolute cannot be a thing . . .

MR. GABRIEL MARCEL: Yes, but I see the possible problems with the word, and I am not sure that I see its advantages. I do not see what we gain by returning into the dangerous and difficult circle of the absolute and the relative.

Of course I am basically in agreement with you, I think, that indeed one can and should move from the relative to the absolute (for the moment I shall use this language, though I do not like it), and that, on the other hand, the idea of a kind of deduction— for it would be that—a deduction of the relative from the absolute is not practicable. This is how Brunschvicg saw things, by the way. But I wonder if this really puts us on the ground I am trying to stake out or to mine, or if we are not rather slipping back, so to speak, toward plateaus of philosophical thought which I find it absolutely necessary to go beyond. We remain with Hamilton and others who, it seems to me, were as far as possible from what I have in mind.

For me what remains the most important thing to consider is that kind of untenable duality, but a duality which seems, all the same, to be inevitable, between what I call the "foundation" [*soubassement*] (a word both of us have used) and what I call the "pleroma," that is, the perfect consummation.

I would say that if the word "absolute" could be used (and again, I shrink from it), it would not be for the foundation taken in itself, and perhaps not even quite suitably for the pleroma (thought this may be more arguable), but rather for what I have called that mysterious conjunction of the two which, as I said, I am not sure lends itself to reflection—and again this is a point on which we probably are not wholly in accord.

I think that here reflection points, so to speak, toward something which is no longer absolutely within its own province. And here I think I am very close to the later Schelling.

MR. BÉNÉZÉ: I think that in rejecting *transdescendance*, we are in agreement.[3]

MR. GABRIEL MARCEL: I am no supporter of *transdescendance*, but I am not at all sure that Jean Wahl would agree with us. I think he is terribly fond of *transdescendance*.

3. The text of Mr. Bénézé's remarks is left unfinished here, with the permission of their author.

Please notice that I do not accept the position you outlined above, because it causes some difficult problems, and would require a different terminology from the one I have used. I do not know whether you and I are fundamentally in agreement, but notice that there is something even more difficult in my position, namely the idea of that foundation which we have assurance of, as I said, but do not have evidence for. It hardly ever lends itself to being *seen*. Once, I even called it "tactile."

MR. BÉNÉZÉ: Yes, you did. But I think that neither word is appropriate . . .

MR. GABRIEL MARCEL: Of course, but in my opinion all words are bad.

MR. BÉNÉZÉ: Even the word "foundation"?

MR. GABRIEL MARCEL: Certainly. There is no doubt that the word "foundation" is even, from a certain point of view, disastrous, and that is why I repeat that it is extraordinarily difficult to speak of what is at issue here, for language is continually working against itself. It is certain that when I use an expression which is so spatial, I completely miss what I want to say.

MR. JEAN WAHL: I quite understand Gabriel Marcel's repugnance at seeing what he has developed for us likened to the classical opposition between the absolute and the relative. You have made an effort, in the *Metaphysical Journal* and since then, to get beyond a certain way of posing problems. Now the old way has just been offered you again, and I can understand that you would be reluctant to adopt it.

I would have one reservation about the use of the word *transdescendance*, which in my mind has never had the meaning given it by Mr. Bénézé. It is probably true that Mr. Marcel and I do not agree about *transdescendance*, but it is not true that I ever use this word to mean descending from the absolute to the relative.

MR. GABRIEL MARCEL: No, that is something entirely different.

MR. JEAN WAHL: Mr. Bénézé has asked whether it was necessary to return to the idea of being. It is very fine to say, as Heidegger does, that we must get "beyond judgment," and certainly I agree with him. But then how is the idea of being to be maintained? The Thomists have rightly pointed out that the idea of being is essentially in the judgment.

I think that you have been speaking of something which indeed I can hardly characterize at all, but which I certainly would not characterize by the word "being." But perhaps we could come to agreement if you would not insist on keeping the word "being."

You have said that it is not qualifiable or characterizable. That depends on the meaning of the word. The quality belonging to being is clearly not definable, and yet it is the most real quality, so that I would say what you have been speaking of is "qualifiable in an unqualifiable way."

MR. GABRIEL MARCEL: I must say that I am quite in agreement with what Jean Wahl has just said, and I believe as he does that the word "being" carries some disastrous consequences for philosophy. If it were possible to do without it, I personally would be delighted. But I think that that is extremely difficult. If someone could come up with a metaphysical terminology which excluded any reference to being, I think that he would be rendering an immense service. But I really think that no one has succeeded in doing that . . .

MR. JEAN WAHL: Bradley, perhaps.

MR. GABRIEL MARCEL: I would like to come back again to this "nonqualifiable" we have been trying to come to grips with.

It seems to me that I expressed what I meant most precisely when I said that basically it is a question of a fundamental situation; this fundamental situation cannot be an object; and it might even be said that it is not to be appraised in terms of the subject-object distinction. I think that there is no more serious error in this respect than the error of subjectifying. Let us call the fundamental situation something other than being, if you wish, though I don't know what.

You spoke of Bradley. There is probably a certain kinship, though not complete similarity, between what I have said and the thought of Bradley. But for Bradley, what is there? There is absolute experience, which obviously cannot be likened to experience in the empiricist sense.

Actually, it is quite illuminating to bring up Bradley here.

There may well be something closely resembling the absolute experience of Bradley in what I have called the liaison, the mysterious junction, between the "foundation" (I am sorry to have to use this word again, but I see no better one), the fundamental assurance, if you wish, which we cannot do without, and on the other hand the aspiration which I have called the pleroma. If we could establish ourselves in this unity—which I do not think we can, because I hold that our thought is essentially itinerant—we would have something like Bradley's absolute experience. My difference with Bradley lies in the fact that I find his philosophy too much removed from what I have called a certain dynamism. His is a philosophy where the itinerant condition of man is too little recognized, at least in my opinion.

Mr. JEAN WAHL: If I had to articulate a view of the world here, it would be Bradley's view, but without his absolute, and that is what you have just been saying.

Mr. GABRIEL MARCEL: I do think that after all Bradley remains very fundamentally absolutist. He would be much more in agreement with the terminology of Mr. Bénézé, whereas for my part I reject it without being at all satisfied, as I said, with my own terminology. What I am presenting, actually, is much more a kind of putting-into-question of the usual language of metaphysics.

Mr. JEAN WAHL: I would like to draw attention to one point which I admit is really a detail. I think that nowadays to prefer the later Schelling to Fichte is a bit unjust to Fichte, in view of some of the extraordinary aspects of his thought.

Mr. GABRIEL MARCEL: That may be. Actually I was not exactly speaking of the later Fichte, but of his philosophy as a whole. Let me say that I referred to these philosophers only as guides in trying to arrive at an understanding of the question at issue. It was the same when I spoke of Schopenhauer.

Mr. GOLDMANN: If I have understood Mr. Marcel correctly, the key idea of his talk to us lies in the distinction between two aspects of being, or perhaps between two levels at which, according to him, the problem of being has to be taken up: there is a hypo-problematic foundation of everyday reality, something which would be the basis of this reality, its ground, and on the other hand there is something very exalted, the ideal, or, ultimately, God. Between these two levels is situated the intermediary plane, that of the distinction between the thinking subject who questions and acts, on the one hand, and on the other hand the objects he thinks about, along with other men who respond to his questioning. This is not only the level of everyday life, but also that of positive research in the human sciences. But it seems to me that Mr. Marcel sees no need to pose the problem of being at this level. If I understand him correctly, he has even opposed Heidegger in saying that for him the question of the relationship between "being" and "beings" has no meaning, since beings are situated on precisely that intermediary plane where the question of being does not arise.

Personally, I would reproach Heidegger in the opposite way, for not dealing with the problem of the relations between being and beings in a sufficiently radical and universal way, since he acknowledges, on the ontic level, the possibility of a science which is not philosophical, but is nonetheless appropriate for dealing with human realities.

In the last analysis it could be said, though this may be something of an oversimplification, that Gabriel Marcel would have us, if I have understood him correctly, take up again the tradition of the nineteenth and early twentieth centuries, in which the positive sciences of man grew further and further away from philosophy, while for its part philosophy continued on the purely metaphysical and religious level, more and more losing contact with positive science.

It seems to me, however, that the most important philosophical event of the last forty years has been the progressive awareness (which is doubtless no longer still dominant, but which is still being expressed by certain thinkers in the positive sciences as well as by some philosophers) of the fact that it is precisely at the level of the positive understanding of beings, especially human beings, that the separation between science and philosophy turns out to be untenable and distorting. A given partial and limited fact can be understood only to the extent that it is seen in the context of the meaningful and structured development of a spatio-temporal totality which embraces at the same time the *object studied* and the *subject who is thinking it;* but that means precisely that we pose the problem of the relations between beings and what Lukács calls the "totality" and Heidegger calls "being."

To illustrate this problem methodologically, I would mention a famous passage where Marx explains that when I see a black man passing in the street, the knowledge I have of him is abstract and inadequate; any progress toward a concrete knowledge can only come through a whole set of mediations in which the black is seen in terms of the totality of social development. Indeed, if he comes from Africa, he is perhaps the chief or the king of a tribe; if he comes from America, he is perhaps a slave; and if we continue this kind of reflection, we shall arrive at the insight that European society, too, participates to a certain extent in the fact that at this time there are slaves in America and tribal chiefs in Africa. But Marx lives in Europe and participates in the life of European society, so that in some measure, minimal no doubt, but real, his behavior contributes to creating the reality of the black he is setting about to study: and inversely, of course, the behavior of the black contributes to constituting the reality of what we call the individual person Marx. That is why human reality cannot legitimately be studied on a scientistic level, where this reality is considered as an object external to the inquirer, to which the inquirer would be related only as a spectator, or rather through an interaction similar to that which, in microphysics, links the investigator to the object of his studies.

You were perfectly right to say that in dealing with the problem of being, the essential thing is to get beyond seeing being as a spectacle, to get beyond the level of the distinction between the subject and the object, the level of the thing. I believe that this is necessary even at the intermediary level of the positive sciences of man, not only at the level of the ultimate foundation and the final end.

Of course this does not mean doing away with the "thing" and the "spectacle" at the level of positive studies, but it means coming to understand them by integrating them into a totality, or if you prefer, into being, which envelops and surpasses them; for only in this way does one truly have science, and not scientism. As a final remark I would add that such an attitude no doubt leads to the reintroduction into positive science of concepts which the nineteenth century practically eliminated from scientific thought, namely value, finality, and even faith. This in no way means faith in God, however. Between faith pure and simple, and faith in God or in the absolute, there is a leap which could only be made after it was justified on the level of the positive understanding of facts.

I think, too, that one must be very careful, again at the level of everyday realities, in claiming that one man cannot be attached to another, that he is a singular, irreducible personality, and so on.

Gabriel Marcel is perfectly right in taking a stand against the danger of a purely quantitative scientism, a thought which reduces man to an interchangeable element, to a cog in an industrial and technological machine. This is the problem which Marx and Lukács have dealt with on the level of the reification and fetishism of merchandise; but while the concrete aspect of human reality must be respected, quantity must also be taken into account. Men in fact do form attachments with one another in innumerable areas of their activity and their behavior. Take the case where ten, a hundred, or a thousand men join to solve a technical problem, to make a joint effort. Here it is not necessary to make an absolute value of the individual. There are some situations where it must be required that he submit himself to general ends, without, however, reducing himself to a simple means, and also without making an absolute value of the general, which would be nothing but the opposite extreme of the same mistake.

In short, I think that the highly interesting analyses we have just heard ought to be complemented by the recognition of another domain, where the concept of being seems to me just as fundamental: the domain of beings, of positive science, of human relations with Pierre, Jean, or Jacques, and with all the other men we try to understand, hoping that they in turn will understand us.

Mr. Gabriel Marcel: This may surprise you a great deal, but I do not think that I am so very much in disagreement with you. It is true that I have not spoken much of the historical. But that does not mean that I do not regard it as an extremely important matter. When I spoke, in passing and very discreetly, of an upward movement, I meant it to involve precisely that whole world of concrete relations which, for me more than for anyone, is of the greatest importance. After all, you are speaking with a dramatist, and a dramatist recognizes the importance of the concrete if anyone does.

I would simply say this: I am not always in agreement with you, but I would agree on the necessity of going beyond the order of the spectacle. I do not know to what extent you would insist on bringing in the word "being" here, the word Jean Wahl and I were just saying is so unfortunate. I would say that in this domain the word "being" is entirely useless.

MR. GOLDMANN: Here we are at the very heart of the problem. It seems to me that one can grasp the concrete facts at the level of life, of the immediate, of empirical data, in a positive manner, only by trying to understand them through a philosophical dialectic of being, or, if you wish, a dialectic of the development of spatio-temporal wholes which simultaneously embrace both what is thought and thinking itself.

MR. GABRIEL MARCEL: Here, you see, I would be a bit skeptical. It is a curious thing, but here I would be a little more of a phenomenalist than you. There are concrete realities to be taken account of, no one could deny that, but is it really necessary to treat these concrete realities in ontological categories?

The point on which we would be in complete disagreement, however, lies in the fact that I would start out from an axiology much more fundamental than yours. If we leave aside questions of terminology, which are not so very interesting, I am not absolutely in disagreement with you, believe it or not, because in fact I find everything you are saying extremely important.

MR. ETIENNE SOURIAU: I hardly need say this, but I think I speak for all of us in voicing my appreciation of the beauty and the depth of what Gabriel Marcel has just said to us. This was particularly striking in the pathos appearing in the development of his theories in the region of the "perhaps." For my part, I do not wish to raise an objection. I simply would like his opinion about one resource which I think might lie in an inquiry of this kind.

I wonder if the very idea of a question, which plays so instrumental and important a role in all this, does not perhaps suggest the resource I have in mind, in that it must be asked, in dealing with this idea, who is questioning and who is questioned.

Alas, there are surely many questions without answers, but there is no answer without a question. But here, who has the initiative in posing the question? Often an apparent question is really only a wish, if it is not a prayer, a supplication. Is not the questioning of being simply the wish for a light from being, a light which would illuminate us about it? Is this a true act? The question is an act only on the condition that it calls forth a response with some authority. We cannot question just anyone, and besides, is everyone we question obliged to answer us?

My problem is this, then: can we question being? And I do not escape the difficulty by saying that it is I who am questioning myself about being. For can I hope for an answer to such a question from myself, except insofar as I more or less take myself for being? Or insofar as I more or less participate in it?

So, is it not necessary to resolutely reverse the order here, and suppose that in every question of this kind we are the questioned, not the questioners; and that we are questioned not by ourselves, but by being?

This is at the same time my difficulty and my hope. If we are questioned by being, we are thereby given a kind of investiture. By this questioning, and in its presence, to the extent that we are able to actively become a response, we are invested with being, and with an existence which is both correlative to and distinct (though not separate) from being. In entitling me to respond, being gives me a kind of consecration of my existence, an existence not merely to be received, but to be actively taken hold of.

The key to all this would be in that experience (which seems to me at the same time direct, immediate, and perhaps of primordial metaphysical importance) of feeling ourselves questioned, of feeling ourselves more questioned than questioning, whenever any question about being is posed.

MR. GABRIEL MARCEL: This is basically very close to the question Mr. Césari asked me in a recent letter.

I would say that I find what you have just said very seductive poetically. But on the level of pure philosophical reflection, it seems to me that you immediately run into the difficulty I mentioned. You say "Is it not *being* which is questioning me?" In what sense are you taking being here? Actually it is in the sense of *a* being. Mr. Césari, too, says in his letter: "One must listen to being." But these formulas which, I repeat, please me poetically, call forth a philosophical doubt. I would ask, "But who is being?"

I would say that all this becomes perfectly satisfying on a religious and Christian level. If one says "It is Christ who is questioning me," that means something absolutely precise, and from a certain point of view it would satisfy me completely. But outside this wholly specific and revealed religious datum, I am not sure that the sentence "It is being who is questioning me" has any meaning, because you are immediately exposed to all the critical questions I spoke of earlier, which are so troublesome.

I would like to know what you would answer to this question: "Who is being?"

MR. ETIENNE SOURIAU: Here is what "I hope" can answer. I know perfectly well that I am using an expression open to formal criticism when I say, in order to express my situation briefly and problematically, "It is being who is questioning me."

Actually, of course, I do not know who is questioning me. The experience I am speaking of, which I think is primordial, amounts to *suffering* the question. If I knew who is questioning me—if that were given, even implicitly, in the question—I would have the solution to all metaphysical problems. What I experience carries with it only the instigation to march in the direction of response, and to make of myself a response to the question.

Pardon me if perhaps I am misusing words, but the possibility of establishing myself through my response is connected with this question. If I manage to be an adequate response to the question, I will know what being is. It is the quest for being which I find we are drawn into by this feeling of being questioned. Thus being is hypothetically, or rather problematically, at the end of the long search we are drawn into in this way. That is what I am expressing, apparently inadequately, when I say that being is questioning me. Perhaps it would be better to say that I suffer being questioned in the intention of being; or perhaps even that I suffer being questioned in the intention to be.

MR. GABRIEL MARCEL: Well, here I would like to return to what Jean Wahl was just saying. I think that what you are saying has real significance on the level of experience, which, for me, is the only one which is unquestionably important. I think that it is perfectly true that we can experience ourselves as questioned, as summoned. I do not see what you gain by using the word "being" to designate the unknown summoner, and it seems to me that if you use this word, which I too find unfortunate, you get yourself involved in antimonies from which you cannot escape.

Once again, we are continually faced with the problem of language.

MR. ETIENNE SOURIAU: Apparently I am taking somewhat too easy a position, because I speak of attraction, of incipient movement, of inquiry in an inchoate stage, and so forth, and I do feel that in certain respects it is too easy to put all that into the data of experience. But anyway, I use the word "being" because I think that by doing so I manage to discover in myself that I am a being. We are all midway in existence, between the minimum and the maximum of being. Well, to the extent that I am questioned and to the extent that I respond, I find that I gain a little more "being," I am more "a being"; consequently, thanks to that *élan* which comes from the question, not from me, I discover the possibility of entering into relation with something I experience, even within myself, insofar as I am more a being.

All of this, obviously, is purely problematic. What is required is to advance further along this path. I willingly grant the formal illegitimacy of everything which presupposes the accomplishment of what has yet to be accomplished. But to accomplish it is my task, and it is only as a task to be accomplished that it is given to me.

MR. GABRIEL MARCEL: Once more, I think that from a certain point of view you are entirely right, and I think that you are expressing something which is very close to the fundamental experience of the artist, even though the artist himself would be absolutely incapable of seeing that. Here we must recall Heidegger's expression, *Entfernung*. But I must say that this expression has to be regarded with caution.

I think that here you have an experience which I myself regard as perfectly genuine and even very important philosophically, metaphysically, but I think that by giving it this ontological value you are in danger of spoiling it, distorting it, rendering it suspect.

Let me say again that I am not contradicting you. I would be if I said that for me the experience you speak of has no meaning, but actually I am quite sure that this is an entirely positive, entirely essential experience, an experience, finally, which does contribute to the growth of a being (*a* being exists more by it, is nourished by it, as it were). But it does seem to me that, almost inevitably, you are going to find yourself launched onto an ontology from which there can be no escape.

It may well be that we have now come to the end of ontology. This is very possible. Once again, up to a certain point I wholly accept Jean Wahl's "objection," his "question"; and I say up to a certain point only because I have yet to hear of a terminology which would allow us completely to do without the word "being." So far I do not see this anywhere, and I wonder if it is possible. I wonder if we are not finally reduced to the very embarrassing situation of perpetually having to struggle, in some way, against the very words we are obliged to use, knowing that at any moment these words are liable to involve us in error.

Mr. Sandoz: I would like to say first how interesting I found Gabriel Marcel's talk, especially what he said at the beginning about the absence of an intuition of being, and about the way the questioning of being is carried out.

I am deeply convinced that there is no intuition of being. We grasp being only to the extent that we speak of it, we grasp it only in speech, in discourse, in sentences, and finally in dialogue; and I think that it is precisely this "dialectical" character of thinking which is subjacent to the difficulty discussed with respect to questioning.

I should like to suggest that perhaps the way you posed the problem of questioning, once again in answering Mr. Souriau, is not the best way. Is the primary difficulty to know *who* is questioning, or *who* is being questioned? Is not questioning born more radically out of that ambiguity we find ourselves in with respect to the word, which can enunciate the true as well as the false, because it can be affirmative as well as negative? And to go at once to the heart of the problem, does the questioning of being bear primarily on what being is or what it is to be, as you say? On the contrary, does not this questioning quite simply come down to "Is it true?" or "Has Paul returned, or has he not?" or "Is it raining, yes or no?" In short, it seems to me that one is questioned first of all about the truth (or the falsity) of speech.

It may well be that in analyzing the structure of speech, concerned to see whether it is true, we may discover a sense of being even more primary than those you have outlined. Please excuse me for whatever presumption I show in attempting to go beyond the distinction you propose, with the Greek and the German, between the participle and the infinitive, between ὄν and εἶναι, between *seiend* and *sein*. In the absolutely primary questioning, which bears on the truth of the sentence or of the proposition, being takes an even more verbal form, as it were, than the infinitive (which is a little like the abstract name of the verb, while the participle would be its concrete name).

In fact it is remarkable that the verb involved in a sentence is always in a *personal* form, that is, it always has reference to a subject—I, you, or he. It cannot be isolated from this reference to the subject by which we "conjugate" it, as the grammarians so surprisingly say.

If we try to clarify what the fully verbal form signifies, the personal form of the verb, then we shall perhaps see that it adds to the infinitive (which amounts essentially to a designation of the nature of an action) the expression of the very *exercise* of this action, an exercise necessarily related to a subject (whereas the designation of the nature does not imply this actual reference to a subject). That is why this exercise as such is beyond any particular determination, and I wonder if indeed it is not being in its purest and most actual sense, that with which the primary questioning is concerned.

Following this line of thought, we shall discover not two but three aspects of being.

The first aspect would be that which we have just outlined, being as exercise, in the process of being exercised, expressed by the personal form of the verb.

Closely connected with this would be the "subject" aspect, expressed by the participle. This would be the German *seiend,* the Latin *ens.* This subject would be, in a way, the bearer of the exercise, or better yet, this subject *is* precisely insofar as it participates in that exercise. In this sense, being is *"the one who* is."

Finally, inseparable from the two others, would come the aspect "essence" or "nature," the specifying determination, which would refer to the subject (which it names) and to the verb (which it defines), and which would be expressed by the radical, what linguists call the semantic root. This aspect would become explicit in the definition *"what* who is, is."

Would not this analysis make clear the very meaning of the questioning of being? Of course it is hard to show this in such a short exposition.

What I think can be seen, however, is that being in the primary sense is not beneath all specification, but rather beyond it, like the completion which all "definite" perfections require and count on in order to become actual. And here I would insist on that extremely important point you made at the end of your talk, namely that being is a gift which the subject does not receive from himself. But I would not hesitate to maintain that this gift lifts out of nothingness the subject who receives it, so that it seems to me that the idea of "thing" need not be absolutely disregarded. It signifies precisely that subject without which we cannot think the exercise of being.

Obviously all this must be related to man and to the experience we have of being. I shall be content with raising the problem of whether we ever experience ourselves other than as ordered by something other than ourselves.

MR. GABRIEL MARCEL: I am not sure I understand, Mr. Sandoz, what it is you wish to add to what I have said. It is quite possible that you are right, I do not deny that. But would you mind perhaps taking an example? That is always my method. I would like to take a very simple example, of your choosing, and to have you show, in relation to it, how your view differs from mine, because I am not at all sure that there is any real disagreement between us. What you said at the beginning, about the intuition of being, pleased me very much.

MR. SANDOZ: Let me return to the two examples I have just used: "Has Paul returned?" "Is it raining?" In both cases, what is at issue is always the truth of the proposition, but the structure of the proposition is not the same in the two cases. In "Has Paul returned?" what interests me is knowing if Paul is in the house and not outside; it is this kind of qualification or localization of Paul which concerns me, but not Paul's existence, which stands outside the question and is presupposed by it. However, when I ask "Is it raining?" it is the very existence of the rain I am concerned about. Thus, in relation to these two examples, one can distinguish the two senses of the word "being" you spoke about: being as "qualification," which would be tending toward being as plenitude, and being in the sense of the "fact of being."

But what I see as important is that in neither case does the question have to do with *what it is to be*, or *what being is*, but rather with the *truth of the attribution* of being (expressed by a verb) to its subject. I find it impossible to stress too much this reference of the act to its exercising subject; it is in this sense that the notion of subject seems to me essential to the understanding of being.

MR. GABRIEL MARCEL: But what is this subject in your other example—"Is it raining?"

MR. SANDOZ: We could analyze it in various ways. But let us say generally that it is "rain."

MR. GABRIEL MARCEL: I must say that I simply do not understand that. Let me take your two examples. "Has Paul returned?" You are right in saying that the question concerns a certain qualification of Paul. Actually, in this particular case, the word "qualification" is not quite right, but I don't see a better one. Is Paul in the house at this moment? Can I picture Paul to myself as really being in the house, and above all can I act accordingly— call out to him, for example? A concrete analysis would require bringing in some elements which probably would not come into play in the other example. But in the first example there is one existence which is Paul, and in the other an existence which is the rain. I do not see the difference in register between these two examples. Besides, I do not see very clearly where this distinction would lead.

MR. SANDOZ: In the first example I do not question myself about the existence of Paul, whereas in the second I question myself directly about the existence of the rain. What I think is remarkable is that in both cases there is nonetheless a subject which exercises the act signified by the verb. I think, at least, that this is what results from the very structure of the sentence, which is at the same time discursive and dialectical. I repeat that I do not think these remarks run counter to what you have said.

MR. GABRIEL MARCEL: What bothers me is that you are obviously seeing something which I am not clearly seeing. Again, I am not absolutely sure we are in disagreement, but I apologize for not clearly seeing just what you actually mean to propose.

I think we shall have to discuss this at more length.

MR. PATRI: In listening to Gabriel Marcel, and then to the discussion afterwards, I have had the feeling that the classical philosophical problems which everyone would like to think are overcome remain lurking in the background in spite of everything.

At first, Mr. Marcel proposes an argument which seems to dissolve definitively the question of being: he says, in effect, that since the notion of being is a presupposition of any question whatever, it is absurd to raise the question of being.

But then he introduces the notion of nothingness, quoting Claudel in an altogether remarkable way.

I wonder, then, whether the question of being does not arise precisely because we conceive the notion of nothingness in opposition to that of being. Nothingness arises as a sort of foil or contrast for being. From the moment we oppose being and nothingness, we have the right to ask what being is, what nothingness is, and what distinguishes them from each other. If we then want to do away with the question of being, as apparently some would like to do—Jean Wahl, for example—we would first have to be sure we could do away with the question of nothingness. From the moment we oppose being and nothingness, there is no longer a single presupposition, and it is as if being were opposed to nothingness as something to something else, something whose distinguishing characteristics it would be legitimate to inquire into. Are we not reviving the *aporia* of Plato here? If we are asking "What is nothingness?" then nothingness must not be as devoid of being as it seems, and being itself "is" not as much as it seems.

Thus we are back to the problem of legitimizing the question of being, an archaeo-problem which, after all, does not seem to be settled. Everyone who speaks of being does so by presenting it in opposition to nothingness. I must admit, however, that I have never quite understood what Kant meant when he held that being was only a logical predicate and not a real predicate, with his example of the one hundred thalers. The logical predicate adds nothing to its subject, whereas the real predicate does add something since it takes us beyond the mere concept. Thus it seems that being must constitute a real predicate rather than a logical predicate.

Now, when we say that the square circle does not exist, we undeniably introduce the notion of nothingness. This means, in effect, that by virtue of its defining idea, the class of square circles cannot be represented by any member.

What I am going to say now will surely revive all the old problems. It seems to me that it could be said that being is the class of all classes which can be represented by members. In this interpretation, the notion of being would not be that of the class of all classes pure and simple, for in fact we know classes, such as that of square circles, which do not belong to being because they are not represented by any members. This is what gives birth to our problem, the question of being, which cannot be separated from that of nothingness.

I do not claim in the least to have provided a solution to this problem, but I have had the feeling that it was an old question which needed reawakening, because it has never been resolved.

MR. GABRIEL MARCEL: You bring up a difficulty, Mr. Patri, because with the example of the one hundred thalers you introduce the problem of existence.

I do not say that there is no relation between the problem of being and that of existence. In fact I am certain that such a relation does exist, but one cannot say that there is one thing that is being and another thing that is existence. That would be contrary to everything I have said today. In any case, I think that perhaps it would not be wise, given the point of view I have taken, to bring in these existential references.

MR. PATRI: Still, I think that ordinary language authorizes us to do so, because if we completely separate being from existence, philosophical language would entirely lose contact with that of the ordinary man.

MR. GABRIEL MARCEL: But surely we go far beyond ordinary language when we question ourselves about being.

I would like to consider for a moment what you said about nothingness. You referred to the quotation from Claudel. It is obvious that in a certain manner nothingness can indeed be considered as the ground on which being presents itself. On the other hand, we cannot disregard Bergson's critique, either.

I wonder if nothingness does not play a kind of intermediary and suspect role between two positions of being—an initial position and an ultimate one. Certainly I would be hesitant to grant nothingness any kind of primacy—in any case, I obviously cannot develop that possibility now. I do think that it is psychologically false, and metaphysically, I do not think it is at all tenable.

In other words, I do not think that one can seriously say that the problem of being involves a kind of priority for the problem of nothingness. I think that nothingness is a derivative problem.

MR. PATRI: I would say that from the moment we use the term "nothingness" in ordinary language, which means when we use negation, we opt, as it were, in favor of the legitimacy of the notion of nothingness. In order to do away with nothingness, we should have to manage to express ourselves in a language where there would be no negation. But with that we would be doing away with being as well as nothingness.

MR. GABRIEL MARCEL: I do not think that we can proceed quite so expeditiously.

MR. ALQUIÉ: I have a very brief question to ask Mr. Marcel. He has spoken of the problem of being as if it were a new problem. And in fact, many think that modern philosophy poses this problem of being in an entirely new way—new at least, by comparison with classical metaphysics.

I would simply like to ask Mr. Marcel whether he thinks that the various problems he has dealt with this evening are dealt with in essentially different terms by the classical philosophers. For I am very much struck by the fact, just to mention one thing, that a number of the words he has used have equivalents in the writings of the classical thinkers.

I am thinking, for example, of the word "substance," which horrifies everyone, and which has been banished by Mr. Marcel, by Mr. Goldmann, and by many others. But is not the word "foundation," which Mr. Marcel uses, equivalent to the word "substance"? And the problem of substance has been dealt with since ancient times. It is said that beneath extension, there is the extended thing; beneath thought, there is the thinking thing; and this thing, this *res* is substance.

Here, simply, is the question I wanted to ask. Does Mr. Marcel think that in modern philosophy there is a new way of posing the question of being? Or does he think that the classical philosophers posed the same question, in terms which mean essentially the same thing, even if they are slightly different?

MR. GABRIEL MARCEL: No, I am convinced that these are questions which have always, in some way, been present to all philosophers. We should probably have to begin by speaking of Plato, preferably, to my mind, the Plato of the *Sophistes* which I have not reread for some time, but which I am certain would reawaken in me the same admiration that it always has.

Now, when you say that after all "foundation" is "substance," that may be right. But I would say that there is an extremely important difference, namely that the word "substance" is so laden with what I have called "thingish" associations that it is no longer useful. Again, the word "foundation" is not at all satisfying. I would not want to propose that we adopt it. I used it, for better or for worse, to evoke something which it seems to me does not at all correspond to what was meant by Descartes. You, who know Descartes much better than I, could perhaps show us that Descartes himself was not free from these doubts.

But what seems to me important is not the word "foundation," which I used simply as an approximation, but rather what I meant, what I was seeking to indicate in a much more indirect way, when I spoke of a certain fundamental situation, and when I said that this fundamental situation could not be reified. And if I say that, it means discarding the word "substance," and still more definitively the word "absolute," proposed by Mr. Bénézé.

However, I think it would be absurd to pretend that there could be unrestricted innovation in this area. I think that the truth is exceptionally subtle here. We continually encounter the same problems because the problems are eternal. And it must immediately be added that such an inquiry is centered on the unsurpassable.

How often I have said, for example, that it is absurd to think we can surpass Plato! Yet it remains true that for reasons it is not so easy to enunciate, but which are felt, we are forced to deal with these same eternal problems, using our miserable personal resources, in a different context, with a different horizon. I think that even Heidegger, although he is often evasive and imprudent in this matter, would acknowledge that there is an unsurpassable. He makes no claim to go beyond Parmenides or Heraclitus.

In the last analysis, these are not the terms in which the question should be posed. For, in posing them thus, in my opinion, we are guilty of the extremely serious confusion of treating philosophical problems as if they were technical problems. There is no denying that there are technical problems which are absolutely new. The problems which today can be formulated in the field of electronics, for example, probably have no connection with many of the problems which were coming up only thirty years ago. So we have to acknowledge some absolutely new techniques, which themselves presuppose conceptual innovations. But I believe, and I want to say so, expressly, that it is terribly dangerous to liken the fundamental problems of metaphysics to technical problems.

Still, this does not mean that we can be content simply to

repeat what the greatest thinkers have said, even though we realize that we cannot go beyond them.

MR. GASTON BERGER: I would like to ask a question in order to be sure that I have grasped the originality of your thought.

Many philosophers, in different linguistic expressions, have spoken of a point of departure and a point of arrival; they have not, generally speaking, regarded their point of departure as the object of a perfectly clear intuition. In particular, I am thinking of Descartes, but also of many classical philosophers, and the expression "assurance" you used before seems to me entirely right. What we have at one end of the chain is the assurance of an insufficiency. At the other extremity, in what you call the pleroma, we have the assurance of a fulfillment, but a fulfillment which we lack.

MR. GABRIEL MARCEL: That is right.

MR. GASTON BERGER: What I think is characteristic of your thinking, contrary to what Mr. Goldmann was just saying, perhaps, is that you put the emphasis on itinerant thinking, and that the word "being" troubles you because it gives too much importance either to that point of departure which we do not grasp, or to the plenitude which we do not attain. You find that the most important activity of the spirit is in the interval which is actually being traversed, which is not purely relational. That is why you do not use the word "foundation" to suggest that your movement is resting on something. You mean it to designate a condition for explication, in our search for a formula which continually escapes us.

Thus, it seems to me that in your thought there is a kind of option offered between being, which would immediately be realized or given, and an existence which is in search of itself through a personal journey in which the emphasis is precisely on questioning. What is given is the question, even before it is known who is questioning, who must respond, and what the question is about; even before it is known what kind of satisfaction the question is going to provide.

What I discover, in listening to you, are persons "under way," persons who are questioning themselves, their interlocutors, and the situation in which both are immersed. It seems to me that the originality of your thought lies in bringing out this movement, whose extremes are only limits, so that you are not simply offering us the static view of two beings, one lacking and one perfect, which would have to be brought together.

MR. GABRIEL MARCEL: You have expressed my thought admirably, probably much better than I have done.

MR. MICHEL SOURIAU: I have had visits with Mr. Gabriel Marcel, conversations, in which we shared experiences of such a high order that I want to avoid at any cost giving the impression of attacking him. I want to make that clear, because my question may well seem like an attack, being necessarily so brief.

Here it is: I have had the impression that in proposing a purely interrogative thinking, on the one hand, and on the other, the idea of a kind of being which does not lend itself to intuition, you have situated the problem in the one perspective in which it could not possibly be resolved.

Interrogative thinking is a thinking which is always questioning, which questions by definition, like the child who says "Why won't you give me that?" "Because it is not good for you." "And why isn't it good for me?" And so forth: there is no end to it. As you have said, interrogative thinking will always be insinuating itself into its own object, from inquiry to inquiry.

With regard to being, I was surprised to read your statement that you acknowledge no intuition of being. I think that if there were never an intuition of being, it would be better never to speak of being. I think that after all it is only by a kind of intuition that we know being.

If we deny to interrogative thinking the right to make affirmations, if we reject the possibility of an intuition of being, we shall never be able to confront the two sides of the problem.

And I wonder whether you did not have some mental reservations about saying that philosophy cannot resolve the question, so that it is necessary to turn elsewhere.

MR. GABRIEL MARCEL: Not really. Philosophy, as I conceive it, is straining toward something beyond itself, that is absolutely certain. But this does not mean that we can neglect the advisory role of philosophy. On the contrary, I believe it is extraordinarily important, and I would say that those who claim to give answers without philosophical preparation can, in many cases, fall into the most serious error and illusion.

5 / Truth and Freedom

THE TITLE I HAVE GIVEN this study may at first cause some surprise. These two words, truth and freedom, are not one of those inseparable pairs we are accustomed to meeting in ethical and philosophical writings. But for the purposes of an investigation such as I intend to carry out here, I think this freshness is a good thing. Let me illustrate what I mean by an analogy, for something very similar to what I have in mind happens in the physical world. An electric current travels only between two elements of different charges. Anyone who is given to the practice of reflection knows that there are also currents in thought, though of course it is not easy to specify their exact nature. Now as is so often the case, it will be best here to proceed negatively. What in thinking would be the opposite of a current? It would be a kind of lifelessness very much like what we find in stagnant water. But in thinking the stagnation is very often hidden by a surface movement of words, or, what amounts to the same thing, by ready-made ideas which are no longer really thoughts. We constantly find this sort of thing with professional speakers and also too often, I am afraid, with preachers. Sentences are strung together in a merely mechanical way, out of habit. Whereas the current of thinking, on the contrary, begins to move only when the mind develops a certain power of invention or creativity.

In this particular case, if I fix my attention on the two words "truth" and "freedom," I feel no temptation to give in to the laziness of noticing only those connections between the two indicated by old habits of thinking, no temptation to simply run through some effortless mental routine.

Originally I had planned to discuss simply the distinction between true and false freedom, and of course I would still want to
draw attention to this distinction. But on reflection it seems to
me that I must raise my sights and search to see whether there is
not a certain intimate and hidden relationship between truth
and freedom themselves. To do this it is clear that I first have to
deal adequately with these two notions individually, lest they
lack the vitality they ought to display.

As for the notion of freedom, the problem lies in its ambiguous character. Obviously freedom means something quite different depending on whether it is discussed in a political or social
context, for example, or in an ethical or metaphysical one.

At first glance, perhaps, there does not seem to be the same
difficulty with the term "truth." Reflection shows, however, that
this is also an idea with many different meanings. For example,
I want to consider truth above all insofar as it is a value. But
when we speak of truth as a value do we mean truth as such?
Surely if, rightly or wrongly, we represent truth as something
which is *there* independent of whether it is recognized or not,
it will be very difficult to see it as a value. But I would question
whether truth ought to be thought of in this way, whether such a
conception does not perhaps involve a wholly illegitimate objectification of something which is essentially nonobjective.

In line with my usual procedure, rather than beginning with
an abstract analysis of an idea, I shall take a concrete example
rooted in contemporary history and try to see what light this
example can shed on the problem at hand. In fact I would say
that it was probably this example (though I cannot say for sure)
that originally provoked my reflection on the relationship between
truth and freedom.

I am thinking here of two related things which were forced on
my attention during the events in Poland and Hungary in 1956.
Jeanne Hersch, who is perhaps the most remarkable student of
Karl Jaspers and the author of a very important book entitled
Idéologie et réalité, attended the trial of Poznan; she knows the
Polish language perfectly. When she returned she unhesitatingly
asserted in a Paris interview that the revolt of Poznan was above
all a reaction to the lies promulgated by the government and a
subservient press.

A few weeks later I had occasion to speak with a diplomat
who was the French consul in Budapest from 1948 to 1956. His
report is similar to that of Jeanne Hersch. What the Hungarians

could no longer put up with, he told me, were the continual, systematic lies published in the official press on such subjects as, for example, the economic situation of the country. Here and there, consequently, the people began to rise up against the lying. But in the name of what? That is the important question, but it is a question which is not easy to answer precisely. In the particular case of Hungary it is probably necessary to resist the temptation to bring in here some "ism" such as socialism, liberalism, or the like, to indicate what might have served as a revolutionary "program." It is probable that in this case, as in many others, the very idea of a program is to a certain extent fallacious. It corresponds to the way one tries, after the fact and from without, to imagine a certain movement in which one has not participated. There is no doubt whatever that the Hungarian revolutionaries knew infinitely better what they did not want at any price, what they refused with all their being, than what they positively wanted to bring about in putting an end to an abhorred regime. The one point on which they were probably all in agreement was that they wanted to get rid of an occupying force they hated.

But does this clarify in any way the role played by truth as a value in such a situation? In other words, can we now grasp, without becoming the victim of words, some positive counterpart to this vital protest against the lie which in a few days transformed a capital city into a battlefield? I would say that this counterpart, which can only be an inner demand so profound that it is not given directly and clearly to our gaze, is the will to be recognized. It is this will which is violated each time a person is humiliated. No writer has understood this better than Dostoevski: he was able to portray admirably not only the hidden wound suffered by the humiliated person, but also the way this wound can become infected to the point of endangering others.

Surely the lies which were cynically paraded in the official Polish and Hungarian press could not help but be felt as an offense by those who were supposed to accept them day after day. And this offense can be expressed in the simple, indignant question: "What do you take us for?" Here we have penetrated, as if by a shortcut, into the interior of a kind of dense and mammoth forest which I should like to explore.

What I just called the "will to be recognized" will appear to us, if we reflect attentively, as closely allied to truth, provided that we manage to get away from objectifying interpretations of the kind I rejected above. Once again, everything is lost if we confuse truth with fact, and we can see this clearly if we take the trouble to look carefully at that recognition so cynically refused his victims by the tyrant. I say "the tyrant," but it goes without saying that tyranny may be practiced not only by an individual but by a group—a group, moreover, whose members are not always easy to identify.

But what is actually denied the individual in such a situation? It is nothing factual, nothing which could be entered on a computer card, in a police record, or in a dossier in the basement of some station house or government agency. Rather it is a certain quality essential to self-respect. Why is it denied him? Nothing could be clearer: the tyrant wants to transform the individual into a simple instrument which can in no way oppose his oppressive designs. Here one sees the hideous purpose of the techniques used to obtain false confessions from accused persons. These counterfeit confessions are designed precisely to destroy *from within* men who only yesterday were adversaries and now must be reduced to mere tools. Observe that these techniques presuppose an immeasurable contempt for human reality, an unshakable belief that a man can simply be forged as a blacksmith forges soft metal until he becomes *inwardly* incapable of showing any resistance to the will of the tyrant. *"Inwardly,"* I say, but I am not really sure I have the right to use this word here. What actually seems to happen is rather that all inwardness is suppressed, almost as a cocoon is emptied of its contents, so that the victim can subsequently be "refilled" by the will of the master. Here we are actually in the presence of a slavery harder and more implacable than any that has ever been imagined and practiced.

I want to emphasize and try to clarify certain connections here, whose importance is decisive for our study. First of all, let me insist on this: To persist in killing the sense of truth in a man is to attack directly his respect for himself. A morally healthy person is horrified by lying because he regards it as a defilement. Even if I know that my lie will not be found out, I will refuse to lie because I care about preserving my inner integrity. These words must be taken literally—in a way I am my own room or house, where I want a certain order and decency to prevail. But these words "order" and "decency" serve as concrete approaches to the term "truth" in its existential sense, that is, insofar as it affects me as a living reality.

From this same point of view, if we think for example of the representatives of a subservient press in a totalitarian country, we see clearly that these people are, in the deepest sense of the word, alienated. They are morally or spiritually *heimatlos* (homeless). It is also interesting to observe that to a certain extent there is a parallel here between the material situation of an exiled or deported person and the spiritual condition I am trying to describe. There is no doubt that an exile of either kind can much more easily become a tool in the hands of a tyrant.

I think we can now see that there is a whole set of concrete conditions which we commonly call freedom, without always having a perfectly clear idea of what we mean by this name. In any case it is clear that we have to guard ourselves against the primitive idea that a free man is a completely independent man. This would be a purely abstract view which has no basis in actual experience. If we look at what we call a citizen of a free country, we notice that he is subjected to all kinds of obligations—taxes, the military, and so forth. These obligations are part of what it means to be a citizen, and it would be generally agreed that if a man tried to evade them he could do so only in the name of a false or at least childish notion of freedom. It must be added that a country can remain free only if its citizens live up to their obligations. Thus it must be acknowledged that Kant was perfectly right to establish an inner connection between "obligation" and "freedom," in opposition to a purely anarchical theory which identifies obligation with constraint. Of course we must also be on guard against certain overly optimistic simplifications. Certainly the taxpayer feels that having to pay so much is a constraint, which is why he is so often tempted to cheat on his taxes. We might say that a citizen, to the extent that he is conscious of what his citizenship implies, tends to ignore as much as possible this feeling of constraint and to recognize that he cannot flee this obligation, however painful it is, without endangering the community to which he belongs and which, after all, lets him be what he is. This is a very difficult position to maintain, of course, and there are many ways it can be compromised. This is not the place to enter into the extraordinarily complex detail of the questions raised by life in a democracy. But it is necessary—and I mean philosophically necessary—to recognize this complexity and to underscore the dangerous illusions one risks by persisting in an optimism constantly refuted by politcial experience.

It is certain that at every level, whether that of relations between individuals or of relations between nations, the notion of independence appears incompatible with the actual conditions of civilized existence. But we have to ask ourselves how this ties in with what I said earlier about the relationship between truth and self-respect, and for that I shall have to deal more directly with the very notion of a "free man."

In the first place I think it is essential to do away once and for all with the idea that freedom might be some global attribute which could be affirmed or denied of a particular individual or of man in general. To see why I insist on this, simply ask yourself this question: Am I or am I not a free man? You will see immediately that, formulated in such terms, this question really has no precise meaning. Could I at least answer categorically the question whether some particular act of mine has been free or not? Here we must resolutely steer clear of certain prejudices, linked to a wrong-headed manner of doing philosophy, which would consist in thinking that an act is more free the less it is motivated. Beginning in literature, but then spreading into a certain philosophy as well, we find the greatly suspect idea of what André Gide in *The Counterfeiters* has called the "gratuitous act," the act performed not only without constraint or pressure of any kind, but simply "for the fun of it," arbitrarily, as if to prove to oneself that one is free. We also see an example of this in Gide's novel *The Vatican Cellars*, where the protagonist pushes a traveling companion he doesn't even know out of a moving train simply because he thinks it will be amusing.

Here we are in fact at the very heart of what I earlier called "false freedom." For the gratuitous act is by definition empty of any meaning, wholly irresponsible; but that does not prevent it from indulging in the most deceptive pretension of all—that of claiming to be real and free precisely because of its irresponsibility. The absurdity here lies in thinking that an act is more free the less it is motivated, whereas what really matters for freedom is the proper quality of motivation. Let us take a clear example. Imagine a man being intimidated by a blackmailer demanding a large sum of money in exchange for not revealing some circumstance in his life which for some reason he has always kept secret. Here we have a coercion exactly analogous to that which a robber practices on the lone pedestrian he threatens with a gun. Suppose that the blackmailer succeeds in his designs, and the victim gives him the money he demands. It is perfectly clear that this capitulation out of fear can in no way be considered a free act. I would even go so far as to say that in the final analysis it is perhaps not an act at all but rather a mode of passivity which merely has the external appearance of an act. A true act, and this applies to the free act as well, is always situated between two extremes: on the one hand the gratuitous act or, more generally, the insignificant, meaningless act performed without knowing why; and on the other hand the passivity we see in people who are the victims of some fascination, as is the case for example with the gambler, the alcoholic, the drug addict. The terrified holdup victim is perhaps very much like a drugged man. Thus freedom can be defined negatively as the absence of any form of self-alienation. But this can be expressed positively as well: I act freely if the motives of my act are in line with what I can legitimately regard as the structural features of my personality.

However, this needs further clarification, for the word "personality" is still somewhat ambiguous. It is obvious that here it does not mean temperament, nor even character if by character is meant some sort of individual stamp. Here I take as identical the notions personality and person; and I have already tried elsewhere to show that "person is defined above all by its opposition to the sort of anonymous and irresponsible phenomenon designated by the French word *on* or the German word *man*."[1] It is unfortunate that in English the common rendering of this idea is in the word "one," which is terribly ambiguous and in its ordinary usage often means "one of them," which is what the French mean when they say *un* or *l'un*. The indefinite *they* is another frequent English rendering.

Heidegger, in a collection of what I consider to be invaluable analyses, has shown convincingly that the use of this "one" [*on*] is a sign of degraded thinking, but that nonetheless we are all not only surrounded by such thinking but pervaded by it. Most of the time our opinions are nothing but a reflection of the "one" ("they") in an "I" who doesn't know that he is being a reflector. Thus this "one" or "they" is by definition beyond our grasp and impossible to pin down. For example: a rumor is

1. *Du Refus a l'invocation* (Paris: Gallimard, 1940), pp. 146–47; my translation. Cf. the English translation by Robert Rosthal, *Creative Fidelity* (New York: Farrar, Straus & Giroux, 1964), pp. 110, 111.

circulating about a certain person. I ask "Who says that? Who claims that?" I am told simply, "I can't tell you, but 'they' say.
. . ."

The mark of a person is precisely that he sets himself radically against this vague "they." It is characteristic of the person to expose himself, to commit himself, to engage in confrontation. Thus courage appears as the virtue essential to personhood, whereas the "they" appears as the place of flight or evasion. Here courage is above all looking at things as they are; it is opposed to fakery and cheating of all kinds. But as we have seen at the beginning of this investigation, the slave is condemned to fake and cheat. Those of us who have suffered enemy occupation have only to recall the ruses of every kind we were forced to employ because of the presence of the enemy on our soil, and how those ruses appeared not only as excusable but simply as required, as obligations. We see that every enemy occupation is a school of immorality.

We have also seen that where a totalitarian dictator holds absolute sway, the subjugation of the slave is such that he finally ends up incapable even of deceit or trickery. He no longer has even enough inner reality to know how to deceive, and thus he is annihilated.

The various paths of thought I have been exploring are now coming together. It appears that a man can be a person, and thus a free man, only to the extent that he becomes involved, engages in confrontation. And it appears also that what he is called on to confront is precisely *truth*. But we must look at all this more closely.

The connection between courage and freedom does not seem at first to be seriously problematic. At least most people would agree that a coward could not in any way be regarded a free man. This assertion, however, would certainly draw an objection from those I alluded to above, and patricularly from someone like Sartre. For such people freedom is identified with what they call choice. They contend that our condition obliges us perpetually to choose, and Sartre goes so far as to say we are condemned to choose. This view goes back to a metaphysical position whose details I cannot deal with here but which consists in setting up a kind of Hegelian opposition between being-for-itself and being-in-itself, in which being-for-itself is characterized by a principle of negation or "nihilation" without which consciousness itself could not be. This is not the place to criticize this metaphysical theory which, as ingenious as it is, leads to contradiction, as even Sartre seems to have recognized in the conclusion of his great work. Still he would probably not hesitate to say that the coward has chosen to be a coward and that therefore he remains free even through the worst violation of himself. But in my opinion this is a wholly artificial and untenable interpretation. I think that the real opposition is between the man who tries to make himself more and more responsible, and the man who gives up, who wastes himself, and in the last analysis dehumanizes himself. And can it be denied that cowardice is precisely a way of giving up, while courage is essentially positive? The courageous man is the one who tries to live up to a certain image or idea of himself, and perhaps of mankind in general.

Returning to the other relationship we were considering— the relationship between courage and truth—it appears at first sight much more problematic, and no doubt it would be helpful here to introduce a preliminary distinction. There is—or at least we ordinarily think there is—a physical courage which even the animals may have and which seems to be identical with the force or tenacity with which one defends himself or those who are closely related to him, such as his wife and children, against hostile forces. Actually it is not so certain that we are right to use the word "courage" here; perhaps this word is appropriate only where there is complete consciousness of danger, especially of the threat of death. But here we are entering an area where ideas begin to lose their distinctness. I have often said that the word "consciousness" is dangerously equivocal, because it seems to imply self-consciousness. In the English language there is a much better word: "awareness." The faculty of awareness does not in any way seem to be denied to the animal, though the ability to be aware of oneself through reflective consciousness, whatever that is, does not seem to belong to animals. Thus we ought to ask ourselves whether there can be "awareness" of danger or of possible death for an animal, and it certainly does seem so, for an animal is surely subject to fear.

I think it will be well to keep these remarks in mind as we take up an objection which might be raised against the idea of an inner connection between courage and truth. Have we not seen in Germany, for example, an entirely fanaticized young generation, whose courage was undeniable, yet who threw themselves wholeheartedly into the service of a cause that would have to be considered to involve the worst errors? Thus we are seemingly faced with the following dilemma: either we violate the term "truth" in applying it to an abominable cause or doctrine, or else we must acknowledge that courage may be indifferently put to the service of either truth or error. Incidentally, this word "error" does not wholly satisfy me here. I would prefer something like "moral heresy." But in any case it does seem undeniable that a fanatical heretic can be absolutely courageous.

Perhaps making a distinction between physical and moral courage will allow us to escape this dilemma. It may be that the physical courage of the SS, for example, rested after all on a profound intellectual and moral cowardice. But then it is the nature of this cowardice that we must bring to light. What makes such a task difficult is that we almost inevitably think of physical cowardice when we hear the word "cowardice"— cowardice in the face of death, for example. Let me illustrate what I have in mind by reproducing a short passage from one of my plays, *Le Dard*. It might not be a bad thing to bring a very concrete illustration of this kind into these quite abstract reflections.

One of the principal characters of this play is an academic of very modest origins and means. He has been successful in his studies, but above all he has had the good fortune to marry into an influential bourgeois family. His father-in-law, a well-known parliamentarian, is completely at ease with him. But the character, Eustache Soreau, suffers from a bad conscience. It is as if he were ashamed of having lost contact, through his social success, with the world of the simple people which used to be his own. He becomes embittered by success, a resentful man. His wife Beatrice suffers painfully from this situation, and she ends up confiding in a friend of Eustache, Werner Schnee. Schnee is a singer, a refugee who has left Nazi Germany to rejoin his accompanist and friend, a Jewish pianist who has been treated very badly and is later to die in a Swiss sanitarium. But Schnee is unaware of the frustrations troubling Eustache. Eustache, Beatrice tells him, is an extremely scrupulous man. He is convinced that comfort, a certain kind of easy living, dulls the conscience. Werner claims that what Eustache believes to be his conscience is perhaps nothing but a kind of fear. Beatrice protests: "You know very well that Eustache is courageous." "I agree," answers Werner, "but that word has more than one meaning. One can be brave in the face of poverty, in the face of danger, in the face of death, and yet not in the face of judgment."

"What judgment?" asks Beatrice. "It is hard to say. I think that it is a number of things blended together. Perhaps the idea that what he is depends on the judgment of other people. But this idea itself comes from him. He thinks that he scorns the opinion of others and that he has nothing to reproach himself for. But it is as if . . ." [2] Werner breaks off here. But I think that the decisive ending of his last sentence would be this: ". . . one can be brave in the face of death but not in the face of judgment." And here judgment is identical with truth, or more profoundly, with the universal.

But here of course I should repeat the warning I have been making periodically for a quarter of a century: the disastrous mistake men are most tempted to make today is to think of the universal as a function of the masses. This is the confusion Ibsen denounced in *An Enemy of the People* with an enthusiasm that has never been outdone. I cannot refrain from remarking here that when my father read me this play—it must have been in 1898 or 1899—it left a disturbing impression that has had repercussions throughout my life. This is a personal matter, but it does seem pertinent, especially since the commentators on my work seem most often to underestimate the autobiographical aspect in the history of my thought.

Recently as I was reading the excellent lectures given in December, 1967, at Cambridge University by Iris Murdoch, it came to me that in spite of everything that separates me from her agnosticism, something very deep inside me says yes to her Platonic views on the good, on virtue, and on courage.

2. Gabriel Marcel, *Le Dard* (Paris: Plon, 1950); my translation.

6 / Truth and Concrete Situations

A PHILOSOPHY PROFESSOR from the Sorbonne, in the course of a television broadcast designed to orientate young professors, declared that the notion of truth had no specifiable meaning except in the area of scientific thought. This would be tantamount to saying that the values evoked by the moralist or the aesthetician are radically separate from what must be called truth. It would inevitably come down to locating those values in the domain of pure subjectivity—a subjectivity which certainly has nothing to do with that defined by Kierkegaard, but which on the contrary would imply an arbitrariness which could take different forms according to whether one placed oneself in the framework of psychology or of sociology.

But should we not precisely call into question so narrow a way of conceiving truth? The method I intend to follow consists, as always, in beginning from an experience in the broad sense, a sense which goes beyond that employed by traditional empiricism.

In *The Mystery of Being* I tried to bring to light what we mean when we say that someone is or is not "in truth" [*dans la vérité*]. To say that someone is in truth or in error is seemingly to express oneself as if truth or error were comparable to an atmosphere in which the mind, and not the body, were somehow enveloped. I would like to begin now with a particular case which offers what I regard as the great advantage of leading us to distinguish between *being* in truth and *telling* the truth.

Imagine a doctor who has discovered by way of laboratory analysis that his patient is condemned to die in a very short time.

This sick man, who does not know the laboratory results, has asked the doctor to tell him the truth about his condition, whatever it is. But let us say that the doctor is gifted with a certain acuity in psychology which permits him to understand that his patient, if he learns of the short time he has to live, will have his last months or weeks poisoned by anxiety. With that, what should the attitude of the doctor be? Is he not bound to mitigate this cruel truth, to say, for example, "Your state is doubtless very serious, but you have some chance of pulling through"?

We must notice carefully here, as in every other case, the meaning of the words "concrete situation." It is not a question of considering the doctor-patient relationship in its generality, but rather the relation between the doctor and a particular sick person. You will notice that I refrain from saying a particular doctor, for we have to suppose the idea of a medical vocation which is not limited to this particular doctor. But this vocation precisely implies the absolute duty of taking into consideration the singularity of the patient.

It is obvious, however, that what has just been said still involves a simplification. Let us suppose that the sick man is a believer, concerned for his salvation. This is something the doctor cannot dismiss from his consideration. It is possible that the sick man might truly be animated with the desire to settle his accounts with God, and let us say also with his conscience, before he dies. The doctor will be faced with a very difficult, very embarrassing question in deciding whether in his behavior toward the sick man he ought to give priority to easing his ordeal (what is left of it to live) in whatever measure possible, or on the contrary to consider as primarily important the religious aspect of the situation. Let us note that on this point it is no longer the vocation of the doctor as doctor that comes into play, but rather almost inevitably the personality of the doctor, the fact that he himself is or is not a believer. And this will be true no matter what efforts he might very honestly make to abstract himself from his personal point of view.

What we see distinctly here is that the words "being in truth" are applied to a way of being or of acting which is essentially loyal—loyal toward oneself and loyal toward the other—but which can legitimately remain marked by an uncertainty.

Let us remain in the concrete. The doctor will have to call on one of the relatives if possible, but it will not always be easy for him to discern, for example, which member of the family he must confide in and ask advice of. Here again, a faculty of appreciation will have to be exercised which in itself is not of the medical order. It might be desirable for him to contact the priest or pastor whom his patient ordinarily sees and consults. But here too, what difficulties are possible! Who is to guarantee that this priest or this pastor is a sensible man, sufficiently discerning?

What appears to me very important is to notice that here, as is so often the case, seeing what it is to be in error is easier than knowing exactly what it is to be in truth. To attach oneself exclusively to one aspect of the situation, neglecting the others, will certainly mean being in error. But on the other hand, one might fear that if our doctor weighs the opposing arguments too scrupulously, he will remain in a kind of suspension without making any decision. And in fact *not to decide* can be a hypocritical way of deciding negatively. This is something that seems to me important for our purposes. Would it not have to be said in fact that cowardice, which is expressed here by the refusal to choose, is in a certain way flight before truth?

This will be clarified, I think, if we become distinctly aware of the relation, actually very complex, that links subject and situation. On the one hand, it is clear that the situation is presented as being offered to the subject, and that it is offered to him in order to be overcome. Moreover it is this overcoming that matters. But on the other hand, it must be emphasized that the subject is caught up in the situation, is implicated in it almost exactly in the sense in which it could be said that someone is implicated in an affair of some kind. It is in this second perspective that it is possible to give a meaning to the expression "false situation." And here again I will immediately give an example, as I am persuaded that in order not to lose ourselves in words we must always illustrate our thoughts concretely.

The example which comes first to my mind is very simple. Suppose that I have a friendly acquaintance with both the wife and the mistress of one of my friends. Each of the two women confides in me and speaks to me freely of the other. In such circumstances, how could I fail to experience a painful feeling of duplicity? What increases this feeling is the fact that the wife does not know that I know the mistress. I find myself thus in a false situation—a situation which must be overcome. It seems at first that the solution lies in my saying frankly to the wife, for example, that I have a friendly relationship with the mistress.

But by that it is probable that I will create a new situation no less painful than the first. For the wife would reproach me for this friendship, and would no doubt demand that I make a choice. But it may be that I have some humane reasons for not wanting to make a choice. I may feel that in remaining the confidant, the advisor of these two women, I can have a beneficial influence on them.

I will limit myself to saying that the mark of the false situation is precisely the fact that one cannot get out of it without there being ruinous consequences. This, as I shall show further on, is particularly apparent in the domain of international politics. False situations have continued to multiply in the world, whence the horrible imbroglio in which all the powers find themselves implicated today. But, remaining for the moment in the area of private relations, I would like to develop a much more complex example taken from my play *A Man of God*.[1]

The minister Claude Lemoine, a few years after his marriage, has learned from his wife Edmée that she has betrayed him with a certain Michel Sandier, and that this man is the father of their daughter, Osmonde. The pastor has forgiven her, and since then everything appears to have returned to order. Edmée has proven to be a dutiful wife, and the daughter has grown up suspecting nothing of the truth. She is now twenty years old. But now the lover, Michel, knowing that he is afflicted with an incurable illness, asks to see his daughter once before he dies. With that a new situation is created, calling for a decision. Claude does not believe he has the right to deny Michel's request, which appears to him legitimate. Moreover it seems to him that his consent will only be, after all, the corollary of his earlier forgiveness. But Edmée, on the contrary, is revolted by the coolness her husband shows in this circumstance. And his unexpected calm serves to reinforce in her a retrospective suspicion. What really was the value or the import of the forgiveness she received? Was it not simply a professional act which cost almost nothing to the minister Claude, who actually forgave only because he was incapable of loving like a man? Thus it is not only Claude's *act* which is put in question, but his very *being*, and in the end Edmée's accusation finds an echo deep in the soul of Claude, who literally no longer knows *who* he is.

1. In Gabriel Marcel, *Three Plays* (New York: Hill and Wang, 1965).

Now where is the truth in all this? Let us recall what has been said above. The situation calls for a certain overcoming or surpassing. A philosopher of the old school would probably say that what is necessary is that the two spouses, eschewing any kind of self-questioning, agree to act charitably toward the unfortunate Sandier. But it is too clear that this response or solution, even if it is reasonable, does not reach the level of existence, and thus can have no hold on these two beings who are battered by existence itself. Indeed, the development of the play moves toward discovering or rather establishing this truth. But for that to happen, the process of destruction will have to be pushed to the limit, with the wife Edmée being forced also to put herself in question. For her former lover does not hide from Edmée the fact that he despises her for having been a coward, for having fled when he offered to take her away with him. But then what right has she to reproach her husband? Is she not as weak as he? And so now they both stand shivering in a kind of moral nakedness, having stripped themselves of all self-deception.

What appears to me interesting to note is that we are here beyond lucidity. Lucidity reduced to itself is without doubt insufficient to establish a truth. Joined to it must be mutual compassion, and also humility, without which compassion is undoubtedly impossible. Where pride reigns there is no room for mercy. An example like this, to which many others could be added, helps us to better understand that truth on the existential level cannot depend exclusively on intellectual processes. Something else must be added, something belonging to the soul.

I said earlier that in my opinion international problems provided especially significant material for an investigation of the kind we are undertaking here. Recent history offers us some examples on which one cannot meditate too much.

I have in mind, for instance, the situation in which the leaders of the French and English governments found themselves early in 1936 when they were warned by a secret agent that Germany, contrary to the stipulations of the Treaty of Versailles, was preparing to invade the left bank of the Rhine. For Hitler this was truly a roll of the dice; the German headquarters considered the undertaking wholly imprudent. Today it appears clear that military reaction was indispensable in such a situation. But thanks to a kind of blindness, which contained a good deal of cowardice, the occasion was not taken; the future would show that there would not be another. In my opinion, reflection on history shows us very clearly that the passing of events is much like a train journey. In both cases there are moments when one can and must make a choice, just as when there is a stop at a junction. If you miss your stop, you may have to go two hundred miles before you can get off and purchase a return ticket. What loss of time! What useless expense! But in the case of events it may happen that a return is impossible, that the occasion is irretrievably lost. It seems to me that that is just what happened with regard to Hitler's Germany. What we needed in 1936 were leaders who had the lucidity and courage of the surgeon who declares that right now is the moment to operate: yesterday would have been too early, for the abcess was not ripe, but tomorrow would be too late, would bring on the chance of widespread infection.

The result of our leaders' disastrous abstention was that when the crisis in Czechoslovakia came it was too late to react, especially since after the *Anschluss* the Czech military defenses were crushed. Thus I think that those who opposed the Munich agreements were wrong in appearing to believe that the situation in 1938 still allowed for the military reaction which had been possible and even necessary in 1936. This was to forget the irreversible character of the historical process. On the other hand, the joy and relief which welcomed these agreements was simply scandalous. For it was essential to recognize that the Allies had betrayed their commitments, betrayed the confidence the Czechs had placed in them. As for me, I recall having felt distinctly that we ought to be deeply ashamed for this treason.

Here it can be very clearly seen—doubtless more clearly than in the preceding examples—just what the necessary overcoming would be: for France and England it was a matter of working without respite in order to be ready when the supreme test could no longer be avoided. Unfortunately that is not what happened, since the French government placed so much undue confidence in the defense known as the Maginot Line. I remember the excellent letter one of my relatives wrote to President Daladier at that time, to tell him that the capitulation at Munich could be excused, if not justified, only on the condition that the most sustained efforts be demanded from the French from then on. But this appeal was not heard.

Everything that has just been said appears to me hardly contestable. Yet I can very well imagine that a reader might make the following objection: "Have you the right," he will no doubt ask me, "to use the term truth in a case such as the one you were just discussing?"

Let me return to my example. I said that in 1936 an occasion had been lost which would never again be retrieved. But this word "occasion" is neutral. One can imagine bandits lying in wait for the occasion which would permit them to work their mischief with a minimum of risk. In what conditions, then, can we establish a connection between occasion and truth, such that to miss the occasion would amount to being on the side of error? I would say that in this perspective the case of Hitlerism appears privileged in a certain way. For Hitler's enterprise was directed against what could be called human order, or the human community considered in its universality. Consequently the occasion, the *kairos,* here takes on a positive value, since it designates the possibility of stopping short an enterprise founded on contempt for all right. It might also be added that the inertia shown by the governments of London and Paris in these circumstances implies the cowardice and blindness I spoke of above. It is at this point that one can best appreciate that virtue of courage in the service of truth which is perhaps at the core of any ethic worthy of the name. Experience shows, moreover, that too often the fear of risk leads to an indefinite increase of risk, to the point where it becomes the certitude of losing.

Some analogous remarks could be made with regard to the hesitations shown by England's leaders at the end of July, 1914. Fear of getting involved helped to create a situation in which absolute involvement became an unavoidable necessity. If Sir Edward Grey had warned William II at the very beginning of the crisis, through the intermediary of Prince Lichnovski, that there was every chance England could not remain neutral in case of conflict, this information would almost certainly have helped to prevent the war. Does this mean that Sir Edward Grey was chiefly responsible here? I do not believe so, for he could not arrogate to himself the right to engage the entire British cabinet in a commitment when he knew that its members, of which he was one, were divided among themselves on this matter. Rather it would be appropriate to blame members of the cabinet like John Morley, for example, who were opposed to the intervention. Their fault, as is always the case, consisted in an erroneous appreciation of the situation of Europe at that moment. The aversion which Morley and many Liberals felt toward Russia perhaps led them to minimize the danger represented by German imperialism.

I do not at all mean to say that Russia herself was beyond reproach in this crisis. She certainly mobilized much too soon. But to be fair it must be added immediately that Poincaré, along with his ambassador to Saint Petersburg, Paléologue, showed themselves to be imprudent at least. Poincaré should certainly have spoken to the tsar to urge him to moderation. But it seems that in fact he promised Russia unconditional support in the Serbian crisis, which was not at all implied in the terms of the treaty. It is no wonder Nicholas II believed that France would certainly be with him. It is impossible not to ask oneself here whether at heart Poincaré, who probably believed that war between France and Germany was inevitable sooner or later anyway, did not think that now the occasion was in every way favorable for what would become a war of revenge permitting France to win back the territory lost in 1871.

But now, within the framework of my foregoing explanations, I would like to show the difference between these two "occasions," that of 1914 and that of 1936.

I said that in 1936 it was a question of bringing to a halt an enterprise spelling disaster for the human community, even in fact for the German people who found themselves implicated in the enterprise. Let us thus admit that military operations should have been launched by France and England against Germany in 1936. They would almost certainly have put a stop to Hitler's adventure. But it appears evident to me that there is an essential difference between such operations and a war of reconquest breaking out more than fifty years after the Frankfurt treaty. And this difference must be affirmed even if one judges, as I do, that Germany committed a grave injustice in tearing Alsace-Lorraine away from France. To demonstrate this difference, moreover, it is sufficient to note that no French leader, not even Poincaré, would have dared to take the initiative of actually declaring this war of reconquest. All he could do was to hope for a provocation from Germany so that the war would appear as simple retaliation. But the fact that it was necessary to settle for such indirect procedures is enough to show that at the beginning of the century the time had come when a war of revenge undertaken without provocation would be considered a war of aggression. I shall not insist further, but will limit myself to saying that in the light of the documents it appears today that the war of 1914 was born of a situation harboring infinitely more confusion and varied responsibilities than was believed by those who, perhaps in good faith, thought that right was entirely on one side. We see today that this war was actually the first phase of the suicide of Europe.

It would be well, however, to examine carefully a question which may arise in the mind of the reader. Is there not something arbitrary in establishing an a priori correlation between truth and universality and then concluding from this that truth was necessarily on the side of those who opposed Hitler's enterprise? I think it must be answered first of all that in the scientific domain the separation of truth and universality is of no practical use. We must add immediately however that here it is a question of a *de jure* universality, and not necessarily a *de facto* one. It is thus that Galileo for example was right, and his adversaries wrong, even though their number was greater. And so it is with every true pioneer. But unfortunately in the domain of international relations the worst confusion tends to be established between these two types of universality, for here numerical considerations intervene to confound all wisdom. You may suspect that I am referring to the strange arithmetic which prevails in the United Nations, when a people from middle Africa, newly promoted to independence, has the same voting rights as a great power. I am not unaware of the practical reasons for which this obviously absurd equality has been instituted. They are clearly negative reasons, however. In establishing differences there would have been such conflicts that the organization would simply have become chaos. But perhaps, I would even say probably, the future will show that this equality also leads to chaos.

Actually the only justification for this odd arithmetic would consist in saying that with large numbers the upsetting factors involved in each particular case tend to be neutralized, and that thus there is the probability that a kind of good common sense would prevail in the end. But that is a theoretical argument which experience shows us does not at all work out in practice, for it does not take account of one central fact, namely, the seductive allure of collective action. Recent experience shows that in a very great number of diplomatic questions the Afro-Asian bloc, for example, votes unanimously. But this unanimity does not in any degree constitute a sign of wisdom or of truth. I am afraid that on the contrary it very often is on the side of error.

Here however the problem at the heart of all these reflections again arises in a disquieting way. I just spoke of error and truth. Yet these words have meaning only where one can speak of a *de jure* universality. Now who will be qualified to recognize this universality?

I think that here we must introduce some distinctions without which one falls into the worst confusion. First of all, certain facts can be established by means of statistical investigations, especially perhaps in the areas of economics and demography. Let us take the present situation in India, for example. It could be shown in a convincing and objective way that the increasing growth rate of the population must lead within a few years to a catastrophic situation, such as already exists in certain areas of that huge country. This, if you wish, is a truth which can be brought to light by experts. But this truth has an abstract and almost sterile character, for what matters, as we have already seen in other examples, is to find a way of overcoming this catastrophic situation. The experts I referred to will doubtless not hesitate to recommend the massive use of contraceptives. But it is just at this point that the most serious difficulties arise, and the experts are shown to be incapable of dealing with them. For here it is a question of human beings, and one cannot forcibly impose such measures on them the way one imposes, for example, a vaccination (although I would remark that even in the case of vaccination the same problem exists). It is a fact that up to now the vast majority of India's population has rejected the use of contraceptives. That puts our experts in a most embarrassing situation; and at the same time, it becomes extremely difficult to see exactly where the truth does lie. To say that it is on the side of the experts is, as I have said, to hold to an abstraction, for after all it is a question of coming to the aid of human beings, and one has no right to trample on their convictions. All that can be said is that it will be necessary to try to introduce among these masses of people a certain education, and to awaken a certain awareness which does not presently exist. This response appears reasonable, but reflection shows that it is in a certain way illusory, and that it presupposes that the problem is already solved. For who in fact would these educators be? How will they be recruited? And granting that they are intelligently chosen, how will they be accepted by the population? It will all require a great deal of time, trouble, and money, and in the meantime millions of people may be dying of starvation.

These observations may sound quite pessimistic, but I be-

lieve them to be extremely important, for they show how wrong
it is to imagine a ready-made truth in the order of existence we
have been concerned with in our examples. This is even more
true here than in the realm of science, though the difference
is perhaps not absolute. Truth can emerge only by means of an
ordeal which always presents a tragic character. And its emergence can very probably come about, I would add, only through
the intermediary of individuals belonging to a certain elite, by
which I mean persons having that extremely rare faculty of
appreciating experience. One could not insist too much, I believe,
on the rarity of human beings capable of experiences. We have
lived much too long with the mistaken idea that experience is
something given in common to all men, enjoying an unassailable
integrity, whereas it is almost always packed with prejudices
which have never been submitted to discussion.

It is not hard to see that these reflections, so simple yet so
essential, apply to the still unforeseeable destiny of all the
peoples who have recently acceded to independence without yet
having anything resembling maturity.

I think it is now time for us to raise ourselves above the
numerous examples I have found it indispensable to use, in order
to show how the problem of existential truth—by which I mean
truth *in* existence—is difficult not only to resolve but even to
pose.

What stands out especially from what has been said is first
of all that truth cannot be separated from a set of values. Analysis would show, I think, that these values are grounded in a
certain conjunction of order and freedom, and that this conjunction is always difficult to bring about and then to preserve. It is
very close to what we ordinarily call justice, and I have tried to
show in another context that there actually exists between truth
and justice a solidarity which should never fail to be appreciated.

We have just now seen that theoreticians, because they
habitually remain imprisoned by abstractions, are always liable
to substitute what is often only a grotesque caricature for a reality
which is living and, like everything which lives, is threatened.
By nature the theoretician always tends to forget the very important role of circumstances and events, especially when he
projects what the best possible government would be. He then
risks falling into the trap of a fanatic ideology. We see this
difficulty even with Plato.

But what I have above all tried to show is how the question

of truth is posed in a crisis which concerns the destiny of all humanity, such as the crisis of 1914 or that of 1936, or even the situation in the world today, particularly as it appears in the region of Southeast Asia. All the foregoing remarks manifestly apply here. This situation, whose agonizing character no one would deny, is due at least in part to what I believe must be considered an error of appreciation committed by the American government when it refused to recognize the newly constituted government of Communist China. Events have shown without any possible doubt that England, which certainly had no more sympathy than America for communist regimes, acted in a much more sensible way in recognizing this government. It is clear in fact that this recognition, which perhaps can no longer be avoided, is now much more difficult for the United States than it would have been at the outset. Whence a contradiction wholly comparable to the one I spoke of earlier with regard to Munich. We might add that except for a few military men everyone, or almost everyone, agrees that negotiations between these two countries have become indispensable to avoid the risk of widespread conflict. And it must be said that such negotiations presuppose that America recognize Communist China, however painful that may be.

Let me now state the general conclusion this admittedly unacademic study is moving toward. I mean to bring to light the immensely important role reflection ought to play in the life of the political leader—and not only reflection, but courage. Unless courage is confused with an impulsiveness which is merely its most contemptible caricature, it will have to be affirmed that courage and reflection are inseparable, for in a democratic regime nothing is more naturally unpopular than reflection. I believe that this lack of reflection and courage is the principal reason why false situations, or in other words inextricable ones, continue to multiply in the world today, creating the state of general anxiety felt by everyone who is not simply naïve.

It would be sheer stupidity to interpret these severe remarks in a pro-fascist sense. Today it is evident that fascisms of whatever stripe have never been anything but sicknesses of democracy. In them are found considerably aggravated, beyond all limit, the dangers that are perhaps inherent in democratic regimes. However there is no question of anything in my thought supporting a return to some form of nondemocratic regime. One could wish for such a return only in some utopian fairy-tale. But the extreme intricacy of this question shows once again why at the center of this world, threatened at the same time by collective aberrations and technical excesses, what is needed is a reflection decidedly oriented toward truth as I have tried, not perhaps to define it, but at least to approach it.

POSTSCRIPT

I AM REREADING this text in February of 1968, at the moment when the American troops are undergoing furious attacks by the Vietcong and when most of the large cities of Vietnam are reduced to ashes. At this time it is impossible to say whether useful negotiations will be able to take place between Washington and Hanoi. But what is clear is that the American enterprise appears today, leaving aside all ideological partisanship, completely absurd. Or at least the justification offered by the White House is today definitely discredited. While pretending to defend the liberty of South Vietnam, America has in fact condemned her to annihilation. In these conditions it must be recognized that the war waged by Washington against Hanoi and the Vietcong can hardly seem anything now but the defense of Western capitalism against communism, carried out by the most hyperbolic means.

7 / Life and the Sacred

I want first of all to indicate the sense of the following reflections. Clearly, the question of the relation between life and the sacred could occasion a very extensive sociological inquiry of considerable intrinsic interest. But besides the fact that I am not qualified to pursue this kind of inquiry, I am not at all convinced that such an inquiry could in any way illuminate the problem I am concerned with.

My study will be a phenomenological one. I will be inquiring to what degree men today can still accept in some sense Blake's very general affirmation that "every living thing is sacred." The phrase immediately provokes in us a thousand objections. When I say "men today," I have in mind the fact that we are doubtless involved in a kind of prodigious change. I say "involved"; it is certainly inadequate to say that we witness this change. Whether we want it so or not, this change concerns us. It would be artificial and absurd to look for some kind of lifetime protection to shelter us from the radical and more or less direct transformation of everything we value. But to say that this change concerns us does not mean that we have to submit to, much less justify, a fatalistic process. That would be much too simple, and one important purpose of this kind of inquiry lies in distinguishing what is inevitable from what can or must be avoided.

I want to treat what could be called, roughly, the attitude of contemporary man toward life. Here, however, an objection usually arises, often from the kind of Anglo-Saxon neopositivist I met on my travels in the United States. It makes no sense, he might say, to speak of an attitude to life, because life is an abstraction. In the precise sense of this word, there can be no attitude except in the presence of a particular concrete and specifiable reality, for example, a human being, or an animal, or even at the limit an inanimate object.

But the question is precisely whether life is an abstraction. Here, as always, we have to proceed on the basis of a particular experience. Each one of us has said or has met someone who has said "I really love life" or "I don't love life anymore." Now, can we say that these remarks are nonsense? It is better to try to illuminate their meaning.

We will discover very quickly that when we speak of life this way, we evoke something beyond the confines of what might be called the stereotyped framework of discursive thought, for this something is neither a particular thing nor, properly speaking, a general idea. It is tempting to think of Aristotelian transcendentals here, though such an association would probably not survive deeper analysis. If I say that I love life, I am clearly not referring to the pure and simple fact of biological existence. I am referring on the contrary to an entire class of unspecifiable objects or experiences in terms of which biological existence is organized. Here there comes to mind a remark in a study by Professor Tanaki Fujui of the Tokyo Zoological Institute. Fujui observes that when one speaks of life, he never limits himself to considering the living being exclusively; he takes account at the same time of what surrounds this being, that is, of the objects its activity is linked with. Fujui's idea is that this activity involves those objects, and that without them there could be no such activity. At first this observation may seem a simple truism. However, I think it is much more important than it seems, and that we must take careful account of it when we consider the relation between life and the sacred. Clearly, this observation applies directly to the two contrary assertions I referred to earlier. To say "I still love life" means above all that I continue to be interested in everything that occurs.[1] And this interest is linked in a certain fashion with appetite, when that word is used in its ordinary nonphilosophical sense. But someone who says he doesn't love life any longer means that he is now indifferent to

---

1. Unfortunately, the term "occurrence" does not have the same sense in French that it has in English.

everything life presents. There may be an illusion here. Does not the very fact of living involve, however little, an interest or an appetite?

But here again we must anticipate an objection. If we introduce into the notion of life these objects or these occurrences, do we not in some fashion destroy the unity that seems to be implied in the very fact of speaking about life? Do we not substitute for this unity a kind of inconsistent and diffuse multiplicity?

To answer this question, some reference to the experience which in some way underlies affirmation is appropriate. This inarticulated experience is the experience of *my life,* an experience I am hardly able to dissociate myself from without having to treat life as a unity, as for example the unity of a particular path to be traveled. It is this unity, in some sort presupposed, that I project unawares into my affirmation of life.

But this reference to *my life* in some way colors an affirmation that seems to bear on life in general. Nonetheless, I think we can treat as negligible the more or less explicit opinions about the "principle" which the term "life" is supposed to designate. We will have to come back to this point later on.

Before going further, we ought to ask what exactly is the place of biology in this kind of reflection. The question is delicate because the word "biology" can be taken in different senses. When, for example, Bergson used to say—wrongly, I think— that "all morality is biological," he was taking the word in a extraordinarily large sense. But I think we can avoid these tiresome confusions if we take "biological" in a narrow sense to designate everything that has a functional character, everything that can be studied in a strictly objective way. Insofar as it is objective this study claims to abstract from every axiological consideration; that is, it leaves the question open not only whether life is good or bad but, even more profoundly, whether this question has any meaning at all. But, in the light of what we said earlier, this elimination of the axiological element is in some manner arbitrary or even absurd. For it could well be, as I indicated earlier, that the fact of living implies something of interest or of appetite, which itself involves something like an inchoate evaluation. The logic of a science like biology, to the degree that it continually enlarges the role of physico-chemical investigations, minimizes this element to the point of practically doing away with it. Yet philosophers would take this as a kind of axiological retreat. If "pure biologist" refers to someone who would commit himself as totally as possible to this path, then I think that Blake's phrase would make no sense at all to such an individual. But if we are trying to clarify the meaning of those attitudes we have come to adopt when faced with the particuliarities of our own lives and the indeterminate duration of life in general, we cannot situate ourselves inside a strictly biological viewpoint. What still needs questioning is whether this idea of a pure biology, that is, of a biology entirely cut off from every reference to our life and at the same time from an axiology of whatever kind, is, if not a fiction, at least a rather arbitrarily impoverished expression of a science whose basic framework is much broader. Of course biology itself has to decide these matters.

But the idea of a biology that makes no place for value or even for finality weighs on the conscience of contemporary man. Suppose a scientist were able to "manufacture life." Of course, the press would immediately report such an invention in a sensational way. But this discovery would probably cause hardly any astonishment at all to the secular mind. Hearing the continual talk of the "electronic brain" (without being able to understand however just what these words refer to), the man in the street has gotten in the habit of conceding that technology has already more or less completely penetrated the secret of life. The result is that life has undergone a kind of general devaluation. But what benefit has this devaluation produced? The answer must be that the devaluation has been to the benefit of man, of man's intelligence, of human *ingenium* which is manifested by technological development. But people refrain from asking about the roots or the conditions of possibility of this intelligence, of this *ingenium* considered apart from every relation to life, to the individual, and to the affective sphere.[2] But from the moment technical intelligence is made primary, life, no matter how one thinks it necessary to define it, will appear more and more like some kind of energy, essentially the same as other natural forces. Bernard Shaw, we remember, continually used the expression "life-force" in the prefaces to his plays. If, when everything is taken into consideration, there is no natural difference between life and the forces or manifestations studied by the

2. It is interesting to note in passing that a mind of the highest distinction, like that of Paul Valéry, insofar as his thinking is susceptible to popularization, should have contributed on a high level to giving credence to a notion which otherwise seems such as would fill childish minds with enthusiasm.

physical and chemical sciences, extremely serious consequences necessarily follow. I have in mind above all, of course, the idea of rational control, if not of life, at least of its manifestations. The question remains open, I would say, whether this distinction between life and its manifestations is not another version of the traditional and philosophically marginal opposition between substance and accidents. But the idea of birth control is part of a regulatory and technical kind of thinking like the one I have just evoked.

Recall here the general remark I made earlier in passing. When I speak of life, this discourse implies a basic and as it were inarticulated reference to *my life*. I could express more exactly what I mean by saying that the experience *of my life*, which is so difficult to think precisely, in some way secretly irrigates, as it were, the confused notion I tend to form of life independently of any knowledge of biology. Moreover, the biologist seems to think he need not take any account at all of this communication or of this articulation. And to the degree that he is impressed by this attitude of the scientist, the man in the street comes to block the communication in question. When speaking of life, he forgets his condition as a living being.

Phenomenological reflection must question such a situation and the absurd dualism it implies. This dualism is between an experience of the living self, the self which has lived and which has still to live, and what is for the man in the street only a supposed knowledge taken from some article in *Reader's Digest* only remotely connected with the actual science and its research.[3] What the phenomenologist would not allow himself is the a priori devaluation of this experience of *my life*, which after all remains at the origin of all concrete knowledge. In other words, this knowledge is not reducible to a set of propositions formulated in such a way that every adequately educated human being can comprehend it (and while writing these lines I am wondering whether we catch here a glimpse of a centrally important distinction between a knowledge that is taught and one that is not teachable). But the experience of my life as such is something

3. It would be fitting to ask whether the scientist, the biologist himself, does not come to establish something like an unbreachable wall between his science and his own experience as a living being which is, after all, of the same stuff as the living experience of the man in the street.

that could never be taught. Perhaps because of this the experience of my life can in a certain sense open onto the sacred.

And so, after a long journey, we arrive at the fundamental problem. But on the way we have already been able to anticipate how far the development of a soulless biology stretches every interpretation of Blake's phrase, "every living thing is sacred."

However, the facts of this problem are altogether more complicated and disconcerting than they might seem to be at this point of our discussion. The desacralization of life does not operate merely under the pressure of the scientist or the technician and the popularized expressions of their work. Up to now the word "sacred" has been used here in an allusive sense only. But when someone tries to use the word in connection with *his life*, even negatively, the word ought to be made more precise. The term may at first seem to designate a system of rituals that would involve "my life." But I think that these rites belong to the realm of sociology, and that we must consider them only to the extent that they are related to a certain mysterious reality. Thus the question remains open whether in any particular religion these rites are anything other than transitory and necessarily inadequate expressions, or whether they must be regarded on the contrary as revealed institutions. We need not venture further here.

Someone might object that this distinction between a mysterious reality and its contingent expressions is an arbitrary and artificial one. But what justifies the distinction I think is the fact that something sacred, whose nature remains to be determined, can exist for individuals who refuse all ritualism and belong to no church. Someone might reply that the affirmation of the sacred in this case is only a kind of survival which is probably destined to disappear rather quickly. But here, as elsewhere, genetic considerations do not permit any decision about the value and the essential meaning of a judgment. For example, to say that the value of Kant's ethics is its laicized expression of a certain pietism does not suffice as a judgment. Arguments or discussions like this may conceal in this case the essential problem, that is, whether the radical desacralization of life is not in fact its dehumanization. But here again we have to be more precise about the meaning of "dehumanization."

To clarify, I want to cite several lines from my paper "Some Remarks on the Irreligion of Today," in *Being and Having*.

Pure religion, religion as distinct from magic and opposed to it, is the exact contrary of an applied science; for it constitutes a realm where the subject is confronted with something over which he can obtain no hold at all. If the word transcendence describes anything whatever, it must be this—the absolute, impassable gulf which opens between the soul and being whenever being refuses us a hold. No gesture is more significant than the joined hands of the believer, mutely witnessing that nothing can be done and nothing changed, and that he comes simply to give himself up. Whether the gesture is one of dedication or of worship, we can still say that the feeling behind it is the realisation of the holy, and that awe, love and fear all enter into it simultaneously. Notice that there is no question here of a passive state; to assert that would be to imply that the activity of the technician, as he takes, modifies or elaborates, is the only activity worthy of name.[4]

To understand just how inexact it would be to claim that this attitude of adoration implies institutional religion, it is sufficient to think of a mother's adoration of her child. This experience is so simple and so primordial that it seems to present us with something sacred that is immanent not in life but in the living. I use the term "primordial" to indicate how every attempt at a genetic reduction would be, if not impractical, in any case unworkable.

Similarly, all kinds of experiences could be evoked where living nature becomes an object of contemplation. Since one must always try to be as concrete as possible, I would refer personally to what I have experienced in certain gardens or sacred groves in Japan, or even more recently in the surroundings of San Francisco.

Here again we have to anticipate an objection. "When you speak of sacred groves," someone might say, "—for example the one that surrounds the Ise Temple—you cannot avoid referring to Shintoism. In other words here again the sacred cannot be detached from a certain sociological reality."

But, speaking here again as a phenomenologist, I would say that this way of putting the matter reverses the real order of terms. I believe I caught a glimpse of what Shintoism is from within because of this experience of the sacred before the temple of Ise, and not vice versa. It would be false to say that my very vague notions about Shintoism contributed in any way to the

4. *Being and Having,* trans. Katherine Farrer (New York: Harper Torchbooks, 1961), p. 187.

experience of this feeling. But it is unnecessary to go ten or fifteen thousand kilometers to encounter the sacred, that is, a sacred reality directly linked to life. Because it seems important for our inquiry, I will only remark that the Japanese seem to have come farther than Westerners along this path where the sacred can be encountered.

The point of these sketches, even in their discontinuity, is to draw attention as concretely as possible to the connection Blake's phrase implies. Sincerity, I think, would demand of everyone the recognition that there are some resemblances in his own life to this experience. Yet all the forces at work in the world and taking form around us seem united in their encouragement of a kind of thinking that either appraises these experiences as worthless or submits them to a genetic sociology capable of devaluating them.

Here again an important objection might be raised. "Do you not see that if these sporadic and inarticulate experiences are to serve as the bases for your attempt to confer a content on the word 'sacred' in its reference to what each one of us calls *his life,* you are heading for certain failure? To raise questions, as you have claimed to do, about the relation between life and the sacred is to imply at least hypothetically that the sacred exists, that it has a certain consistency. Otherwise, one might be content to ask whether life, with its contingencies, naturally awakens affective reactions which could be thought of as merely the attenuated survivals of a collapsed faith."

As with every genuine objection this one has the merit of constraining me to make more precise what I mean by speaking of a mysterious reality. If the reactions evoked are affective only, then they cannot be regarded as relevant in this context. But we are in fact beyond simple affectivity here. The sacred is such only if it determines a course of action. This course of action is contrary to everything resembling technique or, even more concretely, to everything that might be mere know-how or manipulation. But this negative determination is insufficient. It is particularly appropriate to try to define very carefully the hierarchical meanings of a verb such as "respect." This verb, like so many others (for example, the verb "to serve"), is subject to devaluation. Consider for example just what respect for an order is. To respect an order means quite simply to conform to it, automatically perhaps, or even to avoid the troublesome consequences of not respecting it. This kind of respect, however, is nothing like what we generally call respect. It is not difficult to imagine cases where respect in this general sense is at issue. Take for example a conversation with someone who is undergoing great moral suffering. Here respect will be something entirely different from conformity to an order. This kind of respect, manifest perhaps in silence, implies recognizing a kind of dignity. Without even analyzing this dignity we already find ourselves at the edge of the sacred. Another example is even more significant. Consider a personal relationship with a very young person, quite innocent, whose innocence we must respect by keeping ourselves from any suggestion or allusion that could injure or contaminate this innocence. This innocence, which a certain kind of suspect psychoanalysis seems bent only on shattering, we find primordial. More profoundly, this primordial character seems to be the sign of an integrity. Here again of course we have to weigh our words. The term "integrity" is not used here in the sense in which someone speaks of "a man of integrity," but in an ontological sense. In other words, we would be conscious, perhaps in a very confused way, of being in the presence of a primary and revealing situation. But what is revealed? It is really very difficult and even in a sense impossible to answer this question. The words at our disposal, which will always be taken from particular experiences like those where something seems to break forth like sunshine or spring up like water, could only point in some way toward an intact freshness, like the essence of an absolute principle. Were we to glance in this direction, we might even perceive dimly some possible connection between this kind of virginity and, in a different dimension, sanctity—*sanctitas*.

I have thought about this matter for a long time and I think it is only in this dimension, and exclusively here, that I am able to distinguish something like an articulation of life and the sacred. To pretend that such a position is not extremely difficult to hold is pointless. The position is so difficult because what we call life, precisely in its progression through deterioration and old age, seems to the observer like something turned against its own initial integrity. I think that this is the case, if not in principle, at least in what we know of life in its manifestations; life is engraved with this contradiction. This is where our embarrassment arises when we try to distinguish the relationship between life and the sacred. Everything proceeds as if a kind of initial and invincible assurance in us were ceaselessly opposed by critical judgment based on the observation of what life in fact is, of what life involves not only of expenditure but of waste, of merciless destruction. It is entirely understandable that we might adopt a pessimism as radical as that of Schopenhauer. But pessimism is abandoned, at least superficially, in favor of let us not say a hope but an ambition. This ambition is the one I referred to in the first part of this paper, an ambition which is essentially and purely technocratic. But at the same time and by a kind of a paradox which the technocrats would be very wrong to neglect, to the degree that this enterprise is actualized and develops its rationalistic consequences, a restlessness awakens and grows in us, a protest is articulated. This protest would be incomprehensible if it did not have its origin in the seminal assurance which I have been discussing.

Is the word "integrity," when taken in its strongest sense and associated with the epithet "primordial," the key to a domain that seems under examination curiously defended and not even completely open to someone who tries to discern it? These words, "integrity" and the "primordial," I think, polarize the philosopher's meditative attention. They help us to understand that the spectacle of life can only turn us aside from everything that would permit us to sacralize life. Their intervention implies that life is, as it were, surprised in its center; and must it not be said that this center is revealed only to love? This word is so vague and so burdened with equivocations, its meaning is so diluted, that we are tempted to reject it. I have spoken previously, in *Homo Viator* if I am not mistaken, of the announcement of a certain marriage contract between man and life. These words have found an echo in many readers, but they are meaningless unless we think of a welcoming of life, a welcoming which can only be found in a loving heart. We know well enough that Schopenhauer's experience was different.

"But here," someone might interject, "are you not sacrificing the rigor you wanted to safeguard to a detestable sentimentality?" It might seem that way, particularly if no effort is made to define the term "love" carefully. The term does not refer to a vague effusiveness; it is something very different. I remember a psychiatrist from Tübingen who had heard one of my talks at Freiburg, who said to me in connection with the ideas I have just mentioned that a very young baby, even when surrounded with the best care in a model institution, suffers in its development, in its being, if it is deprived of love or of maternal care. How can we not see this frustration as precisely a weakening of a primordial integrity? What is remarkable, however, is that analogous observations could be made with respect to the taming of animals or the cultivating of flowers. It seems that here and there an art is required whose principle resides precisely in the heart and is not reducible to a technique, to some kind of textbook know-how. This art implies a gift of self, a reverential attitude designated by the term "piety." This attitude is inconsistent with the pretension of mastering something in order to exploit it. I think the German word *Gelassenheit,* a practically untranslatable word that is the title of one of Heidegger's later writings, refers precisely to this disposition which is so contrary to the disposition of the pure technician. *Gelassenheit* finds its most perfect expression in the poet. Consider here not just Blake, but someone much closer to us, Rilke. In the distant past, however, the roles of the poet and the naturalist were sometimes confused. Rationalism, especially the Cartesian variety, helped effect a dissociation that was indispensable for scientific progress. But this does not mean that the dissociation was not in certain respects damaging.[5] Only in the realm of this disposition, which is so difficult to describe, does Blake's affirmation make sense. And, as always in such areas, it is by the negative path that the preliminary work of a reconstructive thinking can realize itself. Even if the thought does not at first seem rationally justifiable, we see today nonetheless that the forces in favor of the desacralization or even simply the devaluation of life are the same as those that tend to dehumanize man, to humiliate him before the products of his own technology.

As I have had the opportunity to say in another context, the basic problem here is axiological. This does not mean returning to the dusty philosophy of value, especially the German strain; the idealist presuppositions of this philosophy have by now been correctly criticized. I mean rather that the problem lies in the fact that values are rooted in the concrete, in life, which we must affirm. And this affirmation must not remain purely theoretical. On the contrary, it must be particularized in the light of precise

5. It is interesting to note that in the work of certain scientists and thinkers from the other side of the Rhine—I am thinking, for example, of the botanist Hans Andre—it seems we are witnessing an effort to reestablish this lost unity in a perspective already to be found in other areas.

instances whose tragic and even agonizing character experience never stops showing us.

SUPPLEMENTARY REMARKS

NOT LONG AGO I received the three large volumes into which had been collected, under the patronage of the Dar es Salaam Study Center, the papers of my friend Louis Massignon. Massignon was undoubtedly one of the great spirits and souls of our time. In going through these writings, which cover an extremely broad field from archaeology to sociology and mysticism, it is impossible not to be struck by the importance he attached to the idea of the sacred, even more than to the idea of sanctity. I am thinking, for example, of a paper first published in volume ten of *Dieu vivant,* in 1948, entitled "Un Nouveau Sacral." Massignon here categorically opposes a correspondent's idea that a broader sacral view is required which would integrate science and technology and which would be elaborated by man making himself the very immediate collaborator of God. The discussion is directly related to the difficult problem I have tried to treat here. The idea of this kind of collaboration could be a temptation for someone who refuses to deny the sacred and yet remains a prisoner of the immanent categories of science. The rather vague idea of man's completion of the work begun by God seems part of our mental atmosphere today and is linked to a more or less deformed version of the ideas of Teilhard de Chardin. But Massignon, the great and deep Christian, reminds us

> that God is not at the root of our acts in such a way as to require his creatures' collaboration. We have resented the appeal of God, and we bitterly resent the buffoonery of this condescending offer of technical artifice to perfect the work of a creator we are united to only by the awareness of our abandonment.[6]

By definition, it is absurd to speak of a "new" sacral reality.

> The truly sacral is made explicit by the natural landscapes of all times and all places, whose symbolism is plain to the common sense of all men. To consider this symbolism is not to exhibit an out-of-date traditionalism, for the symbol is not worth anything

6. Louis Massignon, *Opera Minora,* ed. Y. Moubarac (Paris: Presses universitaires de France, 1969), III, 798.

unless it is explicated. And this constructive liturgical assimilation of the symbols of a collectivity inspired by a church gathers in its unity all the ages of human history.[7]

It is essential to note that, without referring to specifically Christian facts, Massignon tells us in "La Signification du dernier pèlerinage de Gandhi" that

> the sacred is revealed to us in this terrifying world of sin where everything has little by little been desacralized on the counsel of a perversely angelic intelligence which separates the suffering we inflict on others from the instinct of the sacred that alerts us to the divine visitation witnessed in humanity, poverty, sickness, sleep, and death. [The enumeration is from a sentence in the *Shi-ite Kaasibi*.] In default of a metaphysical courage UNESCO has not even dared to define human nature because the attempt seemed contradictory. Thereby, UNESCO testified to a historical plurality of cultures irreconcilable except by momentary compromises. But, reduced to its essential poverty, a definition of human nature could become the pure mirror of divine nature itself.[8]

And, a little farther on:

> In hospitality we find the sacred at the center of the mystery of our destinies, like a beggar, furtive and divine, which no assurance social or otherwise would ever dispense us from. In sheltering and in caring for the soul by caring for the body, hospitality attests to the immortal value of the most humble human life, of the body infinitely venerable in the worn clothing of the worker (seed of glory). Clothing is not to be taken from a man, as Indian frontier guards did in 1947 when they tore the clothing from deported women, their earrings and their foot bracelets, and as Lebanese policemen in 1943 did when they relieved an imprisoned government minister, ridiculously, of his dentures.[9]

And, to conclude, he reminds us of Meister Eckhart's phrase: "The soul will never be saved except in the body which has been assigned to it."

The profundity of these views will escape no one. They go far beyond the rationalistic Kantian idea of respect for the person. They go beyond them because they are centered on the Incarnation.

7. *Ibid.*
8. *Ibid.*, 349.
9. *Ibid.*, 350.

But what might not appear clearly is their possible application to life properly speaking. Must we say "to life in general?" But I have already put my readers on guard at the beginning of this study about the use of this term "general." If we stress generality, almost inevitably we come on the idea of vital force. But why this force should be any more sacred than any other energy—electricity, for example—is not clear. Attention must be centered not on life but on the living being. Perhaps there is room for thinking that "being" is as important as the term "living." It would be difficult to determine the exact relationship between the two terms in the expression "living being." For I do not think that "living" can be considered simply as a predicate of "being," as classical logic might have it. Rather, the adjective "living" clarifies something in the word "being" that remains an obscure possibility.

I insist on this to emphasize that the question raised here refers not only to an axiology but also, and more essentially, to an ontology. Axiology and ontology here are probably inseparable.

Another objection might arise here. "You spoke of a living being. But at bottom it is clear that all the time you were thinking of man. What happens in this perspective to those living beings which seem to be situated at the very opposite pole from man, living beings such as insects or mollusks?"

This needs attention. We have spontaneous reactions not just in the presence of fellow men, higher animals, and plants, but also in the presence of these lower animals which can seem insignificant to us or awaken in us something like disgust. But here it is important to think of the naturalist. For him, the word "insignificant" has no sense. In the passionate study of a particular species he has triumphed for all time over such reactions. The living organism he considers subsists in a dimension of being to which we, the profane, have access only with difficulty. Even leaving aside any belief in a divine creator, the naturalist experiences a kind of wonder before the fineness and the complexity of the structure he observes. Here, in a very unexpected way, beyond our world of the profane and ignorant, some connection is realized between the scientist and someone who must perhaps be called the saint. But we have to specify what we mean by the word "saint." "Sanctity" here does not refer to a quality or a moral disposition in the properly rational sense of this word. We are rather on the level of ontology. The saint is someone who has arrived at a way of being that overcomes the current separation between man and nature. Perhaps the example of non-Christian saints is just as instructive here as that of the calendar saints. I recall what I saw and heard and felt in Japan. The landscape became manifest to whoever would contemplate it in such a way that a living exchange was established between the two. The word "contemplation" is important because it is at the level of the poet's contemplation that Blake's phrase makes sense. The artist too is on this level, the artist as he was conceived during the great periods of art. The current aberrations are, I think, consequences of the fact that the artist, in his need to be himself and express himself, has broken the unity that strikes us in the very greatest artists, the unity that is particularly evident in the great art of the Orient.

But what relationship can there be between the kinds of values related to contemplation and those embodied in the kind of hospitality Massignon referred to?

Again, I would refer to a memory of a trip. Some years ago, when I visited Medina for the second time, I noticed that every passerby, however miserable he was, seemed truly endowed with a kind of dignity. I was astonished by this, and I admired the people for it; I felt I was moving at the center of a *mirabile*. I contrasted my walk in Medina with what a walk can be like in a modern city, where people are continually brushing by one another in general anonymity. In this depersonalized world, where animals can no longer be seen except in cages, that is to say outside their natural context, Blake's phrase "every living thing is sacred" no longer has any real meaning. My friend Max Picard, who has written two very profound books on the human face, thought that, as a result of social conditions and especially the progress of disbelief, even faces have undergone a kind of fatal erosion. But in Medina, as very many years ago in Damascus, I saw myself outside this desacralizing evolution. There, human beings presented themselves to me as beings, as *mirabilia*. If hospitality has a meaning, it is precisely because the unknown guest who has come to ask a resting place partakes of what one would be tempted to call the incorruptible. It is quite evident that here again, but more imaginatively and affectively, we touch on that primordial integrity I spoke about in the first part of this study.

Granted, this collection of apparently discontinuous but converging remarks might disconcert those who pursue traditional scientific or philosophical research. But if we wish to get at the sources welling beneath worn-out structures, I think it is appropriate to break with the usual frameworks of thinking. Ontology itself is nothing if not a return to sources, and even to the sacred. But we must be careful. The return to sources does not mean the return to chronological origins. Here a particular mistake about evolution must be denounced once and for all. I do not mean that the idea of evolution must be rejected; that would be absurd. I mean that frequently it is a mistake to imagine that origins are illuminating in themselves. Origins are always obscure, hidden, and perhaps never illuminated except by what follows them. How can they be illuminated? That is the problem. From Aristotle to Hegel and Bergson, the greatest minds are agreed in thinking that the higher allows us to explain the lower and not the other way around.

At first, these very general views can seem unrelated to the problem that has occupied us in the course of this study. But I think this is an illusion, and that it is sufficient to reflect on what the word "higher" means to understand that this impression is mistaken. I think that the higher is meaningful only for someone who has arrived by recollection at a certain sanctuary. Does recollection have a sacralizing value? Life tends to be desacralized because it is somehow involved in disorder, a disorder which affects human existence from the moment it is delivered over to vital powers which are in some way only the metastasis of life.

The meaning of my work, even and especially of my dramatic work which must not be separated from my philosophical writings, consists above all in trying to bring entities back toward the living center, toward the heart of man and of the world, where everything is mysteriously in order and where the word "sacred" rises to our lips like praise and a blessing.

8 / My Death

THE PROBLEM I want to discuss here, certainly not for the first time but in a perspective somewhat different from that I have previously adopted, is the problem of the relationship between the human being and his own death. I have used the terms "problem" and "relation," but these words may not be appropriate here. What is certain, however, is that any relation here can only be in an existential and not in an objective mode. If there were an objective relation at issue here, it could be discovered inductively. But this is absurd. What is in question is beyond the grasp of every possible inquiry. And the question here is not about man's describability, but about man insofar as he exists. I cannot separate the existing being from the relationship he has with himself, from the fact that he is concerned with himself.

But, of course, I immediately encounter on my path the assertions presented by Heidegger in the most dogmatic fashion in *Being and Time*. And these are the assertions I want here to examine critically.

We should recall how and at what point the consideration on *Sein zum Tode* [being-toward-death] intervenes. I am not translating here on purpose, and I will come back later on to the reasons why the Heideggerian expression is not adequately translatable into French.

The expression *ein existenzielles Sein zum Tode* appears for the first time in section forty-five. This section opens the second division of the book, which is entitled "Dasein und Zeitlichkeit" ["*Dasein* and Temporality."]. Here again I must preserve for the moment the German term. However, despite Heidegger's protestations, I think *Dasein* can be translated roughly in French as *existence humaine* [human existence].

After he has quickly reviewed the existential analysis in the six parts of the first division, Heidegger recognizes that this analysis cannot claim what he calls *"Ursprunglichkeit"* [primordialness]. However, I am not sure that this word adequately expresses Heidegger's thought. Heidegger is more precise when he says that a primordial ontological interpretation participates in what he calls a hermeneutic situation assured *"in phenomenaler Anmessung,"* which means "made secure in conformity with the phenomenon."[1] But this interpretation must also expressly determine whether the entirety of the thematic entity has been *"in die Vorhabe gebracht."* The words *in die Vorhabe gebracht* are also very difficult to translate. But I do not think we would be far off were we to translate them in French as *mettre en avant* or *mettre en evidence.* Two lines further on Heidegger says that "if we are to have a fore-sight of being, we must see it in such a way as not to miss the *unity* of those structural items which belong to it and are possible."[2] This language seems to me abominably obscure and uselessly complicated. I remain convinced that all of this could be expressed in an infinitely simpler and clearer fashion.

Heidegger says then that he has determined the idea of existence as the power to be, a power which comprehends and a power which is concerned about its own being. But insofar as it is mine, this power to be is open to authenticity or to inauthenticity, or to a mode where neither is differentiated. The earlier interpretation, which was based on ordinary everydayness, was limited to the analysis of existing indifferently, that is, inauthentically. But in this respect there was something essential missing in this ontological characterization of the structure of existence.

What sort of lack was it, if not with respect to this totality which has just been evoked? Here again we find a terminological difficulty. Perhaps the word *Ganzheit*, which is of course very unusual, must be translated in French as *intégrité* [totality] in the

1. *Sein und Zeit,* 11th ed. (Tubingen: Niemeyer, 1967), p. 232; English translation by J. Macquarrie and E. Robinson, *Being and Time* (New York: Harper, 1962), p. 275.
2. *Ibid.*

etymological and consequently nonethical sense of the word. It was previously asserted,[3] Heidegger remarks, that the concern was *"die Ganzheit des Strukturganzen der Daseinsverfassung,"* [the totality of the structural whole of *Dasein*'s constitution], literally, in French, *l'intégrité du tout structural de la constitution de l'être humain comme Ganzheit.* Again, it is quite clear that *Ganzheit* cannot be translated in French by *totalité* and that the word *ensemble*, although a little better, is hardly an improvement. But, Heidegger remarks, doesn't this involve the impossibility of putting *Dasein als Ganzes*, human existence as a whole, in its visual field? For everydayness is being between birth and death. And if existence determines the being of *Dasein*, and if *Dasein*'s power to be contributes to constituting its own essence, then as a capacity to be in some way *Dasein* may not yet exist. The entity whose existence constitutes its essence is naturally opposed to the entity whose being can be grasped as a *ganzes Seiendes*, as a complete entity or an entity in its "completedness."

Thus, Heidegger hopes to illuminate here by a negative argument a connection between authenticity and totality or completedness. So it is a question of highlighting *Dasein*'s completedness, and consequently, rather than considering *Dasein*'s position midway between life and death, considering instead the end, *das Ende*. The end of being in the world is death. This end to the power to be, that is, existence, delimits and determines the possible completedness of *Dasein*. This fact, that *Dasein* is at an end (*zu Ende*) in death, can adequately come into the consideration of possible completedness only if there is an adequate ontological concept, that is, an existential concept of death. I cite in German the following centrally important sentence: *"Daseinsmässig aber ist der Tod nur in einem existenziellen Sein zum Tode."* [4] It seems to me that I would translate *daseinsmässig* in French by *dans son application* or *dans son affectation au Dasein."* But we must be particularly attentive to the fact that the preposition *zu* here is extremely ambiguous. This preposition had a well-defined and simple meaning when it was a question just earlier of *zu Ende Sein*, because these words mean in French *être à son terme*, *être au bout de soi-même.* But I think that this little word *zu*, which is apparently insignificant and harmless, takes on a com-

3. *Ibid.*, p. 191 (Eng. trans., p. 235). Throughout this discussion Marcel interprets Heidegger's text somewhat freely.—Translator.
4. *Ibid.*, p. 234 (Eng. trans., p. 277).

pletely different meaning when it is a question of *Sein zum Tode*. For the moment I leave aside the difficulties when Heidegger dares to introduce *das Gewissen*, that is, conscience, where that word—to follow the translation and commentary of de Waehlens—means the power of radical challenge addressed to us when we are lost in worldly distractions. I intend to remain with the immediate implications of *Sein zum Tode*. I think Heidegger slips, with the help of some sort of magician's trick, from the initial meaning of this preposition *zu* to a completely different and very ambiguous one. The French translators have noticed this. And, hoping to avoid the equivocations that burden the French word *pour* [for], they have tried to introduce here the preposition *vers* [toward]. But I think that the words *être vers la mort* have no meaning whatsoever. To forget that *vers* implies the verb *aller* [to go] is to forget the elementary facts of the French language. Whatever may be the unlimited resources at the disposal of metaphysical jugglers, the verb *être* will never become a verb of motion. Recourse to the preposition *vers* is, therefore, a dishonest expedient. Moreover, it is unhelpful because it actually illuminates, contrary to Heidegger's own intentions, the uncertainty which the words *Sein zum Tode* cover over. If we wish to translate these words into French we must come back, whether we like it or not, to the word *pour*.

The truth is that the preposition *zu* conceals here different possibilities which, if one took the trouble to explicate, would be expressed by different verbs. I will cite several.

Etre pour la mort can mean *être livré à la mort* [to be delivered up to death], but also *être destiné à mourir* [to be destined to die], or *être condemné à mourir* [to be condemned to die]. If he is forced to choose, the commentator on Heidegger would probably prefer "to be destined to die." But, if this translation seems the best, or the least unsatisfactory, it is precisely because the translation itself remains equivocal because of the equivocation between "destined" and "destination." Fidelity to Heidegger's thinking, to the degree that his thought can be comprehended, requires, I think, removing completely the notion of finality from the word *pour*. But it is impossible to use the words "destined to" without preserving some tint of finality.

On the other hand we must come back to a word that is constantly used in the text, which I have sometimes translated and at other times paraphrased, the word *Ganzheit*.

Heidegger must have had to ask himself a prejudicial question, whether the term *Ganzheit* is applicable to *Dasein*. Let us reflect on the implications of what I have designated by the rather barbarous word *complétude,* "completedness."

To begin with, one might be tempted to say that there can be a completedness only of what is countable. But however it is defined, *Dasein* cannot be related to any kind of enumeration. Suppose however we grant that this implication is not necessary. I would say then that something can be complete only to the degree that it presents itself as compact, as *Lückenlos*. But reflection on what I am is sufficient to reveal that what is missing is precisely this feature. When I question myself about it, my being seems extremely intermittant. It seems to involve all kinds of drives, inclinations, or attempts which come to nothing. Perhaps the somewhat unusual term "dishevelment" expresses most exactly what I want to say: my being seems disheveled. I am thinking here of a comparison. I recall those urban sprawls, like São Paulo, for example, which extend in every direction and are circumscribed by nothing—a fact that radically differentiates these cities from earlier ones. The city is *ein Ganzes;* the modern agglomeration is of its very nature *ein Unganzes*. And here, in strict contradiction to what Heidegger says, death changes absolutely nothing. It modifies in no way at all the inner incompleteness I just referred to. Death cannot even be called an end—which Heidegger himself seems to recognize from time to time, but not without contradicting himself. For example, he says that in death *Dasein* is neither accomplished nor has simply disappeared nor has terminated nor has become manageable (*Verfügbar*) again like something at hand (*Zuhandenen*).[5] I think that death appears as an end only when life is seen as a kind of journey. But life appears this way only when I consider it from outside—and to the degree I consider it this way, I no longer experience life as my life. Here we come back to someone I think Heidegger has misunderstood, Bergson.[6]

But someone will say here that I am neglecting something essential. Why have I not referred to a text like the one where Heidegger writes that *Dasein*, insofar as it is thrown into being-in-the-world, is already delivered up (*überantwortet*) to its

5. *Ibid.,* p. 234 (Eng. trans., p. 277).
6. Cf. *ibid.,* pp. 432–33, n. (Eng. trans., pp. 483–84), where it is said that Bergson's conception, despite the different basis for his theory, ties up with Hegelian thought.

death? [7] "Being *zu seinem Tode*"—we have already seen why these words for all practical purposes cannot be translated. *Dasein* in fact dies and dies continually so long as it does not suffer its "demise" ([*dé-vivre*], *Ableben*).

As has often been remarked, there is an idea here which Rilke has translated into incomparably more fitting language. But nothing in all this eliminates the equivocation I pointed out earlier. All we can say, I think, is that Heidegger, with the help of a terminology which is infinitely less precise than the superficial reader thinks, is at pains to express a certain existential experience of death in life. This experience does not have to be rejected; but it need not be treated as an absolute either. I am hardly accustomed to refer to Spinoza's thought. But it is incontestable that in Spinoza there is also an existential experience which is totally irreducible to Heidegger's experience. Would it make any sense at all to claim that Spinoza's experience is inauthentic? Moreover, the expression *Freiheit zum Tode* (literally, in French, *liberté pour la mort,* a freedom to die) is also equivocal, for it would be just as applicable to Spinoza's attitude. But could one imagine for one second Spinoza being able to use the expression *Sein zum Tode* as his own?

I think an alternative is possible here, and that this alternative need not be reduced to Heidegger's distinction between the inauthentic and the authentic. In fact, Heidegger has forced the issue here, and reflection ought to resist.

After this long introduction I want to take up again what I said more than thirty years ago at the 1937 International Philosophy Convention in Paris. The text is in *Creative Fidelity,* and here is the essential passage.

> At every moment I am able to abstract sufficiently from my life so as to regard it as a series of draws in a lottery. Some of these draws have already been made; other numbers still have to be drawn. But I have to realize that, as soon as I participate in this lottery, I am given a ticket with a death sentence. The place, the date, and the manner of execution are left blank.
>
> On the other hand, when I consider the lots that have already fallen due, I notice that I cannot juxtapose them. These instances of good luck and bad luck interact. I cannot even assign fixed values to them. They can vary as a function of the lots I still have to draw. Moreover, the way in which I am to make the remaining

7. *Ibid.*, p. 259 (Eng. trans., p. 303).

draws can seem to be determined by lot as well. Here matters are indistinct, for it may seem that I must *be* before I am to *receive*. I can scarcely hope to distinguish precisely between what I will roughly call my nature, and the gifts or trials dispensed to me. . . . In addition, I am not excluding the possibility that "my nature" here may include an act that constitutes my very self, as Kant and Schopenhauer thought.

But in the midst of so many clouds, which somehow accumulate and descend from the unknown future to the depths of the problematic past, an invariable assurance remains—I will die. Among the things that await me death alone is not problematic. It is enough of a problem that death imposes itself on me like a star fixed in the scintillating universe of possibilities. But I can overcome death by imagining it as already come full term only on condition of putting myself in someone else's place, someone who will survive me and who will experience *my death* as if it were *his* death. This kind of possibility can invest my death with an obsessive and petrifying power. In this case there will be nothing left in my life that cannot be dried up by this presence of my death. I may even be stricken with vertigo and yield to the temptation of terminating this wait, this miserable respite whose duration remains unknown. In such a situation I am like someone condemned to death who, from one day to another and from one moment to the next, can see himself taken to the execution chamber.

This possibility constitutes for me a metaproblematic of being no more which can degenerate into a systematic despair.[8]

If I restrict myself to these texts, it is tempting to distinguish between death as something *implied* by being-in-the-world, and the manner of this death. In this case, I would say that the kind of death is connected with the order of events, for example, an auto accident I may be a victim of, or a sickness I may contract somewhere, and so on. But death *in itself* surely cannot be reduced to an event. This would amount to saying that my death is not something that will happen to me.

But two words here stimulate my reflection: first of all, the word "implied." Do I have grounds for saying that the "must die" is truly implied by being-in-the-world? I could, it is true, construct for myself an *a posteriori* account to the effect that my being-in-the-world is assured by mechanical functions which, just because they are mechanisms, cannot function perpetually. The

8. *Creative Fidelity*, trans. Robert Rosthal (New York: Farrar, Straus & Giroux, 1964), pp. 140–42.

inevitable breakdown of such mechanisms would be what I am calling death. Such an argument—even though the term "implication" is not perfectly relevant—seems to point out a necessary relation between being-in-the-world and having to die.

But there is a catch. The argument presupposes that I can detach myself sufficiently from my being-in-the-world to substitute for it something else, which would first have to have been divested of what I would readily call its experiential weight. I would have to effect a kind of ideal disincarnation of myself and to imagine the material factors necessary for this presupposed entity to be in the world. This might be expressed by saying that I would have to represent myself as riveted in some way to what I am calling the world.

But what I have always called secondary reflection must be exercised on this imaginative operation of prior disincarnation, if not for doing away with it, at least for making it problematic. When I say "make it problematic," I mean *putting into question* the legitimacy of this dissociation between a prior *self* and an instantiation of this self by material means which secondarily would render this self present to the world. In another idiom we could say that the priority of essence to existence is problematic —which does not mean, of course, that one must blindly assert the contrary, that existence is prior to essence.

But clearly this kind of interrogation undermines the argument that claims to establish a necessary connection between being-in-the-world and having to die. Perhaps just what the words "being-in-the-world" mean is much less clear than they seem at first sight. After all, mechanisms whose existence no one doubts may be operative between entities in the world and not operative at all between the world itself and an entity supposedly alien to the world.

Perhaps this having to die is immediately apprehended, not inferred, so that I would have to avow that I perceive or experience myself as mortal, as having to die. But here again we meet Spinoza. Spinoza affirms that we perceive and experience ourselves as immortal. All our experiences of fullness, experiences like love, creation, and contemplation, where we are aware of attaining being, testify in Spinoza's behalf. These experiences, at least for the average man, can of course be transitory or intermittent, and every man can reach the point of refusing these experiences when his vitality is blunted, when fatigue and depression intervene. No one would doubt that there are moments when each man not only seems to himself mortal, but seems to aspire to die, to let himself go to pieces, to dissolve himself.

Heidegger would protest here in the most formal way against a reference to what he would call, very disdainfully, psychological states. But whatever certain phenomenologists might say, it is extremely difficult to demarcate precisely the psychological from, let us say, the "experiential." I am using here Henry Bugbee's term from his fine book, *The Inward Morning*, as I did in my paper before the Académie des sciences morales in 1955. To the degree that it is experiential, Spinoza's adage is radically opposed to Heidegger's *zum Tode Sein*. Spinoza maintains that the finite being I am is ordained to eternity—others would say to eternal life.

I would be the first to concede that what is true in moments of fullness ceases to be true when vitality is blunted, when depression appears, when a fatigue that seems an aspiration to an eternal sleep carries the day. When things are this way, *sentimus experimurque nos mortales esse*. But the question remains open whether this relativist determination of an "at one time . . . at another time" can be maintained. Nothing is less certain. Here the metaphysician has the floor; he would surely refuse this idea of a simple oscillation, but he also has the best reasons for contesting the claim that truth lies in the kind of self-repudiation which always implies fatigue, because fatigue inevitably inclines toward resignation.

Besides "implied," there is another word I used above that invites debate. I spoke of "death in itself." But it is quite doubtful whether one can legitimately speak of an in-itself or an ipseity of death.

Without encumbering ourselves any longer with Heideggerian assertions, let us summarize. Since my childhood I have been aware that I will die even though I have been unable to learn when and how I will die. Hence, I am certain about my inevitable death, even though something irresistible and unreasonable in me rebels against this death. But I come back inexorably to denying that, one after another, all human beings succumb by chance. Dying requires a reason, a reason connected with our nature or with our condition. But does this requirement allow me in any way at all to pronounce on the relation that binds me to my death (and even to pronounce on whether this term "relation" is applicable here)? Recall the alternative I formulated earlier. Am I

delivered up to a fate? Am I called to die? The second case remains ambiguous because the meaning of the term "call" remains
radically undetermined. Am I then condemned to die? This is
clearer, on condition that "condemned" is taken in its precise
sense and that there is in fact a judge who condemns, who condemns *us*. But this case opens before me the indefinite contesta-
tion at the base of Kafka's work. Why are we condemned? Where
is the fault or the offense in what we are alleged to be guilty of?
This side of, or beyond, revelation, the question is destined to remain without an answer. In the final analysis, the question somehow disappears. For something in me finally will refuse the
question. Someone might object that, if the idea of death is condemnation is linked to revelation, then the philosopher does not
have to give an account of this idea at all. I think this viewpoint is
simplistic, and I cannot accept it. Even if I were an unbeliever I
live in a world impregnated with thoughts that owe something to
revelation. Hence, it is by abstraction and to whatever degree I
can separate myself from this existential context that I can treat
revelation and its associated propositions as foreign to the debate
and consequently as not having to intervene. Moreover, it is quite
difficult not to discern behind the assertion of the *zum Tode Sein*
the indistinct shadow of a *Verurteilung*, a condemnation. To the
degree that one decides to eliminate this shadow completely, he
will find himself in a dilemma. Either he will go very far beyond
the existential toward the naturalistic and scientific affirmation
of a pure and simple law of determinism, or else he will have to
stress as strongly as possible the provocative bareness of the
scandal of death, this time of course without being able to cover
up the scandal with any kind of internal finality. But in this
direction there is no affirmation of *zum Tode Sein*, but an affirmation of being *despite* and *against* death.

We must be wary here of yielding to the dangerous attraction
of something that could be nothing but a phrase. Can I describe
myself, my existence, as *being-against-death*? This phrase involves the risk of falling into a simplification just as arbitrary as
the one I reproached Heidegger with. Should the truth be sought
in the direction of a dramatic structure in my being? The almost
insurmountable difficulty here, I think, is the fact that every recourse to contradictory tendencies or instincts, like that of Freud,
for example, may involve a schematization whose artificial character needs to be formally recognized. If it is true to say that I
am or, more exactly, that I tend to constitute myself over against

my death and despite it, it is also true that something in me can be or can become an accomplice of this death which I have ranged myself against. I think we meet here again that kind of confusion I mentioned at the beginning of my analysis.

So long as we immediately introduce the necessary precision, perhaps we can say that each of us is called in some way to determine himself at the core of this confusion and to deal with it in such a way that his future death can have a meaning for him. But here too all these terms would need weighing, particularly the term "call." Have I not said in effect that each one of us can be called to something? Should I say now that it depends on me to constitute a world where this term "call" has a positive meaning? Of course. But here too we must be wary, because the nature of this dependence, or rather independence, is also questionable. And if I find here again, here on my path, the notions I have so much insisted on elsewhere, especially the notion of a creative receptivity, then these notions are radically opposed to everything connected with constitution. It is on this point that modern idealism has defaulted. In other words, there is no question at all of my being able to construct the world, both personal and suprapersonal, at the heart of which my future death can take on a meaning. I cannot even will this world, unless "will" is understood as acquiescing in a concrete order which I have almost had to awaken myself to.

As very often in my work, I find the words for what I am trying to say in the mouth of one of the characters in my plays, words which are summoned by the secret necessities of the dramatic context and which have a concrete precision the pure philosopher can hardly pretend to. I think one of the most revealing moments in my entire work is when Antoine Sorgue speaks in the final scene of *L'Emissaire*. This play has never been performed in France; and it will never be performed until the ferment of hatred that goes back to the Liberation has ended.

> There is one thing I discovered after the death of my parents— that which summons us to survive [*survivre*] is actually what sustains us [*sous-vivre*]. And those whom we have never stopped loving with the best of ourselves become like an immense skyscape, invisible yet somehow felt, under which we move forward, always more divided from ourselves, toward the instant where everything will be enveloped in love.[9]

9. In *Le Secret est dans les îles* (Paris: Plon, 1969), p. 269; my translation.

Here philosophical consciousness, that is reflexive consciousness reduced to its own resources only, makes room for what must perhaps be called prophetic consciousness. "The moment when everything will be enveloped in love" is not *like an event;* it is essentially *jenseitig,* on the other side. It is a moment in which our existence can take on shape; without such a moment this existence risks foundering in the absurd and, in the strong sense of the word, in the unnamable.

These remarks lead to a recognition of something basic which Heidegger has in no way suspected because, despite appearances, he remains the prisoner not of a theoretical but of an existential solipsism. (I would say almost the same for Sartre.) This is the fact that, most profoundly, the consideration of one's own death is surpassed by the consideration of the death of a loved one.

I have already insisted too much on this preemminence, in my 1937 paper and especially in *Presence and Immortality,* for it to be necessary to come back to it here. I will recall here only the brief but profoundly meaningful dispute at the 1937 International Philosophy Convention between myself and Léon Brunschvicg. When Brunschvicg remarked that the death of Gabriel Marcel seemed to preoccupy Gabriel Marcel much more than the death of Léon Brunschvicg preoccupied Léon Brunschvicg, I replied that he had posed the question very badly; the only thing worth preoccupying either one of us was the death of someone we loved. On this point my thinking since 1937 has not changed at all. On the contrary: experience has confirmed my thought in the most sorrowful and inexorable way. It is at this point that I am most radically opposed not only to Heidegger and Sartre but to most earlier philosophers as well. One notable exception ought to be mentioned, and, as so often, it is Schelling, the author of that extraordinary and profound text, *Clara,* which appeared after the death of his wife.

9 / The Encounter with Evil

I WOULD LIKE FIRST OF ALL to specify my perspective in this paper.

It is quite clear that I intend to speak as a philosopher and not as a theologian. Yet I do think that with the problem of evil—I would rather say the mystery of evil—the philosopher's line of thought and that of the theologian curiously approach one another.

I think that in dealing with the question of evil, philosophers have in the course of history shown their impotence more than anywhere else. It has too often happened that in their effort to rid themselves of an irritating problem they have actually evaded it by substituting for the reality of evil mere concepts which they could easily manipulate the way a magician does his tricks. Fortunately there are exceptions. I will cite at least two: Kant, with his notion of radical evil, escapes the criticism I have just formulated; and of course so does Schelling—in his *Of Human Freedom.*

I now want to attempt to develop what I have often called a thought experiment, carried out in the spirit of an existential philosophy; I do not say "of existentialism," for everyone knows, or ought to know, that for a number of years now I have struck this word out of my vocabulary. "In the spirit of an existential philosophy"—this means that I will not carry out an analysis of some concept, but that I will be asking myself how it is that we human beings encounter evil, and what it is possible to say of this encounter. I do not think that we are capable of speaking of evil without taking account of this encounter. This could be put in

another way by saying that if we abstract from this possible encounter or from this possibility of encounter, we are perhaps no
longer speaking of evil but of something else, from which it
would be very simple to liberate ourselves. Generally speaking,
here more than anywhere else, that which is easy is suspect, and
that is my basic objection against the facile literature of edifica-
tion. Anyone who wishes to reflect honestly on evil has to keep in
continual and accurate touch with concrete situations precisely in
their agonizing and, it must even be said, their excruciating character. Without this he is lost in the clouds, in words. Kant's
famous phrase about the dove has an unexpected application
here. Thought, or let us say reflection, is not only inconsequential
but without any weight at all unless it remains very close to that
which is most wounding and suffering about experience. When I
used to reflect with students who came to me for some direction
in approaching the central problems of ethics, I would always
invite them, after they had read short papers, to try an exercise
they were unaccustomed to, a dramatic exercise. "Let us imagine
a particular human being who finds himself in the grip of a problem like the one you have spoken about—a problem, for example,
of responsibility—and let us ask ourselves if what you have just
said could be of any help at all to him, that is, could help him
find himself in the kind of night in which he is groping. But
to reply to this question you will have to put yourself in the
place of this particular being. You will have to stop being simply
a lecturer speaking in a university classroom, which we may as
well admit is an unreal context. Only if you do this will you be in
a position to judge whether in your presentation you have said
anything real at all or have been satisfied simply with words." I
must say that this recommendation could also be usefully addressed to those preachers too prone to be enthralled with their
own phrases without asking themselves anxiously, as they ought
to do, just what echo these phrases might awaken in wounded
hearts. As is so often (if not always) the case, reflection cannot
operate where there is no imagination. And I would add that
without imagination, there is no charity, no *agapē* worthy of the
name.

These general observations apply directly to the problem of
reflecting on evil; they show the extreme difficulty of such a task.
For it is quite evident that for our purposes the imagination of
concrete evil situations cannot suffice, that it must be in a certain way overcome, and yet all the while it must remain present,

intimately present to the thought of the inquirer. If I were to express myself in German here, I would not use the verb *aufheben,* which Hegel and his successors have often, in my opinion, used imprudently. I am entirely convinced that for the kind of beings we are, beings on the way, what we call evil can never be *aufgehoben.*

In order now to get underway with our thought experiment, it seems desirable to begin with the experience of threat. There can be evil, if I am not mistaken, only for a being who is susceptible of being threatened. Of course, this threat does not have to be verbalized; the verbal threat is only a particular kind. We have to ask ourselves just what are the structural conditions without which any threat is impossible, and what are the general forms, whether precise or indistinct, explicit or inarticulated, that threat can assume. One thing we can say is that the only being open to threat is one whose integrity is capable of being compromised or injured. I am intentionally using the term "integrity" because of its generality: it can mean organic integrity, but also moral or spiritual integrity.

Must it be said, as one might first be tempted to claim, that threat as such is always external to the being who is threatened? Reflection seems to suggest that the word "external" is inappropriate here, at least if it is interpreted spatially. I can feel myself threatened from within, where "within" is taken in an organic sense or perhaps as meaning some force or forces over which I do not have *control* but which I am unable to localize outside myself. It is precisely this impossibility of control that is important here and that appears as an essential characteristic of threat.

But let us notice that threat is all the more a threat the *more* diffuse it is, the less it can be isolated. And in this respect it seems to involve a certain confusion of the outside and the inside. The threatened man is in this way comparable to the defender of a besieged city. The defender is unsure whether the besieger has collaborators inside the city or not. He feels betrayed, and the very uneasiness he experiences because of this suspected but unproven treason only adds to his trouble.

This word "trouble" is very important here. It seems to me that we must put considerable emphasis on this word if we intend to raise questions about evil. If we ignore this word, we place ourselves outside the concrete situation endured by human beings who are actually in the grip of evil.

I said "in the grip of evil." Certainly this suggests what I referred to earlier when I spoke of an encounter without which it seems that evil loses its proper character. But the preceding remarks already allow us to see that this encounter has something special about it. I would say that it is an encounter in the night, quite different from encounters that can be had during the day with someone who is clearly visible. Recall the episode in *Sous le soleil de Satan* by Georges Bernanos, where Abbé Donisson encounters the devil. Precisely because this encounter takes place in the night, it cannot occur without the human being hesitating and losing (or being on the point of losing) his equilibrium.

My approach here is perhaps unusual enough to give rise to the following kind of objection. "What is important," someone might say, "is not threat taken in itself, but knowing whence it emanates. Who threatens? It must be that this threat is the manifestation of something, that it is the doing of a particular agent who can be discovered. Who is this agent? What is his intention in threatening? This is what must be determined. But it seems that the only way to characterize this intention is as evil, and that brings you back to asking what evil is—the very question you hoped to begin *answering* by your discussion of threat."

But the thought experiment I am leading us up to here may offer a way out of this traditional dilemma. Indeed, what is particularly interesting about threat or the threatening in this experience is that evil appears as wholly unsusceptible of being characterized and classified like an object, which we control to the extent that we describe it. Free of our control in this way, evil takes us unawares, it surprises us with its treachery, and does so in such a radical way that we are quite unable to locate who or what is to blame.

Obviously it would be completely useless to think of treating evil like the character in a detective story where Inspector X, by his tenacity and shrewdness, finally manages to identify the criminal. Even to speak of the criminal is again to introduce a certain duality between agent and act. Every investigation at bottom postulates this duality, for it is meant only to solve the question "Who is it who . . . ?" Once this question is resolved, the detective can and must consider his task finished. He does not have to question himself about the intimate, perhaps metaphysical relationship between agent and act. The judge or the jury are in a somewhat different situation, of course, because they have to ask themselves whether or not there have been extenuating circumstances, whether there was full responsibility or not, and so forth. We know only too well the confusion jurists and psychologists fall into in the face of such questions.

After this digression, intended to help specify what is distinctive in my approach, I return to trying to explain by a concrete example what I have called the encounter with evil.

Imagine a child who has always had complete confidence in his parents, particularly in his mother. His mother has taught him that lying is wrong. He has never questioned the truth of this commandment, even if he has sometimes transgressed it. If he has lied, it was with the conviction that lying was not good. But this more or less distinct awareness of doing evil has nothing in common with what I am calling the encounter with evil. Suppose now that one day he catches his mother lying. Here all of the remarks I made above about threat as being taken unawares by treachery are strictly applicable. The boy will literally not know where he is, because he will have to admit that the very being in whom he placed his confidence has betrayed him, that this source of values is polluted. As a result the child may be in a quandary. Is his mother guilty because she has transgressed a rule whose value she still affirms? Or must this rule itself be insignificant, so that breaking the rule is also trivial? But then why has this very rule been presented as an absolute one? On the other hand, if the mother is guilty, how can the child reconcile this discovery with the sentiments of respect and admiration he has had for her? Must he say to himself that really his mother is just as fallible as he is? If so, can he continue to feel the respect she once inspired in him, or does her fault actually prevent her from being his mother?

What I have just done is to articulate a certain felt distress, but of course part of the essence of this distress for the one who suffers it is precisely its resistance to such articulation.

I said earlier that the child, even while knowing that he did evil, had certainly not encountered evil. If he had been questioned, and if he had been able to tell us in an intelligible way what he was thinking or feeling, he would doubtless have answered something like this: "I have never pretended to be perfect. I know myself as the kind of person who has considerable difficulty following the rules of conduct which have been taught me. Thus it seems to me perfectly natural to break these rules sometimes even though I know that I am in the wrong. On the other hand I have always thought of my mother as a person beyond reproach. This does not necessarily mean that she has told me she is irreproachable. But for me it goes without saying that she conforms, perhaps without effort and naturally, to those same rules she intended to inculcate in me. Now I have discovered that this is not so. I am therefore in a presence of a genuine treason, and I do not know at all how to interpret this treason. I am disoriented. I am plunged into darkness, whereas before everything seemed to be full of light."

It seems to me that here we have as precise an example as possible of what I call the encounter with evil, where it is impossible to locate exactly or interpret the evil encountered. This comes down to saying that here we are in what might be called pure existence, that is, in an element the domination of which is in some way refused to us, without of course our being able to say by whom or by what.

I shall now take a completely different example which will in some degree complement the first one.

Several months ago I heard about a young man bursting with energy and intelligence who seemed to be assured of a happy and fruitful life. Returning from a vacation, he felt a bit ill and, although he thought it could be nothing serious, he went to see his doctor. He went through certain tests, an X ray examination, and so forth. The tests showed that he had been stricken by an exceptionally virulent cancer, that it was already too late for any kind of surgery, and that he would probably die in just a few months.

Here perhaps even more clearly than in the preceding example we find an encounter with evil. And again evil presents itself as treason, as an unexpected treachery. Obviously it is not easy here to say exactly what takes the place of the mother in the earlier example. The precise designation however is not very important. It is not even necessary to know whether the young man was a believer in the strict and confessional sense of this word. But we can certainly say that his life was ordered by a kind of implicit confidence in those powers which he perhaps felt no need to name but whose harmonious cooperation assured the exercise of his faculties. And this cooperation was required whether the man was a sportsman or a man of action, a scientist or an artist. The feeling of fullness which accompanied his smallest efforts was nothing other than the implicit assurance that this cooperation was in order. He did not have the slightest reason to suppose that it would fail him. I would repeat here what I said earlier. It is evident that here the distinction between what is external and what is not has hardly any meaning at all. One can say equally that everything is external or that nothing is. But now in unforseen conditions and in a scandalous way that cooperation is revoked. One thinks irresistibly of a comparison with a student whose upkeep has been taken care of by someone who suddenly, without any discernible motive, stops his financial aid. The comparison will be all the more striking if we suppose that the benefactor remains anonymous. Suddenly nothing more. The student wants to write, but to whom? The money came through the intermediary of a lawyer who says that he is not authorized to give the name of the donor. Thus, abruptly, an incomprehensible void. In both these cases there is the failure of an indispensable help which was thought to be assured. In both cases every explanation fails, and the very absence of explanation carries to the ultimate the disarray of the being who has been deprived of the indispensable aid.

Let us try to penetrate the tragic and in some ways unfathomable sense of this word "disarray." In both the above examples we see the same radical absence of recourse. In the case of the sick person, it is not simply that there is no known treatment that can stop the progress of the disease. What is missing is any response at all to the terrible question "why?" How should I understand the fact that so many promises, which seem surely to have been made even though I do not know by whom or by what, are suddenly reduced to nothing? Not only do I fail to understand what meaning this terrible situation can have, but I am not even sure it has any meaning at all.

It is on the basis of this situation, whose poignant and even agonizing character I have certainly not tried to attenuate, that we must not ask how evil must be overcome.

It will be fitting first of all to make a preliminary remark which seems to me to be of the very greatest importance. As so often in cases like this, its formulation is negative. It would be contrary to all reason, and one could also say to all possible wisdom, to imagine that there could exist a technology capable of resolving this problem—and perhaps we will have occasion to see that this word "problem" is itself improper here. I have in mind primarily the procedure adopted by Christian Science, which consists in saying that evil does not exist and that one's duty is purely and simply to deny it. This applies of course to sickness. Thus medical treatment is condemned as a sin because it presupposes the existence of evil, thereby contributing to the birth of evil.

Notice however that even in this theory evil exists in a certain way. It is the erroneous or sacrilegious belief in the existence of evil.

Actually, we are dealing here with a claim which is untrue and even strictly *heretical*. It is only too clear, in fact, that the adherents of Christian Science, as well as those of the de Montfavet Christ, arbitrarily isolate and seriously deform an essential part of the evangelical message. In no way does the traditional doctrine of faith imply anything like the proclamation of the non-reality of evil. Generally speaking, Christian realism is radically opposed to this illusory idea, which most often turns out to be a crude borrowing from certain elements of Hindu thought. This explains quite well how alliances can be set up, on the basis however of an almost total confusion, between Christian Science and theosophy. This creates a false spirituality which can become a serious temptation for people who have broken with the strongest Christian traditions but who nonetheless refuse to let themselves sink into a materialism which they identify with positive science.

All of this, however, must not be taken lightly or simply ridiculed. It can never be said strongly enough that these aberrations are possible only to the degree to which not only Christian preaching but theology itself is in default. And it is precisely with regard to evil considered *non in abstracto* but existentially that this failing of Christianity is often the most apparent. I am unable to forget one discussion on divine causality I took part in at the Institut catholique of Paris. When I cited the case of the young man stricken with an incurable disease that I mentioned above, it happened that a religious was there who said that this sick person after all had only to adore the power and the wisdom of God through the determinism of those natural forces of which his case was really just a simple example. I have to say that all of the theologians who were there protested strongly against this remark. Nonetheless, the remark is quite characteristic of a certain type of abstract thinking which is totally blind to concrete human realities, a kind of thinking that is still unfortunately present in many seminaries and faculties of theology. What we have here, and let us not conceal it for a moment, is a laziness of mind which is content to follow paths traced out a long time ago, avoiding that imaginative effort which, no matter what one might think, is inseparable from authentic charity.

What clearly emerges from all of this is that anyone who attempts to reflect on evil philosophically without taking into account the irreducible fact of the encounter with evil condemns himself to remaining outside the subject he claims to be dealing with. Thus whatever he says will have no weight; it will be in contact not with reality but only with vague concepts.

How does one avoid having his thought etherealized in this way? Here I would like to be as concrete and as direct as possible. What I have in mind is really very elementary, and yet I am quite aware that it may appear revolutionary to those accustomed to a certain kind of speculation whose legitimacy they have never questioned. It seems to me that what is called, no doubt improperly, the problem of evil cannot be dealt with except in the context of a concrete communication of one person with another. This problem disintegrates, loses all meaning, the moment it is transformed into an academic question. This might be expressed in a more technical way by saying that the problem of evil is not related to what Kant and others after him have called "thought in general." It could also be clarified negatively, in the following way: It is not only the classical metaphysician or the theologian, but also the technician who operates on the level of what I have called thinking in general, and he does so to the degree that his research deals with perceptible objects which can be modified in some particular way. Let me take an example. I notice something out of the ordinary in the sound of my car motor. I go to a garage and consult the mechanic, who dismantles the motor and finds the indisputable explanation of the unusual noise that was bothering me. Now it is certain that any experienced mechanic whatever would have arrived at the same result. And verification of the result would be easy to obtain: the mechanic replaces a particular part and the noise stops.

Up to a certain point a similar procedure can be carried out with regard to psychological disorders. We can in any case postulate that the problem posed by the existence of this disorder is susceptible of a precise objective solution, and an empirical confirmation ought to be possible.

But I would like to make it clear that there is an abyss between questions of this order, which always have to do with some function, and the problem of evil. Of course it is a permanent temptation for human intelligence, especially in our world which is more and more completely pervaded by technology, to regard evil as a malfunction. A certain kind of psychoanalysis tends irresistibly to interpret what we are calling—quite improperly, according to it—evil or sin as a lack of conditioning, or perhaps a bad adaptation following some distress or trauma. It may not be inevitable that psychoanalysis results merely in mechanistic facts, but it is surely open to this temptation, as I have often said before. On the other hand it might be suggested that the relation beween the psychoanalyst and his patient constitutes after all an example of the intersubjective relation on the basis of which the problem of evil becomes actually meaningful. But this could be true only to the uncertain and precarious degree that this relation comes to resemble the religious one which pertains between a spiritual director and his penitent. Of course even in this domain the dangers are serious, the director of conscience being exposed to the temptation to speak as an expert, as a man who has seen very many other cases, so that he treats the penitent merely as one case among others, without becoming personally involved.

But from the moment evil appears, it is no longer proper to speak of a "case." This is already true to some degree for a physical illness. A doctor worthy of the name will have a relationship with his patient which is individual and in a certain way irreducible. But how much more true this ought to be where it is a question of moral or metaphysical evil.

Thus we arrive, after some necessary detours, at the philosophically unusual idea that we cannot effectively deal with a being visited by evil except on condition of entering into a relationship with him which is in the last analysis a participation or a communion. This means at least that evil cannot in any way be taken as a paradox which has to be explained or solved.

Approaching the problem of evil is not merely a matter of showing sympathy. This word "sympathy" is in any case quite imprecise.

To see a little more clearly what we are dealing with, let us try to go beyond our negative formulation that evil cannot be reduced to a simple malfunction. Even in such an attempt, of course, we can hardly hope to escape the temptation to objectify to a certain extent, for intellectual knowledge always seems to involve a certain objectification.

Here I believe I must stop to consider a remark made to me recently by a man who is not a professional philosopher but who has always seemed to me exceptionally gifted. The substance of the remark was this: "In the depths where evil appears, death invariably begins its work; evil announces death, evil is already death." But here again we have to be careful of those deformative reductions which technological thinking almost inevitably leads to—regarding death, for example, as an integral part of a certain economy or of an order which requires it. But here we see very clearly the falsifying substitution I have so often described. Instead of taking death *hic et nunc* as it comes to devastate a particular concrete life, to ruin a particular love, to interrupt brutally a particular communion, death is taken in general, where it concerns no one in particular and thus can be conveniently discussed at all levels, from biochemistry right up to a certain type of moral philosophy. But this is not all. The way is opened here for a kind of systematic sweetening or comforting of the sort expressed in a spiritualism which thinks it can domesticate death, take away its sting, or transform it into a simple game of hide and seek or blindman's buff.

However, please do not mistake my intention here. In my view there are powerful reasons for admitting that certain communions which are apparently shattered can be reestablished beyond "the shallow slandered brook: death," as Mallarmé says. But I believe also that graces are at work here, certain unforeseeable epiphanies. It would be wholly wrong to think that such reestablishment is anything like a technological success which could be accomplished by anyone who worked at it with enough persistence. There is a balance here which is extraordinarily difficult to maintain—and one might ask whether the Church has succeeded—between an infantile credulity on the one hand, and on the other a systematic suspiciousness which can degenerate into a veritable obstructionism.

I spoke of epiphanies.[1] These liberating flashes of lightning serve to assure us or to confirm us in the assurance that no matter how much a proud and blind philosophy claims that there exists only an emptiness, a nothing, there is on the contrary a fullness of life, the marvelous resources of a world where promises abound, where everything that exists is called to universal communion, where no possibility, no chance, is ever irretrievably lost.

1. I would like to point out here as a fascinating example of such an epiphany the overwhelming witness Rosamond Lehmann brings us in her latest book, *A Swan in the Evening* (New York: Harcourt, Brace, 1968).

In any case our human structure is such that we can only intimate this immense creative consensus. Unfortunately despair has infinite resources for blocking the paths by which these regenerating assurances can reach us. In view of this it must be strongly insisted that a philosophy which gives in to the complacency of optimism, refusing to make a place for the temptation to despair, dangerously misunderstands a basic fact of our situation. In a certain way the temptation to despair resides at the very center of our condition. We need not decide here whether ours is the condition of a sinful and fallen humanity. But certainly questioning despair can help to bring about, if not a solution, at least an infinitely more precise formulation of some of the more agonizing problems I have always kept at the center of my reflection.

Triumph of evil—triumph of death—triumph of despair: these are actually the diverse modalities of a unique and formidable possibility which is inscribed on the horizon of *homo viator*, of man making his way along that very narrow path which runs along a high and dangerous mountain ridge.

Now it would be wholly wrong to think that this looming possibility could be combatted by a completely solitary reflection; indeed it is in the presence of the threat of despair that the inadequacy of such reflection can be seen most clearly. No doubt the solitary consciousness can achieve resignation, but it may well be that here this word actually means nothing but spiritual fatigue. For hope, which is just the opposite of resignation, something more is required. As I first tried to show during what were perhaps the darkest hours of our history, there can be no hope which does not constitute itself through a *we* and for a *we*. I would be very tempted to say that all hope is at bottom choral. But for this we have only mysterious evidence which, in this world of ours, changes its character if it is rationalized. The choir I have in mind here would probably not allow itself to be reduced to the mere intoxication of a collectivity with itself; for if it were regarded in this way, there would be great danger of confusing hope with a kind of exuberance which is after all nothing but an exultation of the vital powers, powers which seem to be inhibited or paralyzed in the presence of death and cannot transcend death. The choir's mission can be accomplished only where the choir itself becomes a propitiatory invocation.

Surely nothing is more difficult to understand—this I think we have to recognize in all humility—than the meaning and the efficacy of this invocation. Obviously we have to refuse in principle every anthropomorphic and mythological interpretation. And I experience as much as anyone the uneasiness that an idea like that of God's anger inspires in modern man. No, here as elsewhere the method required is that of a reflection which exercises itself on and against itself, a secondary reflection. Even if the notion of an impassive God is accepted by certain thinkers, such as the Stoics, Spinoza, and perhaps even Goethe, even if this notion has something intellectually attractive about it, it nonetheless fails quite badly to satisfy a certain kind of mystical need which cannot simply be refused.

I do not want to get further involved in this question, which is one of the most difficult there is, lest I go beyond the limits I have assigned myself in this inquiry.

Yet we do have to appeal here to certain sudden and illuminating experiences in which, beyond the kind of fullness I spoke of earlier, the very heart of God seems to open up to some predestined persons, showing them a mysterious but also in certain respects extremely perilous path.

Surely we must anticipate an objection here, from the man who is not privileged to enjoy such experiences and who can hardly imagine them because they do not fit into any of our ordinary categories. "I follow what you have said about the encounter with evil," such a man might say. "I can even see that a philosophy that thinks it can dialectically manipulate what it calls evil will invariably be guilty of an unwitting fraud. But what I do not see is how those references to a *we* which unifies itself in propitiatory invocation, or to experiences so unusual and strange we can hardly believe they happen, could allow us to escape from the impasse where it seems we are forever blocked up."

What makes any response to this objection embarrassing is the fact that the question itself is put in such a way that it cancels itself out, rendering a response unnecessary.

It is very clear first of all that these "references" can in no way be regarded as means for obtaining some goal. This would be to open the way for a kind of solution I have always insisted we must formally reject. I would say that the term "reference" is itself inappropriate and can only lead to error. Perhaps the only way of proceeding here is by that method of dramatization I spoke of earlier.

If I am in the grip of evil, that is, if I am tempted to despair of myself or of men or of God himself, it is not by turning in on myself that I will manage to overcome this temptation; for solipsism cannot be a liberation. My only recourse is to open myself to a wider communion, perhaps an infinite one, at the heart of which this evil which has come on me in some way changes its nature. For in becoming *our* evil it ceases to be a blow struck at a self-centered love. But this does not say enough. It becomes the evil over which *you, you have triumphed*. Who is this "you"? It can be anyone whose image glows on the horizon of my memory, and of course here we are reminded of the communion of saints, whose value for our salvation can never be too explicitly acknowledged. But it may also be—and in the final analysis these are doubtless only two ways of expressing the same truth—that above and beyond any particular order there is the One who remains for us the archetypal witness, the One whom every witness invokes, whether explicitly or not.

"But," someone may protest, "do you not simply admit the bankruptcy of philosophy in making it depend in the last analysis on the fact of Christianity?" Surely this objection deserves to be considered carefully, but the words "fact of Christianity" could present an ambiguity which ought to be cleared up immediately. Is Christianity merely a certain miraculous history whose authenticity could never seem convincing to anyone who is not a believer? I would answer in the following way: What appears quite clearly to anyone who has meditated on the human condition, on human existence, is the fact that nowhere so much as in Christian teaching has the mystery of this condition been so profoundly illuminated. For this reason no phenomenology of human existence can dispense itself finally from acknowledging the double mystery of crucifixion and resurrection, which alone can shed on our life a light which gives it meaning.

The word "mystery" which I have just used is surely the key word. We have to substitute the words "mystery of evil" for the words "problem of evil" which I said at the beginning we would have to recognize finally as inadequate. Mystery of evil—this means that it is useless and illusory to think that evil will somehow be overcome in history; and no less illusory to resort to some kind of dialectical artifice for integrating evil into a higher synthesis. Here I would say without the least hesitation is one of the absolute limits of Hegelianism and its Marxist successors. But there is another temptation which we also have to resist, one which can sometimes seem almost irresistible. This is the temptation to a Manicheanism, perhaps distorted, which converts evil into a principle opposed to the good and engaged in an endless struggle with it. Nothing deserves our attention more than the heroic effort with which theology from the very first centuries, especially in St. Augustine, has triumphed over this temptation.

Many ways of facing the mystery of evil have proven to be misguided. Only one way really remains, and that is the acceptance of paradox in Kierkegaard's sense, of a double affirmation whose tension must be maintained. Evil is real. We cannot deny its reality without diminishing the basic seriousness of existence and thus falling into a kind of nonsense, a dreadful buffoonery. And yet evil is not real absolutely speaking. We have to arrive not so much at a certitude, but rather a faith in the possibility of overcoming it—not abstractly, of course, by adhering to a theory or theodicy, but *hic et nunc*. And this faith is not without grace. It *is* grace. And what would we be, and what would the difficult journeying which is our very way of existing be, without the light which is so easy both to see and to miss, and which lights every man who comes into the world?

10 / Man and His Future

IN THIS STUDY I shall do my best to refrain not only from playing the prophet, which would be absurd, but even from the more modest pretension of simply working out a prediction as to what the future holds for the human race. On the contrary, I think what needs to be emphasized, at least at the beginning, are the unknowns involved in our present situation—this situation which must be reconnoitered in the sense that one reconnoiters an area in wartime. Probably the main unknown is whether and to what extent nuclear weapons will be used in the near future. It seems to me that on this question one can only wager, and the way one wagers will be determined by certain affective motives. Thus the optimist will take the position that it is unimaginable that men would do something which would endanger the whole race, threatening its very existence. Others who are more pessimistic or cynical would figure that there is no limit to the folly men will commit when they are blinded by their passions.

Another unknown is just how much of the earth might be destroyed. A few weeks ago at a Chinese propaganda film I heard an envoy of the Peking government insist that the imperialists, in their intimidation tactics, were grossly exaggerating the destructive effects of nuclear war. However, it goes almost without saying that such claims designed to reassure the compatriots of Mao Tse-tung are tendentious and deeply suspect.

For my part I do not intend to take a position on these controversial questions, where hypocrisy is rife on both sides. Yet it must be remarked that these unknowns do work their way into the consciousness or the subconscious of men today, and in this

way leave their mark on the general situation we all find ourselves in.

"Mutation" is perhaps the general term which best characterizes this situation as a whole. For there is a certain stability
in it, but this stability is experienced as threatened, not only by
external forces over which one can obviously have no control, but
also from within. It will be worthwhile now to stop for a moment
to see exactly what is meant by these words "from within."

The example that comes to mind immediately is that of the
family. How many parents, at every social level, are bewildered
to see their children escaping them; and not only do the children
repudiate their authority, but more profoundly they seem to live
in a dimension to which the parents have no access. Thus a
process of dissolution gets underway which even the greatest
good will and patience on the part of the elders cannot arrest.
This process deeply and inevitably affects the consciousness of
those who formerly believed they had arrived at some certitudes
which gave their existence some permanent consistency and stability. Now experience seems to show that this permanence was
an illusion, and thus the world of the parents themselves begins
to totter; or to put it another way, it begins to be affected by a
doubt which probably is not acknowledged at first but whose cor-
rosive action will make itself felt more and more. All of this is too
obvious to have to insist on, but as it is my custom to be explicit
and concrete, I shall try to make my example more specific.
Imagine Christian, even devoutly Christian parents whose
children announce when they are seventeen or eighteen years
old that they no longer want to go to church, and with the priest's
approval (supposing he is intelligent) it is decided that no coercion of any kind should be used. Thus a kind of modus vivendi is
established which may well be inevitable but whose effects may
also be harmful: first for the other children in the family who
come to think that assistance at Mass must be simply a matter
of arbitrary whim, and eventually perhaps for the parents too,
if in spite of themselves they begin to doubt the absolutely normative character of rules which have always appeared inviolable to
them.

But it must be recognized that the feeling of change in itself
has something intolerable about it. There is something absolutely
true about this, but it is true in any case for individuals living
in society. That is why there seems to be an almost biological
necessity for a human being to put up defenses against this ex-

perience, which directly threatens what might be called his integrity. I recall one very painful encounter of my own with the kind of uneasiness associated with change. It came when, having just moved out of my old apartment, I realized that I was not yet set up in the new one either. I felt a little as if the earth had dropped from under my feet in an earthquake.

It is easy to see that men today experience an insecurity so fundamental that they seek at all costs to protect themselves, even though they are most often only vaguely aware of what is threatening them. Thus reassurances of every kind take on more and more importance, regardless of how ineffective they might be against such threats as natural catastrophes and wars. But notice that such assurances are invariably technical in character; they are mechanisms which are supposed to intervene to save a given situation clearly determined in advance. These mechanisms appear to have taken the place of the confidence which until very recently men used to put in Divine Providence and in the results expected from prayers addressed to the omnipotent will of a more or less anthropomorphic God. I think that these observations are very important for anyone who sets out to determine how contemporary man stands in relation to an imagined future.

Generally speaking it seems that with few exceptions our contemporaries are not very much concerned about the future, precisely because they are conscious of the change in which they are involved. However, there is one important exception to this lack of concern, and that is the unprecedented effort made by the planners today. The governments of the last quarter century are retrospectively criticized for having so inadequately prepared for the future which constitutes our present, and there is great determination not to make the same mistakes again, especially perhaps in the areas of demography and urban problems. Let me take a specific example. It is generally acknowledged that twenty years from now Paris will have some fifteen million inhabitants, and that it is important to decide on preparations for this enormous extension of our city. But I think we ought to notice that this concern with planning is encountered only in higher circles, among men who somehow feel responsible for the future; it does not effectively reach into the wider population. Everything seems to go along as if people feel obscurely that they can get on with their daily tasks, which might be quite difficult or frustrating, only if they confine their anticipation of the future to one approaching date, which date is generally the beginning of their vacation when at last they can breathe, both literally and figuratively. Thus there seems to be an inevitable gulf between people at the ground level and people at the heights of society, so that the planners can never really feel sure of any mass support. They are perpetually doomed to a kind of uneasy aloofness.

But I think the real problem we ought to be dealing with arises at another level, the level of reflection, or more precisely philosophical reflection, to the extent that philosophy does not evade (as unfortunately it too often does) a certain responsibility toward the human situation it is supposed to explore and comprehend. The word "comprehend" should be taken in its widest sense here. To comprehend is perhaps first and foremost to feel with, to have compassion for. The more I reflect the more it seems to me that compassion is demanded of any philosopher worthy of the name in today's world. I know very well that in expressing myself in this way I am running counter to a venerable philosophical tradition which, with the Stoics and Spinoza, would insist that the thinker's duty is to be dispassionate. But I personally think that while this duty is essential to the vocation of the scholar, the philosopher who is aware of the precise character of his task must refuse this radical separation of knowledge and affectivity which is naturally required in scientific research. I shall not take the time to discuss it here, but I cannot help at least referring the reader to the distinction between existence and objectivity which I formulated very early and which serves as the point of departure for all my works.

The idea that compassion can be enlightening and that this enlightenment is especially demanded in times like ours where the hegemony of technology becomes more entrenched every day is the starting point for the following reflections, which deal with the way in which the philosopher aware of his responsibilities ought to consider that future which man seems to be preparing for himself.

The philosopher of existence does not proceed like a philosopher of the classical type, beginning with a universal principle and then drawing out its consequences. Rather he concentrates his attention especially on a fundamental situation in which, as a man, he is involved enough to live, yet from which he can achieve enough philosophical distance to reflect on it. It is in this spirit that I indicated before how daily life, which is what living in order to subsist is called, appears, at least to urbanized people, as less and less livable, by which I mean that it carries with it less and less of its own justification. For the most part, perhaps even for many genuine believers, this daily life is directed less and less toward an eschatologically conceived beyond, and more and more toward the anticipation of leisure for self-recovery, be it on the weekend, on yearly vacations, or on periodic retreats when one can lay down the oppressive burden of work. But the central question here is precisely whether or not in such circumstances the words "self-recovery" are still meaningful. Many of us know from experience how one can come to grips with himself in calm and solitude. But that happens only if one enjoys a certain inner permanence, and present conditions of life, the influence of radio and television especially, tend to obliterate any permanence of this kind and, as Max Picard has seen so clearly, replace it with a discontinuity to which one may at first merely *submit* but which one ends up *demanding*. Why? Because above all each of us wants to be distracted. We want our attention diverted. From what? To say "from ourselves" would probably be wrong. I would rather say it is from a certain emptiness experienced in an agonizing way as an anticipation of death. Here of course we have something very close to Pascal's notion of diversion [*divertissement*]. But the leisure time everyone is working for, if it is not sufficiently occupied, is likely to bring about just that dreaded emptiness. This explains the fact, which could surprise only a superficial observer, that people on vacation seem to feel the need to group together, rather than seeking out calm, silence, and solitude.

My readers may be wondering impatiently what such remarks, which are no doubt correct but still only partially satisfying, can have to do with an investigation into the relationship of man to his future. I would answer first of all that the big city, not only in the West but everywhere on the earth, is exercising an almost irresistible attraction even on those who formerly would have been happy with a rural life conforming more or less to the rhythms of the seasons. In France a sociologist recently defended a thesis at the Sorbonne in which he proclaimed the death of the peasantry and announced the end of rural civilization as imminent. It is surely possible that this end or disappearance is not quite so near as he thinks it is; but there is no point in denying the fact that for many reasons a kind of tropism is bearing an ever increasing number of people toward the cities, while at the same time, ironically, the cities are becoming unfit for human habitation.

In order to evoke the full meaning of "uninhabitable," I am tempted to recall Heidegger's richly significant discussion of the implications of the verb "to dwell" in his *Vorträge und Aufsätze*. I am thinking especially of the initially disconcerting formula *"Die Sterblichen wohnen, insofern sie die Erde retten"* [literally, "mortals dwell to the extent that they redeem the earth"].[1] The redemption referred to here is certainly nothing like a conquest or exploitation of the world. Heidegger tells us, for example, that mortals are recipients of the heavens as such. In other words, he thinks a dwelling has anthropocosmic value, and certainly this value is entirely lost in the type of civilization prevailing today.

In these conditions it is perhaps not so surprising that I have given such importance to the transformation taking place before our eyes and, more precisely, to the substitution of an agglomeration for what was yesterday the city. It would be entirely wrong to think that this transformation is merely external or superficial. No, what is actually happening under our eyes is a degradation of the very idea of man.

Certainly I can easily imagine an objection which might be raised here by people who think that they see in the present change a sublime emancipation of the human race. They might object as follows: "Instead of hypnotizing yourself with such minor problems as questions about the dwellings or the structure of new towns, would it not be better to emphasize the prodigious conquest of the cosmos that has been taking place in our time, the obliteration of the boundaries in which man was imprisoned up to the beginning of this century? Doesn't this progress offer us an indication of the grandiose future men are working out for themselves?"

I am perfectly well aware how the imagination and even the intelligence can be enthralled with the fantastic exploits of the astronauts, or even more (as in my own case) with the mathematical calculations which permit these exploits to happen. I think the triumph of mathematical thinking deserves special admiration. But there is nothing about mathematical thought which guarantees that the prodigies it produces will have a

1. See Martin Heidegger, "Bauen, Wohnen, Denken," in *Vorträge und Aufsätze* (Pfullingen: Neske, 1967), II, 24.

beneficial effect on the development of humanity itself, and for the philosopher of existence, it is this development alone which counts in the last analysis. In a remarkable novel recently published by a Czech writing in French, I found this profound observation: "Today it is only the verb 'produce' that is still conjugated in the future tense; this is no longer done with the verb 'be.'" I personally would include the verb "have" with "produce."

Here we may return to our earlier remarks on urban civilization. With the contractors who are putting up the huge barracks where the people of tomorrow will be huddled—it is contractors, not architects, who are most often responsible for our buildings today—one no longer finds that essential concern for knowing *what kind of humanity* is being prepared for, and yet no one can deny that a man's existence is molded by his dwelling. It is very hard to see, on the other hand, how the adventures of the astronauts contribute to enriching human nature. In fact everything proceeds as if this nature were more and more being ignored. I would say that here we have the true meaning of atheistic existentialism, no doubt the only doctrine that can be called existentialism without causing confusion. It is well known that for almost twenty years I have consistenly rejected this label which some misguided spirits have mistakenly pinned on me.

I would like to be sure that no one misunderstands the true import of the preceding remarks, and thus I refer to what I said at the beginning about having no intention to play the prophet. This applies especially to what I said about the astronauts. For no one, it seems to me, can make a true or even reasonable prediction as to the range of investigation that will be opened by their adventures. On the other hand, what we can say now is that the astronomical amount of money presently being spent for the conquest of space is detrimental to projects designed to secure the welfare or at least the satisfaction of basic needs of the disadvantaged people of the world. This priority given to activities which are certainly of secondary importance (if not wholly superfluous) unfortunately appears explicable only by certain considerations related to space adventure which are deeply suspect. Can it be denied that this adventure is ultimately based on motives very closely allied to what Nietzsche called the will to power? This judgment could be relaxed only if the great powers who are dividing the world would enter into a collaboration marked not only by consistency but by real good will. We are far from such a development, since it would have to include China, whose cooperation at the moment it is foolish to expect. As things stand now world cooperation is an absurd dream.

The situation of the world being what it is, the ever worsening degradation of those who inhabit the "third world" is at least temporarily beyond hope of alleviation. As Pope Paul VI said in a speech a few weeks ago, the chances of violence seem to be multiplying uncontrollably today. In this regard the dreadful impasse in Vietnam appears as the sign or manifestation of an inner contradiction infecting our world. It is hard to see how this contradiction could be resolved in some kind of Hegelian synthesis. And certainly one cannot fail to remark today the general impotence of good will in the sense intended by Kant and all those who believe in the efficacy of practical reason.

At this point I should like to examine the notion of progress which, beginning with the Encyclopedists, has stirred the hope of so many noble minds. We shall see how degraded this notion has become in our present-day world of 1968.

Long ago I came to the conclusion that there is only one place where the idea of progress remains meaningful and can even be applied in a fully justifiable way, and that is the realm of technology. Incidentally, that is probably one of the main reasons for the increasing fascination technology holds for our generation. But let me be a bit more precise about what I have in mind here. It is undeniable that certain new technical procedures designed for a given purpose are preferable to the procedures they replace. And this word "preferable" should not be taken here in a subjective sense. The new procedure is more economical, for example, or it yields a higher output (i.e., is more efficient). And the result is that it is unthinkable to return to the previous procedures, which have literally been dethroned. Here we find the irreversibility essential to the notion of progress.

On the other hand it would be important, though beyond the scope of this study, to ask oneself what are the negative consequences of such progress. No doubt it would be found that these disadvantages remain negligible, so long as one remains strictly beneath the level of life, and of psychological and social reality. But the more we move in the direction of complexity and, even more essentially, interiority—ultimately, in other words, toward the spiritual—the more these disadvantages assume a threatening aspect. This is no doubt due to the fact that at its outer limits technology loses its self-sufficiency, which is the same as saying that it finds itself up against what must be called a metatechnology, whose presence may of course be verbally denied (everything is possible with words) but which in fact coincides with what I would call the sanctuary of human reality and freedom.

The word "freedom" is of course the key word for anyone who sets out to reflect on the future which men seem to be constructing for themselves. And I am perfectly aware that the confusion that prevails today about the meaning of the term "freedom," perhaps especially among philosophers, contributes in large measure to muddying our view.

For my own part I have always thought that this word "freedom" has precise meaning only where it refers to some development of the person. In my view, freedom can in no way be taken as some attribute which might or might not belong to a human being. I believe that it can only be a conquest, albeit often very imperfect and probably always precarious. From this point of view all the forces of depersonalization work against freedom. There is no need here to go through all the factors involved in the notion of depersonalization. What is important to emphasize is the responsibility incurred these days by those who in the name of a so-called structuralism (this label is as ambiguous as the label "existentialism") are bringing about a devaluation of the person and ultimately moving toward an undeniably extreme positivism.

I shall refrain here from any prediction as to how long such a doctrine will last, a doctrine which appears to me a mingling of several quite distinct tendencies. But unfortunately it seems impossible to deny that the circumstances of existence today militate against the person, and this becomes more evident the more one considers that among these circumstances is the unfortunate state of public information resulting from developments in the communications media. It seems that the media become inevitably more and more standardized, and with that inevitably comes an increasingly marked neutralization of the individuality of human beings. Under our very eyes the prophetic intuitions recorded by the clever Samuel Butler in his *Erewhon* are being verified.

Even if one refuses to engage in risky speculations about the future, a little reflection on the implications of our present experience forces us to recognize that certain very alarming prospects threaten. For *unless there is some cataclysmic interrup-*

tion, the immanent logic of the demographic situation on the one hand and of the uncontrolled spread of technology on the other seems inevitably to lead to a situation inimical to the person and thus to freedom. Unless there is some catastrophe, I say, and this is not just an exercise in style. I am thinking of real cataclysms, not only atomic war, but also the unforeseeable release of telluric or other forces such as we see in terrifying examples every year. We simply do not know what extent these disasters could reach, nor can we in any way intellectually antici-pate what consequences they might have on the ultimate develop-ment of humanity. But let me make a remark here which may seem paradoxical: however emotionally distressing, even stag-gering, such catastrophes may be, pure reflection may nonethe-less find in them the benefit of warning man against a pride, a *hubris* which wise men of every age have seen can only lead to the worst. "Wise men," I say, but where are such men today? As I have had occasion to say elsewhere, the very notion of wisdom has been withdrawn from circulation, generally speaking; but in my view each of us, if he has kept the sense of his responsi-bility despite all threats, must react in his own way against this disappearance or withdrawal.

This is the conclusion of my remarks here, and I apologize for their sober and alarming character. But however terrible the out-look, we must regard defeatism as a trap to be avoided; we have no right to accept the worst as certain: its certainty is what must above all be rejected. And here we must refer to the theological virtues which are situated in what must be called another dimen-sion—the dimension of the instant or of the eternal, whichever you wish. Here I stand with St. Paul, Pascal, and Kierkegaard; and I think we must regard with the utmost suspicion Teilhard de Chardin's attempt, admittedly noble, to unify these dimensions, for he has done it, I fear, at the price of a disastrous confusion between optimism and hope.

The proof of this confusion is the very success his work has found with certain communists who ignore the essentially Chris-tian dimension without which the work loses its thrust and mean-ing. Teilhard de Chardin himself, in *The Hymn of the Universe,* for example, has come out indignantly against any interpretation which would make him the prophet for a future understood as a kind of universal material well-being. But I think that in effect he invites this kind of mistaken interpretation when he seems to sanctify technological progress, and also, I would add, in appearing to underestimate the reality of evil in the history of humanity. Thus, no doubt without wanting to in any way and without foreseeing it, he has prepared the way for a vulgarization of his thought which deprives it of its essential originality.

Obviously one may still wonder whether he has not at least been a great pioneer and whether the task of reconciliation between science and Christianity he has worked so hard at will not be taken up by others who are perhaps better equipped philosophically. Certainly this is a possibility that cannot be excluded a priori. But it would have to be determined—and this is a job which only the philosopher could do—exactly what conditions would be required if such an attempt were to have any chance of success. It would demand a reconsideration of science and religion, or more precisely of the fact of Christianity, based on a direct or immediate insight which would apply to both the theories of science and theological constructions. But it is probably the spirit of Blondel rather than Teilhard de Chardin which would be most conducive to success in such an effort. I am thinking especially of the early Blondel, before he seemed to return to a Thomism from which he had originally freed himself.

I apologize for the rapid and necessarily somewhat obscure character of this sketch. But I do think my remarks may serve at least the negative function of signaling some of the obstacles through which, some day perhaps, human thought will be able to clear a way for itself on the road to a better future.

11 / Philosophical Atheism

ANYONE WHO TRIES TO REFLECT on philosophical atheism must first of all ask himself exactly what basis there is for the term. The kind of agnosticism, with its negative or atheistic tendencies, which flourished in the second half of the nineteenth century is not what is meant. Philosophical atheism involves a formal and explicit negation of God. (I do not just say of the existence of God, for a theology is conceivable that without denying God can refrain from affirming that God exists.)

However, an atheism is philosophical only if it involves a certain pretension. And here, at least at the beginning, we have to keep from taking this word in a pejorative sense. An atheistic philosopher like Sartre, whom I will have to refer to in detail in what follows, undertakes to show or establish not only that God does not exist, but that he cannot exist, and that an assertion of his existence is a contradiction.

But this is still not enough to enable us to speak of philosophical atheism. The atheistic philosopher must in addition attempt to break down the illusions of those who not only affirm that God exists, but even claim some special connection with God in what they regard or seem to regard as an undeniable experience. Thus an authentic philosophical atheism seems to require something like a demystifying enterprise. This is particularly clear in the case of Marxism. But it is just as true for currents of thought like some deriving from Nietzsche which are oriented in a different direction.

The atheistic philosopher must therefore be seen as a man

who says to anyone who believes in God or who in any way affirms God's reality: "I put myself in your place, that is, I am in some degree able to reconstitute what you call your experience. But in addition I have the capacity, which you do not seem to possess, of correctly interpreting whether this is a real or merely an illusory experience."

It seems then that the atheistic philosopher claims to undertake something like what the Copernican astronomer does when he says to someone who still holds to a geocentric theory: "When you say that the sun turns around the earth, you are falsely interpreting a phenomenon which in itself is indisputable. It is true that you believe you see the sun moving around the earth. But as an astronomer I am able to explain this phenomenon. If you are content to say 'I see, or I believe I see, the sun moving around the earth,' no one will reproach you. Your mistake is in the inference you make on the basis of this fact."

And yet a very important remark must be made here, a remark which shows that this comparison might be completely misleading. What the Copernican astronomer does is to substitute for the geocentric hypothesis another hypothesis which accounts for many otherwise unexplainable facts. But it is not at all certain that the affirmation of divine reality is anything like a hypothesis. If, as there is every room for thinking, it is not, then the comparison becomes sophistic and impractical. I do not want to push this point further, but its importance in the present context is extreme.

Another question inevitably arises for anyone who reflects on the basic pretensions of philosophical atheism. What is the basis of these pretensions? Or, more precisely, what evidence justifies these pretensions?

Everything would be simple if it were just that the atheistic philosopher had discovered some new facts so that he had some advantage in making judgments. Then, being in possession of these facts, he could say to the believer: "It is because you are unaware of these decisive facts that you can still think God exists. But look. There are only two possibilities: either you agree to look hard at the facts, and in that case you will see that these facts entail your affirming the unreality of God; or you take refuge in bad faith, either by arbitrarily rejecting the facts or by refusing to draw from the facts all their consequences."

But is this interpretation, in which the atheistic philosopher is seen as justifying his position in an essentially objective way, tenable? Can any decision be made on the factual level here? Is such a factual decision ever conceivable?

Certainly it cannot be denied that the materialistic evolutionary scientism of the nineteenth century led to an atheism of this kind. And if we go back farther to Gassendi, or even to Epicurus, it seems that we do have men who claimed to see the existence of a certain objective structure in things and to have established the incompatibility of this structure with any traditional type of affirmation of the reality of God. And I think that even today the dogmatic atheist is still haunted by the idea of an incompatibility of this kind. However, it can be shown very easily that such a position is philosophically untenable. The more we become aware of the specific character of the affirmation of God, where this affirmation is understood as involving reference to a transcendent reality, the more we shall have to account for the puzzle that no fact and no objective structure of any kind can even be situated on the level of this reality, much less count as evidence against it. In fact we have to admit that there are scientists in every field who are at the same time believers. It is quite evident that between these believing scientists, whether astronomers, physicists, or biologists, and their unbelieving colleagues there can be no objective dividing line. In other words, the atheistic biologist who is also an atheistic philosopher can in no way claim that he knows of facts which the believing biologist does not. All he can say is that the biologist who is a believer is in some way guilty of bad faith, that his reason is clouded by some irrational traditions, habits, feelings, and so forth, so that he does not draw all the consequences from the facts.

Of course, here I am speaking of the scientist who is not only an atheist but who adopts a philosophical position (as was the case, for example, with Félix Le Dantec). But it can very well happen that the atheistic scientist takes a different and much more confused position, by saying: "The word 'God' does not correspond to anything for me, but I see that it is otherwise for certain of my colleagues. Nonetheless, I communicate on the scientific level with these colleagues without any difficulty. I do not know what to think of this difference between us. I abstain from characterizing it since I am not a philosopher." But in such a situation the philosopher's task would be to go beyond simple observation, which remains empty, and to formulate judgments regarding the truth and value in the observation.

In this perspective, it seems that the atheistic philosopher will invariably be brought to denounce in his adversaries what he sees as a bad faith, whose character can of course vary from case to case.

This enables us to recognize that the assurance we spoke of earlier is certainly not a declaration that one possesses certain objective facts that can function as criteria. This assurance is much more a matter of attributing to oneself a lucidity which one intends to show is lacking in the believer. I think we can take as a principle the supposition that the atheistic philosopher as such wants to be, and believes himself to be, perfectly lucid. Let us pause here to consider the term "lucid." What does it mean? Can this term be interpreted in a visual sense? In other words, does the atheistic philosopher actually claim to *see* what his adversary does not see or does not want to see? This kind of simplistic interpretation is too farfetched. Belief in the widest sense, or even simply the philosophical affirmation of God's existence, is certainly not a matter of physical vision. Moreover, we must not forget that philosophical atheism consists in positing an absence, a privation, a negation. But a privation or negation cannot be seen; it can only be thought or inferred. Hence we are constrained to abandon our visual metaphor. Lucidity becomes less a penetrating view than a correct or rigorous thinking.

But new difficulties arise here for the atheistic philosopher. For correctness or rigor cannot after all be defined except in terms of specific criteria such as those of mathematical reasoning, or of experimentation, or of inductive reasoning. But however one conceives of the affirmation of the reality of God or the fundamental act of faith, it is very clear that they are situated in a very different dimension. It is also clear that the notions of exactness and rigor here must be reinterpreted or applied differently.

This is not all. It hardly seems possible to speak of lucidity without referring at the same time to the idea of certain optimal conditions which could be and must be realized by the lucid mind. Doubtless, the atheistic philosopher, whether explicitly or not, attempts not only to benefit from these optimal conditions— for they do not in fact already exist in a finished form for him— but also to set them up to his own profit. The most important of these conditions could consist in abstracting from desires, aspirations, or simply prejudices which he is convinced can only disturb the exercise of thought.

But when we think about this a while we will discover that we are not only faced with a problem here but with a basic difficulty. The difficulty is that the adversary, here the believer, would doubtless refuse to consider the climate the atheistic philosopher claims to set up as normal or, a fortiori, as optimum. He would probably even accuse the atheistic philosopher of a *metabasis eis allo genos*, which is the worst sophism. "To be sure," the believer would say, "if I take up an experiment which deals for example with a chemical or biological process, I must totally abstract from whatever my hidden motives might be. It could be that I am expecting this experiment to confirm a theory I hold. But the most elementary honesty keeps me from letting my expectation interfere with the experimental results which I have to record accurately. With these experimental results I have to act as if I were a *tabula rasa*. But here the situation is very different. For the affirmation in question here can be presented only as transcending or being able to transcend every given objective experience."

Here we meet again what was indicated earlier. An affirmation about God cannot be reduced to any kind of hypothesis at all. But we have to go much further. Someone might think, with the inspiration of an existential theology, that this affirmation is inseparable from a certain passionate interest, or from what Paul Tillich has very well called "ultimate concern," and that where this passionate interest is missing, the affirmation is weakened to the point of losing its meaning.

Thus, when the atheistic philosopher stresses what he calls lucidity, he is on a different level than the one on which the affirmation he contests is situated.

Of course, William James's phrase "the will to believe" can be criticized because it can always be interpreted in a pragmatic sense which neither the metaphysician nor the believer could accept. But it is very doubtful that faith can be thought of without interjecting a volitional and subjective aspect. Faith, it seems, is realized in a paradoxical synthesis of "intelligence" and "will," words which are inadequate here.

If the atheistic philosopher does not want to pursue a meaningless dialogue with the believer, he will have to follow him on the existential level and even go beyond this notion of radical lucidity behind which he pretends to barricade himself. More simply, the atheistic philosopher will come to recognize for himself that his denial is grounded, not in a warrant or anything resembling one, but in passion.

In his book *Chemins vers Dieu,* De Lubac writes: "The psychoanalysis of mythologies has been undertaken with more or less success. More and more the psychoanalysis of atheism must be undertaken. One will always fail, however, to psychoanalyze faith."

Clearly, an atheistic philosopher must take this last assertion as false. Could he admit that his atheism could be psychoanalyzed? I expect that this question can only annoy him, insofar as he remains convinced that he alone has the truth. The consequence is that the passage from the objective to the existential remains difficult. However, beginning with Nietzsche, atheistic philosophy really undertook this kind of migration; but it was never able to free itself from a basic ambiguity. Hence, the deep sense of Nietzsche's phrase "God is dead" is this: On the one hand, it seems impossible to claim that this assertion is a simple observation, for clearly the phrase implies a passionate will to go beyond what is observable. But on the other hand, it seems difficult to eliminate completely from this assertion the element of observation which it contains insofar as it represents a particular judgment on man's development. This kind of oscillation, often hardly perceptible, is an essential characteristic of contemporary atheism.

Perhaps atheism has no force except at the level of a naïve thought, and by "force" I mean simplicity. Philosophical atheism inevitably loses this simplicity when it reaches the level of reflection. It then becomes simultaneously much more virulent and much more precarious. Perhaps the two are strangely linked here. How can philosophical atheism be an antitheism, a hatred of God, without discreditably recognizing what it claims to deny? A kind of despairing dialectic arises here which is quite perceptible in Sartre, less perhaps in *Being and Nothingness* than in *The Flies* and in *The Devil and the Good Lord.*

In this new perspective it is important to reconsider the fundamental question I raised at the outset of this inquiry: what is the nature of that assurance at the basis of the claim of philosophical atheism? For an atheism which calls itself existentialist, this assurance can only be conceived as passion. But we will have to ask whether this passion is not ambiguous. The whole question is whether this existentialist atheism is or is not nihilistic.

The term "nihilism" of course is vague. I have often referred to Besme's words in *The City* by Paul Claudel. These words communicate to me with unsurpassed expressive force what nihilism can be for someone today.

> The evil of death, the knowledge of death.
> It was while I was working, peacefully inscribing
>   a row of figures on the page,
> That this thought for the first time filled me,
>   like a sombre lightning.
> Now I do this, and in a little while I shall
>   do something else.
> In a little while I shall be gay, or I shall be sad, good,
>   wicked, greedy, prodigal, patient, captious,
> And I am living till I am no more.
> But as each of these adjectives reposes upon that
>   permanent verb, in what does my identity continue?
> A torpor invades me, dissolution divides
>   my fingers from the pen.
> The desire for work, the motive for work, have left me
>   and I remain inert and motionless.
> I exist. I think.
> O that I could not think! [1]

And a little further on:

> Nothing is.
>
> . . . . .
>
> I have seen and I have touched
> The horror of uselessness, in what does not exist,
>   adding the proof of my hands.
> Nothingness does not lack the power to proclaim
>   itself through a mouth that can say, "I am."
> This is my spoil and such is my sole discovery. [2]

Nihilism is presented here as a fact, the kind the scientist moves toward, the scientist who has seen everything dissipated or rather reduced to a kind of vain accounting.

But this fact is inseparable from a certain consent, and this consent, by a process whose secret remains unknown, can become passion, destructive passion. In these conditions nihilism ceases

1. *The City*, trans. J. S. Newberry (New Haven, Conn.: Yale University Press, 1920), p. 25.
2. *Ibid.*, pp. 39–40 (translation modified).

to be a simple fascination produced by the consideration of nothingness, and is transformed into the will for annihiliation.

However, this is only a possibility. It seems difficult to defend
the thesis that philosophical atheism entails this nihilistic aspect
or, more exactly, that it conceives of itself as nihilistic. In a general way philosophical atheism even claims to be animated by
a positive, Promethean will. Particularly for the Marxists, but not
only for them, philosophical atheism seems to be the negative
and necessary counterpart of a humanism, even a constructive
humanism. If God is attacked, he is attacked only as an obstacle
man encounters on his path, which must be overcome if man is
to arrive at complete self-mastery.

Does defining atheism in this way involve a dialectic that
leads still further? We have to recognize that atheistic humanism
exalts man much less as he is than as he must become. The risk
here is in conceiving man as Rilke does in some parts of *The
Book of Hours*.

Here again we find an ambiguity we have not succeeded in
liberating ourselves from since we began considering philosophical atheism existentially. This ambiguity is especially clear in
Nietzsche. In general, the atheistic philosopher does not insist
on denying that he may be moving toward deifying man.
Sartre's position in *Being and Nothingness*, particularly in the
conclusion, is very important here.

> Precisely because we adopt the point of view of this ideal being in
> order to judge the *real* being which we call *holon*, we must estab-
> lish that the real is an abortive effort to attain to the dignity of the
> self-cause. Everything happens as if the world, man, and man-in-
> the-world succeeded in realizing only a missing God. Everything
> happens therefore as if the in-itself and the for-itself were pre-
> sented in a state of disintegration in relation to an ideal synthesis.
> Not that the integration has ever *taken place* but on the contrary
> precisely because it is always indicated and always impossible.[3]

(By way of parenthesis, it would be interesting to know
whether Sartre holds these conclusions today. They seem difficult to reconcile with the optimism at the root of communist
ideology.)

But it would be appropriate to criticize the idea of this God-
obstacle which atheistic humanism claims to help man over-

3. *Being and Nothingness*, trans. H. Barnes (New York: Simon &
Schuster, Washington Square Press, 1966), p. 762.

come. The conclusion would be that the atheistic philosopher claims to do away with a God who can be nothing but a corpse, out of fidelity to something more authentically divine which he cannot conceptualize. In this perspective some Christians today, somewhat imprudently, take a position in favor of a professedly atheistic philosophy which seems to them capable of becoming a resource for renewal which religion must undergo if it is not to die.

It is not inappropriate to recognize the purity of intention of these leftist Christians. But such intentions are imprudent. We find ourselves here before the extremely confused situation of the Christian conscience today.

Some years ago I went to Canada, and I noticed at least at Montreal that some lucid and generous thinkers were reacting violently against an indefensible clericalism while adopting a quasi-progressive attitude. I felt they were ready to rebel each time I said something anticommunist. When faced with this kind of situation we need to refrain from what I have often called fraudulent terms. We do not have to ascribe to communism what we legitimately ascribe to an obtuse and reactionary clericalism. However, these practical inconsistencies, which happen every day on the right as well as on the left, betray mental confusions which are becoming more serious.

Some may think I am wandering into politics here and that I am tending to lose sight of what is essential in this inquiry. This suspicion is not very well founded. In our concrete situation it seems completely impossible to dissociate the social from the religious aspect of a unique problem. The essential point is this: philosophical atheism constructs a serious argument from the fact that those who present themselves as God's representatives on earth often conclude deplorable compromises with secular powers. Of course it would be quite legitimate to reply that these representatives testify to their own unworthiness. But in whose presence? Here the problem becomes tragic. It is difficult not to think of the followers these representatives pretend to guide. Representatives like these are liable to deform the conscience of these people, to corrupt them or to scandalize them or perhaps even to cut them off from religion. These simple souls seem incapable of making any kind of distinction at all between God and his unworthy representatives. This tends to create an intolerable situation today for faith.

This again is a much too simple and unjust way of evaluating a state of affairs which actually is extremely complex. The confusion I am speaking about almost always exists in the unworthy representatives themselves. This amounts to saying that this unworthiness is probably not absolute. Certainly he who reads the hearts of men will discover some pure gold, some faith and charity even in those who have concluded scandalous compromises with the powers of this world. In deepening the analysis here one comes up against an ambiguity which has such weighty consequences, an ambiguity implied by the idea of social order. We know only too well what abuses and what crimes those who set themselves up as the defenders of social order can be guilty of; but on the other hand it would be extremely imprudent to misunderstand the values in the social order. It is easy to imagine a genuinely pious man who, ignorant of the world and its doings, collaborates in good faith with those who seem to him the representatives of order.

Inversely, we need to be suspicious of those who declare they do not believe in God but who say that, were they believers, they would tolerate no compromise. This conditional purity has no spiritual meaning at all.

These remarks aim to show how difficult it is in such an area to judge absolutely. Here more than elsewhere we need to refrain from global judgment.

But consideration of the extraordinarily confused situation of humanity today suggests the following distinction, which may perhaps illuminate that situation.

It could be said that there is a philosophical atheism which actually is nothing but a philosophy of lived atheism. This lived atheism is what needs definition. Can it not be said that the United States or a European country such as Sweden—even more than Russia (whatever statistics say)—is tending to become the theater of this lived atheism? This atheism is the basis of the complacency and numbness of a world more and more given over to a technology that ends by functioning only for itself. And numbness tends toward spiritual death. I would agree, of course, that a global judgment here would be unjust or even absurd. But it seems right to say that such a manner of existing and conceiving of life implies atheism as its corollary, even if those who have adopted it and who are moreover numbed by it adhere to a church or to some sect, whatever it may be. Moreever, there would be no difficulty in distinguishing the usual characteristics of this philosophy of lived atheism—a mitigated pragmatism of a biosociological character resting on a psychology and an ethics of conditioning. Every disquiet and, even more, every anxiety would be regarded in such a perspective as the sign of psychosomatic disorder. And psychoanalysis and certain techniques related to it would be counted on to remedy this disturbance, which would be taken as perfectly analogous to the disturbances that affect the digestive system or the kidneys. There might be a mental sciences building which would have a religious department—a chapel equipped with comfortable chairs and provided with a microphone—because some people might think they could establish that a reasonable religious practice presents advantages on a biosociological level. But this model reduces belief to a behavior very much more offensive to the religious conscience than a radical or a declared atheism, because this modernization implies the negation of every transcendence, something which in the most rigorous sense is sacrilege.

This atheism based on complacency can be contrasted with an atheism based on revolt. The latter, we have seen, certainly can be nihilistic, but it is not inevitably so. For it can constitute the negative pole of a thinking which can be oriented finally toward God. In this sense the problem of revolt, as Albert Camus perceived it without however being gifted with the necessary force of mind to discern its philosophical implications, can become not only a fundamental problem but a properly religious one. Revolt can become the initial act of a purifying dialectic. Again the limits within which this revolt is to operate without becoming absurd must be determined. I have indicated along the way how the question can arise with relation to a social order which can be neither canonized nor purely and simply opposed.[4] It would be important to show that the question can and must arise with respect to what we call—or rather what we hardly call anymore—order in nature. It is curious to observe that the consideration of cosmic order hardly seems capable anymore of bringing man today to anything that resembles the pantheism of the past, the pantheism for example of a Spinoza. This is a result of several factors that would require detailed investigation, and I would, moreover, raise against myself the objection that Einstein seems to have adhered to pantheistic conceptions.

4. These remarks are strikingly illustrated by the events of May, 1968, in Paris.

But it seems generally true that this order, in its disproportion to every human measure, is more an object of scandal than of adoration. If the believer finds in it an expression of divine glory, he does so by introducing the reference to a Fall, which would have concerned not only man but nature as a whole. Would it be a mistake to say that, on the religious level, the reference to the Incarnation is so fundamental that the world, considered apart from man and his appearance in the course of the cosmic process, can only give rise to what I would dare to call a negative witness? Here again we find this opposition between the objective and the existential, an opposition which contemporary thought has certainly not yet succeeded in reabsorbing or transcending, even though Heidegger's efforts in his most recent writings are perhaps oriented in this direction. I doubt that this attempt, grandiose as it may be, will succeed; it may very well wind up being a regression rather than an advance.

Although I am not very satisfied with this formulation, I think that rebellious consciousness, which is the threshold of the only philosophical atheism worthy of consideration, ought to be regarded even in the most authentic religious perspective as the starting point for a decisive advance, and the theologian must take as his task the elucidation of the nature of this advance. His responsibility here is the heaviest one possible. For the seriousness and the charity which he will show or not show in his explanation of evil and suffering will determine finally the value and even the destiny of his theology. If it in any way conjures away the tragic, if it substitutes for real suffering and for real evil only a chimera or an effigy that accommodates all the logical manipulations, his theology decisively reinforces atheism. Despite all the arguments that theologians and philosophers have used, atheism finds its permanent base of supply in the existence of evil and in the suffering of the innocent. However, it could be that we are on the verge of important changes. I would not be surprised if we would have to witntess, even in the West, a resurrection of Manichaeanism, a doctrine which remains after all the heretic's major temptation and which is philosophically more interesting than atheism. I will not venture on this ground in order not to go beyond the limits I have set myself. I will limit myself to suggesting that the theologian is bound today, as at the time of St. Augustine, to specify for himself and in contemporary terms not just the clear reasons why he rejects Manichaeanism, but the rationality of this objection.

To conclude, I would recall that an existential theology, insofar as it questions, if not the possibility of attributing existence to God, at least the possibility of interpreting this existence in an objectivist fashion, can confuse some of its initial moves with those of philosophical atheism. A traditional theology of divine attributes sees this confusion clearly. This accounts for the seriousness with which the Roman Catholic hierarchy considers those who are confused in this way.

Doctrinal atheism to me is like a war machine at the service of certain passions embodied in ideologies. But on analysis this kind of thinking proves ambiguous. Its philosophical precariousness is evident because, when submitted to reflection, it falls apart. For, on the one hand, it marks the lowest limit toward which a humanity that has become prisoner of its own conquests can tend; and on the other it attests to this spirit of restlessness, this will to go beyond, which in a perspective of faith, hope, and charity, can be the very mark of our election. But even when understood this way, philosophical atheism, far from being complacent and self-enclosing, must appear as a simple moment in a purifying dialectic. Here there is a serious trap which Hegelianism has set for Christian consciousness. I mean the idea that religion would find its highest and most authentic expression in the thought of the philosopher. Every true Christian would see a simplification in this, even a serious perversion of the necessary relationship between faith and reflection. Moreover, the history of Hegelianism seems to show that this path, like many others, leads to atheism.

But let us know how to act so that what appears as an obstacle becomes the resource of a renewed spiritual dynamism.

12 / Philosophy, Negative Theology, and Atheism

THE SOURCE OF THIS MEDITATION is the crisis which today is threatening to shake not only the institutions of belief but belief itself, and with that, no doubt, all of civilization. I shall be concerned less with the solution of any specific problem than with the exploration of a general situation whose complexity seems to defy analysis. This has been my approach in much of what I have written since the end of the Second World War.

I have also decided to forego any detailed discussion of this or that contemporary theologian or antitheologian, for that would require a course of a year or more. What I shall do is try to make clear a position of my own. I expect this to be rather difficult, and if I do succeed in any measure it will be, as is usual in my work, by a series of convergent approaches, or better yet by a spiral movement of reflection, which is likely to be disconcerting to readers accustomed to a more straightforward development.

Let me begin with this observation: How far we are today from the time when Fichte felt it necessary to clear himself of the reproach of atheism as if it were a slanderous accusation! It would be arbitrary and unjust, I think, to suppose that he simply meant to appease some authorities. However unsatisfactory the great majority of theologians may have found or may still find Fichte's thinking on this particular point, he sees the atheism often ascribed to him as incompatible with the very dignity of philosophy, at least of any philosophy worthy of the name.

But today we find even at the heart of the Roman Church men who tend to accord atheism the value of a necessary test, a kind of purgatory of the Faith, and they suggest that any belief which does not involve an encounter with atheism is too likely to fall prey to a kind of theological dogmatism no longer viable today.

I would say that on a certain level this is an understandable and even justifiable attitude, but we must inquire whether at the level of existence it might not be fatal. Consider the example of the French philosophy professor I know who used to set out at the beginning of his course to tear down the beliefs of his students, claiming that this would help them later to rebuild on a more solid foundation, or more correctly—for this professor was not a believer—on a soil better prepared for the growth of an acceptable religion. But acceptable to whom? To himself, of course, that is, to a nonbeliever. The result was too often just what might have been expected—a catastrophe. It is so much easier to destroy than to reconstruct, especially in a young person in whom the spirit of contradiction and rebellion is raging. Very often it is a suicide attempt which finally shows the danger in such reckless gardening. The idea of a tentative or methodological atheism, which one is inevitably tempted to compare to the methodical doubt of Descartes, will always seem somewhat distressing and even revolting to the naïve believer. Of course it is precisely the idea of a naïve faith that is meant to be attacked by such doubt, so that what is still perhaps wrongly called faith would be perfected or dissolved through the encounter with critical reflection. But can such doubting reflection, however philosophically justifiable, be fruitfully grafted onto the life of a soul unencumbered by philosophical sophistication? Nothing could be less certain. I do think, however, that it is extremely important to locate precisely the position of the philosopher with regard to naïve faith, especially the position of the existential philosopher who is, strictly speaking, not a dialectical thinker.

First, however, I would like to examine the atheism we seem constrained more and more to breathe, except in certain protected places where it might be said that the crucial test has not yet been encountered. I shall begin by looking at the notion of lived atheism, and then see if philosophical atheism might not be regarded as a philosophy of lived atheism.

The words "lived atheism" refer not to any professed opinions but to a certain way of living and of feeling (as opposed to thinking) which has no apparent reference to what is more or less clearly meant when atheism is spoken of as a doctrine.[1] One might be tempted to say that this lived atheism is a mode of existence where everything is subordinated to a kind of individual self-interest or the satisfaction of the appetites. In such an interpretation individual self-interest is obviously taken in its narrowest meaning, signifying acquisitiveness, as, for example, a preoccupation with amassing goods for oneself or obtaining honors. Here the heaviest emphasis is on the words "for oneself," to show that all generosity is lacking, as would not be the case, for example, with the father of a family who works furiously with the intention of leaving his children the fruits of his labor. Admittedly it could be argued that such a man's children are in a certain sense still himself; but it cannot be denied that a life of labor dedicated to one's children implies a certain kind of transcendence.

Lived atheism seems to imply the total absence of scruples, a ruthless single-mindedness in the struggle to possess material goods or reputation. Indeed what appears to define lived atheism is this kind of systematic moral occlusion, which may come about from avarice or greed but also perhaps from licentiousness and lust. In every case there seems to be a kind of asphyxiation of the conscience.

But what would a philosophy of such an atheism be like? Let us remark at once that here the word "philosophy" is not without a certain ambiguity. It does not seem to mean a simple phenomenology which would consist in describing this atheism; it seems to have a further meaning which we shall have to try to uncover. If philosophy is taken here to mean a justification, then it would have to be a cynical kind of justification, something like the extreme doctrines of La Rochefoucauld and perhaps Nietzsche in the transition period when he wrote *Human, All-Too-Human*. It would have to show that in fact human reality is structured in such a way that it is a prisoner of itself, of its tendencies and desires, so that any attempt at generosity or genuine disinterestedness of any kind must be condemned as trickery or more exactly as a camouflage people use to give themselves a deceptive moral comfort. Of course it is difficult to see how anyone could muster a will to lucidity heroic enough to let him unmask all his deception and cure so comforting a blindness.

But in fact it is extremely unlikely that many who actually

1. Cf. the discussion in chapter 11, above.

profess lived atheism would be in the slightest disposed to accept my interpretation of their attitude. Moreover, it must be carefully observed that among atheists one meets many examples of generosity and actual brotherly fellowship of a kind certainly not always found among those who claim to be Christians and who even believe they are practicing what they call their religion. Particularly among Marxists, though not exclusively there, one very often finds a close adherence to values based on concern for the other, or at least for the collectivity, yet there is no question of those values in any way depending on a transcendent or divine principle. For the Marxist, God appears as just one more hypothesis—one which can be done without, however, and which must in fact be rejected in any sensible view. Surely the lives of such men, if taken on their own interpretation or even simply by outward appearance, seem to be irreproachable. But do we have the right to call this kind of existence lived atheism? It seems much rather that we are here in the presence of a *professed* atheism whose significance or thrust is purely negative since it is the refusal of an alleged hypothesis. Is it possible to live a refusal that bears only on an idea considered fictitious?

Certainly a refusal or denial can give rise to a proselytism, itself negative, such as we find embodied in certain organized displays in the communist countries. Here, surely, we are dealing with a militant atheism. But can such militant atheism be identified with lived atheism? Experience shows that it is possible to yield to intense propaganda for something one cannot actually live—for what one calls ideas, for example, which turn out in fact to be merely some intoxicating words. Yet, it might legitimately be objected, one gets drunk on such words only because they are charged with a certain impassioned force. And does not atheism present itself as a passion? Yes, but we must look more closely at what is meant by the word here. It must mean the passion of hate, indignation, or contempt. But what is its object? Does it not look as if the atheist here gives the God he denies just enough existence to be able to hate him, to revolt against him, to have contempt for him? For a man to have such reactions against what he declares not to exist is obviously absurd, or at least it is certain that here we move from atheism to antitheism. I would remind you that, in France, De Lubac, in his fine book *The Drama of Atheist Humanism*, has brought this very important distinction to light.

It may be objected that perhaps the passion of atheism is

unleashed not at all against a God known to be unreal, but rather against people who maintain and propagate a delusive belief. But if this were the case, further questions would arise. What kind of judgment is hiding behind such animosity? Is the atheist reproaching his opponents for being victims of a fraud or swindle which is consciously and intentionally being practiced on them? In this case atheism comes down to being the crudest sort of anticlericalism. Its champions will probably distinguish between the real scoundrels who draw personal profit from these lies and the poor dupes, the "imbeciles" who are simply uninteresting victims of the purely vicious swindlers.

In fact I do not think that an intelligent atheist (I am thinking especially of the Marxist) would hold such a simplistic view, whatever difficulty he might have in admitting that a believer can be at the same time sincere and intelligent. But in any case what is lived in such a case is anticlericalism, not atheism, for atheism appears here as something purely abstract and incidental.

Taken together these reflections seem to indicate that the notion of lived atheism is a pseudo-notion. But in a related perspective it would be useful to note that some men and women who regard themselves as Christians because they continue to go to church can in fact be living as atheists in the sense that they go about their lives as if God did not exist. No doubt they would be astonished, though, if they were accused of being atheists.

These various observations seem to point to an idea I developed some years ago—the idea that belief and disbelief are not necessarily conscious of themselves; thus they are essentially different from what we ordinarily call thinking.

But if philosophical atheism cannot rightly be considered a philosophy of lived atheism, how can it be defined? This becomes an extremely important question, since such a definition would seem to be an integral part of the essence of atheism. Atheistic philosophy as we know it professes atheism. But we must here point out some differences on the existential level. Professed atheism can be presented as a cry of defiance hurled at beliefs regarded as obsolete, as vestiges which could only interest the sociologist. But professed atheism can also—this time in a minor key, not a major one as before—be a lucid and sometimes desolate, brokenhearted declaration which in no way resembles a provocation.

However, it must be admitted that today some atheistic philosophers, Sartre, for example—though one passage in *The Words* might be interpreted otherwise—do not seem to experience anything like a nostalgia for what others might regard as a lost paradise. Or if they do in spite of everything feel something like regret they generally feel constrained to deny it and to attribute it to a lingering childishness which must be gotten rid of as much as possible. Psychoanalysis, where belief in God might be interpreted as a father fixation, is frequently used to accomplish this sort of exorcism.

It appears certain that philosophical atheism involves a certain philosophy of history, the first sketch of which is to be found in the works of Condorcet and Auguste Comte, but which today is encountered in many different forms. In this view it is held that when man arrives at a certain stage of emancipation he can no longer believe in God, so that atheism is seen as a kind of indispensable spiritual weaning. It goes without saying that this idea of a necessary and inevitable weaning can be met today in the continuation of the Hegelian left, especially of course in Marxism, and also in thinkers quite differently oriented, such as Nietzscheans or even, in the final analysis, adherents of Freudian psychoanalysis. In every case atheism is presented as linked to a certain maturity of spirit, and this maturity is seen as the fruit of a preliminary growth, namely history.

Of course it is undeniable that philosophical atheism can develop in certain minds exclusive of any historical mediation. This would be the kind of view which wishes to be pagan and thinks it can turn for inspiration to someone like Epicurus, blithely ignoring two thousand years of Christianity. I think that we ought to regard as a peculiar and isolated fact of contemporary philosophy Sartre's attempt, in *Being and Nothingness*, to demonstrate the very impossibility of God and the purely imaginary character of the totality toward which human reality transcends itself in its existence as "lack." What is meant by the word "God," Sartre says, is a being which at the same time is what it is, in that it is sheer positivity and the very foundation of the world, and which at the same time is not what it is and is what it is not, since it is self-consciousness and the necessary foundation of itself.

The being of human reality is suffering because it rises in being as perpetually haunted by a totality which it is without being able to be it, precisely because it could not attain the in-itself without losing itself as for-itself. Human reality therefore is by nature an unhappy consciousness with no possibility of surpassing its unhappy state.[2]

When one considers the later development of Sartre, it becomes difficult to take this text altogether seriously unless it be admitted—hardly a tenable admission—that the political adventure he has engaged in since he wrote it is to be considered a pure diversion in the sense meant by Pascal. In fact I do not think that Sartre can be made into a Pascalian, but for our purposes this question is not of primary importance.

What is important, however—and here we enter the second part of this study—is to ask ourselves whether, in inquiring into the possibility or impossibility of God as Leibniz did, for example, we do not *ipso facto* place ourselves outside the sphere where the word "God" is still meaningful. Still meaningful for whom? I would say for a believer or for someone whose thinking is situated in an existential philosophy of faith. Here is what I mean: to proceed as one does with a mathematical formula, for example, asking whether or not it implies a contradiction, seems to transform God into an object, thus substituting for him something which is in some sense his opposite. Of course such a suggestion implies a position in which God is viewed as subject or, to use the language of Barth, as the Word speaking to each one of us as creature.

It is true that one could answer, in line with a certain traditional theism, that in creating a free being God is in some way dispossessed to the extent that this being is allowed to dispose of his own affairs. This is an idea which up to a point can be satisfying for a philosophy of the traditional type. But it is highly doubtful that it could be satisfying for the believer or for the existential thinker. As for idealist or dialectical thought, they will generally appear profane and sacrilegious to the existential thinker, not merely because they deny the sacred, but because they in fact seem to view this denial as if it were itself sacred.

This remark brings us to an idea encountered quite often in apologetical writings—the idea that really there is no such thing as atheism. No doubt this idea is at the root of the view I re-

2. *Being and Nothingness*, trans. H. Barnes (New York: Simon & Schuster, Washington Square Press, 1966), p. 140.

ferred to at the beginning of this study, the view that atheism is, after all, a legitimate transitional stage on the way to belief. According to this view, what is denied or rejected in atheism is never God himself, but rather a particular idea or better yet a particular image one has of him, such as the image of a king. But if this image is rejected, it is rejected in the name of an idea which may not be explicitly brought out but which nonetheless refers to what God would have to be in order to be able to be truly recognized for what he is. Now, is not the implicit reference to this idea, this guiding idea, actually a way of believing in God?

It seems to me that this would be a purely theoretical interpretation which has the serious disadvantage of being situated outside existence, outside the concrete life of persons. If one accepts this interpretation, he must see that the upshot of atheism, as I indicated earlier, is revolt. By way of example let me recall the first conversation I had with Albert Camus some fifteen years ago. Like so many others he found the suffering of the innocent, particularly of children, an insuperable impediment to belief. To any theologian who would have tried to explain to him that this suffering is not willed by God but only permitted (it is well known how immoderate a use this distinction has received) he would answer that he rejected a God of this kind. Thus he took his stand, if not with Dostoevski himself, at least with one of the characters in which that author presents himself to us, Ivan Karamazov. Could he have agreed with the argument I outlined above, conceding that his protest or his revolt itself implied a kind of previous acceptance of a God of justice and mercy? I am sure that he would have seen in that a kind of sleight of hand which his integrity would have rejected. He would have been rejecting the idea that it would be possible to hypostatize the sentiment of indignant compassion he felt for so many innocent victims, and for my part I think that, all things considered, he would have been right. It is precisely characteristic of existential thought, it seems to me, to refuse such pseudo-solutions.

Here we must deal with a difficulty. For the moment let us ignore the problems presented by the words "the believer," and take up those surrounding the words "the existential philosopher." The problem is with the definite article.

When I speak of an "existential thinker," such as Kierkegaard, I put the emphasis on his singularity, on the fact that he is one specific man and not another. But if I use the definite article, do

I not imply that this singularity can legitimately be ignored? When I speak of *the* existential philosopher am I not treating him in a way which could be characterized by the German word *überhaupt*, "in general"? But however well this manner of speaking may be applicable to the philosopher of the classical type, or at least to the idea of philosophy which seems to emerge in classical thinking, is it not strictly inapplicable in the existential sphere? What makes the problem poignant and disquieting is that in an inquiry such as this it seems we must either say exactly which philosopher we have in mind (Kierkegaard, for example) or else imply a certain generality in spite of everything. It hardly needs to be pointed out that a very similar problem arises when we wish to inquire about faith. For we are faced with having to make sense out of the relationship between faith as a general subject of inquiry and faith as it belongs to the individual believer himself.

It does seem to me that careful reflection on what I would call the intermediary status of the artist, especially the poet, might allow us to simplify our inquiry, at least to a certain extent, even if we cannot solve the problem entirely.

The poet—and I do not mean the clever rhymer but the authentic poet—is in the last analysis a man of the same stamp as the existential philosopher. And it obviously does not make sense to speak of the poet in general; or, if one does, he must at least refrain carefully from taking the poet as the representative or bearer of an idea which could be called poetry in general. For the truth is that "poetry in general" does not exist. It is perhaps tempting to speak of something like a poetic orbit which any individual poet may travel one part of. But such an expression would also have to be rejected, finally, as inadequate, insofar as it is couched in spatial language. Nonetheless it does help bring us closer to a reality which is beyond the modes of representation by which we ordinarily try to grasp it. Here, as is so often the case, we must avoid the considerable intellectual temptation to think of this reality as a totality. Perhaps this is more evident for music. There is a world of Mozart as there is a world of Beethoven, of Chopin, of Debussy. But what an illusion it would be to think that these worlds could be added to one another to form an ensemble which could be called the musical universe. It is essential to existential philosophy, as I conceive it at least, to take a stand against the pretensions of totalizing thought. I do not at all believe in the possibility of a reconciliation between existential philosophy and Marxism, which remains in principle Hegelian or Hegelianizing.

I believe that these insights have an important bearing on the problem that concerns me here, although it may seem that I have strayed from my subject. The more we try to approach God existentially, that is, from within faith, the more we shall be on guard against any temptation to affirm his reality as totality. Here the uniqueness of the relation which binds the creature and the creator becomes especially important. It is quite possible however that the term "relation" is inappropriate here, precisely because of this *Einzigartigkeit* [uniqueness]. We could speak of a relation only if God could be treated as one term. And that would require, as is always the case in thinking about relations, a thought situated above the two associated terms, a comprehensive thought. But we simply are not capable of all-encompassing comprehension. That is basically what I meant when a long time ago I wrote: "When we speak of God, we should realise that it is not of *God* that we are speaking." [3] To *speak about* implies a designation. But notice that the word *designer* is ambiguous in French. I can free myself from this ambiguity by distinguishing between the German *bezeichnen* [to characterize] and *hindeuten* [to show the way]. What must be avoided here is a *Bezeichnung*, not a *Hindeuten*. Indeed it can be said that a catechesis is precisely *ein Hindeuten*, though this certainly requires some further clarification. A *Bezeichnung* inevitably implies some delimitation, and that is why we cannot practice this operation on what we call God. This comes down finally to saying that God cannot be treated as object or as objectivity.

But what I have just been saying is really the core of what is ordinarily called negative theology. And it is easy to see the inevitable comradeship which develops between negative theology and atheism. Generally speaking, atheistic thought, especially when it proclaims a kinship with science, develops in the domain of objects and attempts to establish some definite relations among them. That is to say that, in its eyes, if God is not an object he does not exist.

Now after half a century I find myself back at the problem that first exercised my thought before the First World War. What do we mean when we say that God exists or when we deny that

3. *Metaphysical Journal,* trans. Bernard Wall (London: Rockliff, 1952), p. 159.

he exists? With Jules Lagneau I asked myself whether denying his existence was in fact refusing him all reality. Here, after many detours, we have come to the central problem. But when I recall all this groping and tormented inquiry, carried out at the time in almost complete solitude, I am forced to admit that I would undoubtedly not have dared to say that I *believed* in that God with regard to whom I was trying to maintain that, even if his existence was denied, his reality could not be taken away.

But it does seem to me that existential inquiry appeared from the outset the only way to follow if I wanted to escape, if not exactly the contradiction, at least the almost unbearable tension experienced by a mind imbued with the idea of a God who was real but *nonexistent, nonobjective.* Could one not escape the tension by finding a way of distinguishing strictly between existence and objectivity? I am quite sure that I was not imitating Kierkegaard, for at that time he was only a name to me. None of his works had as yet been translated into French, nor had I had a chance to look at the German translations. In fact it was reflection on the body-subject and on sensation that led me to think that if I, a human being, exist, I exist to the extent that I have a body, that with this body and through its mediation I maintain contact with the world, which contact can in no way be reduced to a relationship describable in scientific terms.

Without my being wholly aware of it, at least at first, this line of inquiry was actually oriented toward the incarnate God, toward the God who has conferred existence on himself by becoming a man like me. But while philosophical thought was able to lead me toward the incarnate God, it was not enough to make me believe in him. I needed to become personally engaged in a witness that was more than philosophical. I believed in the faith of others before daring to say that this faith was also mine: a threshold had to be crossed, and this threshold is what we call conversion.

"But what possible interest can this story have today?" it may be asked. "Does it not merely stir up a bygone past, which is of interest only to the historian?" But in fact this story is not merely a digression which as such might be inexcusable. What I mean is that the obstacle to be surmounted today remains what it was at the time of my first inquiries. It may even be that it has become still more formidable with the development of science and technology, which in the past half century has reached a dizzying pace. Just recently I read the report of another well-known expert claiming that man is an electronic machine. Is it possible to show a more radical misunderstanding of what we call existence, or, in other words, subjectivity?

It will be well now to return to the term "witness" which I used above, and to answer a possible objection to my employing it in a philosophical register. Is not witness really situated outside the jurisdiction of philosophical thought? Or could we say that there might be two kinds of witness, one of which could be recognized or verified by philosophy and another which operates only in the context provided by an actual conversion of the kind I have mentioned above?

It is evident that if one maintains the classical view of philosophy, such as prevailed not merely in the eighteenth century but even with Kant and most of his followers (although here there are many subtleties which cannot be ignored), the answer can only be negative: it does not belong to philosophy as such to bear witness. Now is this also the case for the existential thinker? This is the crucial question, and I would mention at the outset that in my opinion any appeal here to the expression "Christian existentialist," which I have vigorously rejected as a label for myself these last fifteen years, can only bring the worst confusion into the picture.

Let us look at things closely. Witness implies a commitment. But who is the subject of this commitment? Who is the "I"? It seems evident that it is not simply the empirical "I," not merely the self as an observed fact. Here, are we not literally wedged between the rational domain where the philosopher tries at least to escape the bonds of his individual subjectivity, and the empirical field properly so-called? Existential thought as such, however, involves precisely the refusal to accept such a disjunction. But is this refusal justifiable; can it be defended? What is the status of the thinking which enunciates this refusal?

Let us recall what we said about the poet, for, like the poet, the existential philosopher cannot be considered in purely general terms, as *any philosopher whatever;* he too is defined by a vocation, a vocation for fraternal comprehension. It is this understanding which is at the heart of witness, which permits the philosophical recognition of witness. But such recognition requires an "ear" comparable to the ear of the musician. This ear is not only a faculty; it is a gift. Now one cannot cut a gift to one's own specifications, nor can one do that with a vocation, and the two—gift and vocation—are inseparable. But in the case of fraternal comprehension as in that of "ear," we are not dealing with a simple psychological datum, but rather with a power co-ordinated with a value. I must say, however, that I use the term "value" here with some reservation, because it is ambiguous; we are here at the meeting place of value and being.

Let us now move more quickly beyond this formulation which cannot be wholly satisfying, and attempt to understand what purity of witness would be and how we might recognize it. I think that the key thing to see is that purity here involves the reabsorption of the external relation expressed by the preposition "to" [*de*]—that external relation which is present every time there is witness to an established fact. Would it not have to be said that witness implies what I would call—and please excuse this neologism—the "transpearance" [*transparition*] of what is acknowledged in the witness? But the question of recognition appears immediately. How can I recognize this "transpearance"? It seems that it would be possible only through the reflection of a light. Let us not allow ourselves to be misled here by a metaphor taken from the field of optics. But it is still necessary, it seems to me, to have recourse to what I tried to express earlier when I spoke of a light which would at the same time be consciousness of illuminating, which would be joy at being light. The virtue proper to witness would consist precisely in transmitting this light-joy of which it is itself the bearer.

Here of course we cannot avoid running into objections from critical reflection, which is everywhere on duty to detect possible illusion. A person who bears witness may be both a dupe and a deceiver. It is of little importance what line of development is taken in this enterprise of detection, and of little importance too what partisan inspiration, Marxist or psychoanalytic, for example, lies behind it. In every case the person bearing witness will be finally convicted of fraud, and unwitting fraud at that.

But my evocation of the notions of purity and reabsorption at the start of these final remarks was designed precisely to indicate that all these attempts at detection have their undeniable value only this side of a certain limit, this side of the point at which witness presents itself as transcending every attempt to reduce or invalidate it.

"Still," it may yet be asked, "is it not inevitably some historically defined God who is acknowledged in witness, and is not this historical determination, even if it remains unexpressed, enough to deprive the witness of that character of purity and unconditionality you have insisted on? And on the other hand if you wholly ignore any historical or sociological reference and yet claim that you are still speaking of God, doesn't he become that God of the philosophers (Spinoza's God, for example) to whom there is not much sense in bearing witness since he cannot properly be said to enter into the existential sphere?"

This is a serious objection, and we must stop to consider it. I think I would answer in the following way. In connection with what I have called the purity of witness I believe that we must fully bring to light what is meant in the affirmation of the Holy God, the *Deus Sanctus*. I would point out that this affirmation is not at all reducible to a judgment of predication in which God is assigned the attribute holiness. It is much rather a song of praise or an exaltation surging from a certain central region where the mind and heart are one. But it is clear that a song of praise is witness par excellence, and because it is spontaneous it rejects or drives away the critical and detective reflection I discussed above.

"But does not a certain obscurity or confusion still remain?" it may be asked. "Is the 'I' of praise the 'I' of the philosopher, or if it is not, would you claim that this praise can be justified or discredited by the philosopher?"

To admit this would be to fall back from the position attained in what I said above. It is perfectly clear that when I spoke of fraternal comprehension I did not mean some verification or authentication of the kind which could be established for a phenomenon. The praise affirmed in the *Deus Sanctus* simply cannot be reduced to a phenomenon. It is recognized by the philosopher as transcending any such reduction.

"But have you the right to speak of 'the philosopher' here?" it will doubtless be asked. "Is the use of the definite article justifiable? Are you not in fact thinking about some particular philosopher, some particular kind of philosopher—basically, indeed, about yourself? Does not everything you have just said finally come down to this wholly subjective affirmation that in your individual view the Holy God is metaphenomenal?"

Again I think we are up against an important objection whose value will be in forcing us to steer clear of a certain equivocation or ambiguity. I must interrogate myself, undertake an indispensable examination of conscience as a result of this objection. In speaking of the philosopher, do I really mean myself in the most limited sense—*me myself alone,* the person who is speaking? Certainly I do not mean any philosopher whatever, or the philosopher in general. But I have already suggested that between this "me myself alone" and that "philosopher in general" there is a third possibility which must be taken into consideration.[4] And I have tried to show that this third possibility is defined by a certain vocation, a vocation which is fulfilled in being a voice *in the name of those who* . . . I break off the sentence here, because some reflection is required before going on. Perhaps we could say: in the name of those who through prayerful thought are raised up toward the Holy God, and I have sufficiently indicated that it would have to be a prayer of praise rather than a request, since a request tends to detract from the sanctity of the One appealed to. This third possibility, which I am trying to live, thus appears as a *locum tenens*. It is not enough to say that it is intimately related to a fraternal community, for "relation" would suggest something too loose. What I have in mind is the very voice of that community, which can perhaps be assigned no clearly traceable limits.

But here we must anticipate another attack. "What has happened to philosophy in all this?" it will be demanded. "Have you not left the domain of philosophy and entered that of religion?"

The truth is that this recognition of witness, which moreover must become cowitness, is the farthest limit of an inquiry which as such can only be philosophical. This inquiry has as its goal to determine the conditions in which the affirmation of God can take place, without however crossing the threshold of actual conversion; that is, it remains beneath the level of any acceptance of a specific creed in a certain specific ecclesiastical context.

At this point I think it would be useful to cite a text of Ferdinand Ebner in order to show how in this matter I am in opposition to an existential thinker with whom in many other regards I find myself quite in agreement. I first quoted this passage in a note in my journal which seems to be dated July 16, 1918. Ebner says:

> Philosophical thought seeks God too, but does not find him. The philosopher thinks in the third person, but God must be found in the second person. Thinking that wants to find God must become prayer—not simply ideal or formal prayer, but actual, real prayer.

4. Cf. the discussion in chapter 2, above.

And if it was philosophical thought before becoming prayer, now it is no longer so.[5]

You see that my position here is different from Ebner's. In my view the passage from the third to the second person, to the extent that it must be grounded or justified philosophically, is still situated this side of the religious as such. Moreover it seems to me that here I am in agreement with Martin Buber, for I am certain that he considers as properly philosophical the writings he has included in his book *Between Man and Man*. Indeed, it is reflection itself which marks out the limits of what can be accomplished by thinking exclusively in the third person, and recognizing these limits is what gives the idea of intersubjectivity its full meaning. However, as I believe we have already seen, theory, even discourse as such, always tends to degrade intersubjectivity, by converting it into a relation between beings treated in the third person. For me the consciousness of this kind of antinomy is expressed in the dramaturgical inspiration which is behind a great part of my work. In drama, the subject transcends objectification, since he is treated as a first person, and the other becomes a "thou" for him.

Getting back to what I said earlier about the affirmation of God, I would say that it comes into contact with philosophy, arising at the farthest limit of a philosophical inquiry, where for the philosopher it appears as directed to the Holy God considered in his holiness, beyond any representation which might dedivinize him [*dédiviniser*] (please excuse this slightly barbaric word, but it expresses very well what I want to say). There is still a question as to whether or not this affirmation is something that ought to be dealt with by negative theology, and on this matter I shall not take a categorical stand. I would say however that this is mainly a problem of definition, though I am perfectly aware of how exposed and thus vulnerable such a position can be. But it does seem to me that if one remains, with Ebner, in the third person, if with Ebner one expels from philosophy the entire realm of the "thou," one must probably at the same time deny entirely the philosophical legitimacy of existential thinking as it has developed in the last half century with a fruitfulness which seems to me incontestable.

5. Marcel, "Journal philosophique," V (unpublished). See the listing of Marcel's unpublished materials in Roger Troisfontaines, *De l'existence à l'être* (Paris: Vrin, 1953), p. 423.

13 / Passion and Wisdom in the Context of Existential Philosophy

NOT LONG AGO some students from a neighboring country told me of the uneasiness and even intellectual discouragement they felt at so often hearing their professors come out in favor of compromise solutions to the philosophical problems they were trying to solve. I told them I understood their reaction very well, for I too have often, in retrospect, reproached my own philosophy professor for having proceeded in this way, thus giving the impression to students that truth is something generally colorless and mediocre. My correspondents then asked me if I would accept an invitation to come and speak to them on this delicate subject. I did accept, for reasons of principle, although on the whole I was finding it quite difficult to deal with this problem in precise, intelligible terms. I finally adopted the method of first interpreting the reaction I had noted in my correspondents, and then asking myself whether this reaction could be justified by reflection.

The two adjectives I have used—"colorless" and "mediocre" —did not appear in the letter of my correspondents. However, they do seem to me appropriate, and might allow us to clarify the problem at hand. Those compromises seem to be repudiations of a certain demand blossoming in consciousness, a demand which might be described as the demand for an exalting truth, a truth one could follow passionately and perhaps eventually even sacrifice oneself for. But are we dealing simply with an affective state here? It does not seem so, and in fact the very word "affective" is one of the most ambiguous of words. What needs clarification is precisely the relationship that can be formed between a person—perhaps it has to be a young person—and that truth he would eventually be ready to give himself to and eventually even die for. It is evident—this we must acknowledge in all objectivity—that communism is for its adherents just such a truth. And it goes without saying that Christianity, where it is truly lived, has the same character. But what exalts is the unconditional. Whether it is explicit or not, the affirmation lying behind exaltation is: "It is unconditionally true that . . ." But those professors whose indifference or perhaps even belligerence I mean to criticize will take a stand against this unconditional. For them, *while it is true to a certain extent that . . . it would be no less correct to say that . . . ,* etc. It is as though they are trying to be mediators or judges whose prime responsibility is to give an impression of scrupulous fairness.

I would admit at once that from the point of view of what I have elsewhere called primary reflection, they cannot be faulted for this attitude, precisely because they do appear as committed to the maintenance of a certain kind of justice and because it is actually very rare in any piece of litigation that one or the other party involved is entirely right or entirely wrong. But then would not my protest have to be disallowed on the grounds that it denies the value of the progress which has been made over the primitive conditions in which conflicts were solved by force?

Certainly this is an intelligent riposte. But I think it could be answered in the following way—and now it is secondary reflection which must come into play. The question at issue is one of knowing whether the most important philosophical arguments can be treated as contests between persons which can only be effectively reconciled by giving each his due according to the principle of equity or fairness. Now we can shed light on this problem by focusing our attention on the following point. In ordinary litigation we see distinctly the role arbitration can play, or more precisely we can specify what conditions a judge must fulfill in order to do justice to his office and in order that everyone can see that he actually is doing it justice. But when it comes to deciding on philosophical questions is the matter so clear? Nothing is more doubtful, and of course here I am on ground where my own thinking has tried to clear a path for almost half a century.

No doubt it would be tempting to answer here that a historian of philosophy who has sufficient familiarity with philosophical systems is qualified to practice a kind of reflective balancing which would allow him to pass judgment, to serve as arbitrator between contradictory theories both presenting themselves as true. But in fact nothing is more delicate than moving from the exposition of a doctrine in a historical reconstitution to this kind of evaluation or weighing. Besides, experience shows very clearly that the more deeply the historian enters into the doctrine he is trying to understand and in some measure re-create, the more difficult if not impossible it will be for him to maintain the kind of distance necessary to evaluate it objectively. It is as if the historian, in seeking to identify himself with the philosopher he is treating, *ipso facto* loses the possibility of judging him. Take Victor Delbos, for example, one of the most deeply conscientious historians of philosophy I have known. Nowhere in his book *La Philosophie pratique de Kant* is there a judgment on Kant's thought to be found, and I knew Delbos well enough to know that with him this omission was due to his humility. Such comparative judgments are however quite common in popularizations, which lack that absolute honesty grounded in long years of studying a system in its genesis and structure. Indeed it seems that, contrary to what ought to be the case, comparative judgments are more hasty and categorical the less the person making them has a direct and profound knowledge of what he is talking about.

Moreover it must be admitted that a meting or portioning out, such as is involved in any comparative judgment, always has to do with *things*. But can the thought of an authentic philosopher be in any way regarded as a thing? Here I must refer back to my own very early appreciation of Maurice Blondel's extremely important distinction between *pensée pensante* and *pensée pensée*. Now it is certainly tempting but infinitely dangerous to cut the umbilical cord that binds *pensée pensante* and *pensée pensée*. But that is just the temptation a person yields to (unwittingly at that) when he thinks he can reduce a philosophy to the formulas in which to a certain extent it is embodied. "To a certain extent," I say, for it is infinitely dangerous to think that these formulas can be isolated not merely from their explicit context but from the kind of inner thrust which precedes them and without which they lose the essence of their meaning. It is just such an illusion that lies in the background when a philosophy is treated like some chemical compound which can be manipulated in various ways; weighing, of course, would be just such a manipulation.

I am reminded here of my friend Charles du Bos's declared aversion for comparative literature, and perhaps more generally for any comparison in the literary and artistic order. He had so acute a sense of the unique and incomparable that in his mind the *rapprochements* constantly sought by a certain type of criticism appeared to him as a betrayal of what is essential in literature. Perhaps he carried this scrupulosity too far. But I think that fundamentally he was right, and that what he so sharply condemned in art and literature can be condemned at least as appropriately in philosophy. Thus the very idea of weighing is incompatible with a reflected appreciation of any philosophical doctrine in its profoundly organic character. The necessarily crude operations carried out by the popularizer who claims to give his readers the elements of an evaluation take place in a kind of imaginary space which has nothing in common with that in which the philosopher's own thought grew like a plant, like a living organism.

Bergson, to whom incidentally Charles du Bos owes so much, has shown once and for all, in his memorable work on philosophical intuition, the kind of essential incommensurability that exists between philosophical doctrines:

> In this point is something simple, infinitely simple, so extraordinarily simple that the philosopher has never succeeded in saying it. And that is why he went on talking all his life. He could not formulate what he had in mind without feeling himself obliged to correct his formula, then to correct his correction: thus, from theory to theory, correcting when he thought he was completing, what he has accomplished, by a complication which provoked more complication, by developments heaped upon developments, has been to convey with an increasing approximation the simplicity of his original intuition. . . . What is this intuition? If the philosopher has not been able to give the formula for it, we certainly are not able to do so. But what we shall manage to recapture and to hold is a certain intermediary image between the simplicity of the concrete intuition and the complexity of the abstractions which translate it. . . .
>
> What first of all characterizes this image is the power of *negation* it possesses. You recall how the demon of Socrates proceeded: it checked the philosopher's will at a given moment and prevented him from acting rather than prescribing what he should do. It

seems to me that intuition often behaves in speculative matters like the demon of Socrates in practical life. . . . Faced with currently-accepted ideas, theses which seemed evident, affirmations which had up to that time passed as scientific, it whispers into the philosopher's ear the word: *Impossible!* Impossible, even though the facts and the reasons appeared to invite you to think it possible and real and certain. Impossible, because a certain experience, confused perhaps but decisive, speaks to you through my voice, because it is incompatible with the facts cited and the reasons given, and because hence these facts must have been badly observed, these reasonings false.[1]

I would remind you of Bergson's own experience in this regard. He says that, after having studied a certain number of doctrines which seemed to him at least conceivable, he came to Kant and something in him exclaimed "impossible, that is impossible."

Those who feel that these remarks are meant especially for them may object that this last word does not belong in a truly mature reflection, which would inevitably deny the implied unconditionality and introduce what might be called the *quodammodo*. "By what right," they would ask, "do you reject the authority of a limiting reflection which would come to remedy the abuses of what you call exalting and exalted thought?" Here of course we are at the very heart of the problem we are reflecting on. I would express my thoughts in the following question. If the structure of the real is interpreted not objectively, like some transaction which could be analyzed and arbitrated from without by an expert, but rather as it is revealed from within to beings mysteriously called on to live and die, does not this structure appear somehow inwardly ordered to the demands of exalting or exalted thought? I must return here to what I wrote in *Being and Having* before Sartre's thought had taken shape. I am not first and fundamentally *homo spectator*, but rather *homo particeps*. I have however become aware, since the time when I formulated this distinction, of the ambiguous and in certain respects perhaps fallacious character of the term "participation." Today I would tend to say that basically it has only a negative value; it indicates the kind of natural splitting that seems to take place the moment I say "I am." And here I must refer not to Bergson

1. Henri Bergson, *An Introduction to Metaphysics: The Creative Mind*, trans. Mabelle L. Andison (Totowa, N.J.: Littlefield, Adams, 1965), pp. 108–10.

but rather to Claudel—the early Claudel who is, in my opinion, the greatest. Let me quote for you the beginning of the first scene of *Tête d'or*.

CÉBÈS: Here I am, imbecile, ignorant, a new man before unknown things, and I turn my face towards the year and the rainy arch, I have my heart full of weariness!

I know nothing and I can do nothing. What shall I say? What shall I do? How shall I use these dangling hands, these feet that lead me like a dream by night? The word is only a noise, and books are only paper. There is no one but myself here. And it seems to me that all the misty air, the rich ploughlands, and the trees and the low clouds speak to me doubtfully, in a speech without words. The ploughman returns with his plough, the belated shout is heard. It is the time when the women go to the well. Here is the night.—What am I? What am I doing? What am I waiting for?

And I answer: I do not know! And within myself I desire to weep or shout or laugh or leap and wave my arms! "Who am I?" Some patches of snow still remain, I hold a branch of catkins in my hand. For March is like a woman blowing on a fire of green wood.

—May Summer and the terrible day beneath the sun be forgotten here, O things; I offer myself to you! I do not know! Behold me! I have need, and I know not of what and I could cry endlessly, loudly, softly, like a child heard far away, like children who have stayed all alone by the red embers! O sad sky! Trees, earth! Shadow, rainy evening! Behold me! Let this request that I make not be refused me! [2]

Why did I feel I had to reproduce this admirable text? It is not only because my own thesis is displayed here in a new perspective, but because in Claudel's poem we find expressed with incomparable vigor that fundamental situation, the situation of the "I" on the earth. Now I would say that the more acutely a person becomes aware of this situation, the more he will be repelled by the idea of arbitration in the sense in which we have been considering it. The unconditional is implied in the very fact of being-in-the-world, of having perhaps to love, surely to suffer, and above all in knowing that one is condemned to die. We are thus structurally situated outside the order where it could be said, as if weighing the pros and cons, "it is perhaps true that . . . but it is no less correct to say that . . . ," etc.

2. English translation from *The Penguin Book of French Verse*, ed. Anthony Hartley (Baltimore, Md.: Penguin, 1959), IV, 17–19.

I think that here it would be well to anticipate an objection our opponents will surely raise. "We admit," they will no doubt declare, "that the human situation taken in its brute form, so to speak, actually involves some elements which are situated beyond or, more exactly, beneath any disjunction or any juxtaposition expressible by the word 'also.' But we have the right and even the duty to ask what role ought to be taken by philosophical thought with respect to these brute data. Does not the role of philosophical thought consist in bringing order into this kind of primitive solitude? And to do this must it not precisely put in question any apparent unconditionality? No doubt part of the proper reaction to our fundamental situation, to our bewildered solitude, is the lyrical cry. But is not philosophical thought quite incompatible with lyricism?"

Here we see the field of our inquiry narrowed and delimited. Exaltation belongs to lyricism; can it have a place in metaphysics? At least it is obvious that it could not belong in the same way to both. The real problem is to discover whether song and lyric poetry do not in their own way express an aspect of reality which could also be approached through a different kind of language, but which could never be expressed by concepts designed to allow us to manipulate reality in different ways depending on the field under discussion, through the kind of weighing involved in the arbitration I spoke of above.

Here again I return to what I said a quarter of a century ago in a talk given in 1930 at the Fédération des associations d'étudiants chrétiens, a talk which was later included in *Being and Having*. In a way which today strikes me as too strictly religious—which is explained by the fact that I had just been converted to Catholicism—I described an order which in every respect stands in contrast to the world where technology prevails, an order where the subject finds himself in the presence of something entirely beyond his grasp.[3] I would add that if the word "transcendent" has any meaning it is here—it designates the absolute, unbridgeable chasm yawning between the subject and being, insofar as being evades every attempt to pin it down. Here too is where the experience of the sacred may occur simultaneously with that of fear, respect, and love. My main concern at that time was to assign a place to the act of adoration in a

3. *Being and Having*, trans. Katherine Farrer (New York: Harper Torchbooks, 1961), p. 187.

world which seems more and more determined to banish it. But today after long experience, and also after having grappled with the later Heidegger's thought, I have come to see a broader meaning in what I have called metatechnology. And it seems to me that it is this notion that I must bring to light now in order to make more precise and more intelligible what I said in the first part of this study.

As a matter of fact the present moment in history seems to me especially favorable for achieving an awareness of the intrinsic value of metatechnology. Above all here I have in mind the conquest of space and the foolish ambitions it is bringing about. Does anyone really believe that the chief concern of those responsible for these admittedly stupefying exploits is to extend the limits of our knowledge? No, I fear that we are in the presence here of what might be called an unrestrained, even hyperbolic colonialism. It might also be seen as alienation carried to the absolute extreme, where man appears totally and desperately determined to forget his own condition, to discover or invent the means to break out of this condition altogether. Metatechnology as I conceive it is first and foremost a recapturing of integral selfhood. But notice carefully that I do not mean some strictly psychological phenomenon. The truth is that I can find my true self again only on condition that I become attuned once more to the reality in which I participate.

It is clear that here we are exposing our flank to an immediate attack which we may as well face at once. "The word 'metatechnology,' " it may be objected, "seems etymologically to imply a going beyond. But are you not actually recommending a regression toward a pretechnological stage, where man stood impotently at the mercy of a world beyond him in every sense?"

No, I do not advocate a regression which would ultimately involve abandoning the conquests brought about by technology. What I have in mind is the following: Technology is proceeding in a certain direction, and there is no way to see a priori the limits the mind will encounter in this direction. This is certainly true in the field of interplanetary exploration. We do see obstacles in the way of man's progress here, but certainly we dare not deny that these obstacles might be overcome with the help of technical procedures whose principle still escapes us. We can, however, say without hesitation that in this direction the development is irreversible. Only a cosmic catastrophe or one brought about by the folly of men could halt it. But apart from that it would be wholly unreasonable to think that man could somehow be brought to an about-face where he would slow down or even reverse the progress of technology.

I have been speaking of a "direction." This word is important, and it invites us to consider as its complement the word "dimension." When Rilke said of religion that it is a direction of the heart, he was referring to a dimension in which or according to which technological progress could never happen. But today a considerable temptation exists—we see it in China even more than in Russia—to become enclosed in the dimension of technological thought to the point of denying that there could be any other dimension. The nature of this denial, however, must be more strictly specified. It amounts to the claim that everything that does not lend itself to understanding in terms of technological thought, and thus in terms of observable changes in the material world, must be regarded as illusory. If a philosopher has the effrontery to ask about the nature of this illusion, about its status as being or nonbeing, he would probably be answered by reference to history. "This illusion," it would be answered, "is a vestige, it is something which belongs to the past, which no longer fits in the world we are building with the solid materials of unshakably positive, scientific data."

My dear readers, you must surely be asking yourselves if I have not wholly departed from the question I posed at the beginning of this study. In fact I do not think so, for I have been exposing precisely the kind of middle term, the modus vivendi, which is adopted by those I mean to criticize. Doubtless these compromising spirits would at this point want to suggest the following: "Why not admit that there is a real, objective world, and that of course this world can be controlled and mastered by technological thinking; and then say that on the other hand there is a realm of sentiment, a sort of refuge where the soul, wounded by the spectacle of that pitiless world, can harmlessly get away from it all?" Now I say without hesitation that this false broadmindedness outrages and scandalizes me as much as it should you. The place where metaphysical and religious affirmation occurs is not like a public park, a health spa, or a campground where one spends spare time or vacations.

I am convinced that philosophical thinking worthy of the name must be absolutely uncompromising and must wholly reject any such comfortable pseudo-solution. It must do so even if some people say mockingly that its refusal to compromise is a passion. In my opinion few words are more completely surrounded by confusion than the word "passion," and this is first of all because of the ethymology, the ancestry of the word. If one emphasizes the *being passive* seemingly implied in this expression, there is every chance of wholly misunderstanding the nature of passion, for it is above all an exaltation. It may be tempting to think of passion as a feeling, but this would be wrong. The passion for freedom, for example, or the passion for truth—and these are much more closely related to one another than is commonly believed—certainly cannot be reduced to any feeling whatever. One of the greatest contributions of Kierkegaard (and, much later and in a quite different context, of Nietzsche) is to have brought to light the purely positive dimension of passion. However, we should not imagine that this positive element cannot be degraded into something sterile and even destructive. I think that if we look at an example here we shall have the best chance of seeing clearly. I would like to take the example of the passion for knowing, because it will have the extra advantage of helping to head off any charge of irrationalism that might be leveled against what I am saying. I would remark in passing that this term "irrationalism" ought to be greatly distrusted, for it is very often applied in a confused and unjustified way. I am thinking for example of the unjust and unintelligent criticism Benda dared make of Bergson. It might be noted that Léon Brunschvicg, a thinker of much higher caliber than Benda, always professed an affectionate respect for Bergson's thought.

Recall that a few moments ago I denied that there was any legitimacy in accepting the easy solution of positing, outside the world ruled by technical thought, a kind of small enclosure where sentiment and feeling could take refuge. Now what I have just said about passion ought to help clarify what I meant, and the example of the passion for knowing should be especially illuminating. For in fact the technological world itself is founded on inventive and creative thought, and there is nothing in technology which can account for a passionate creativity, or ground its possibility. Notice that here we are back at that metatechnology I spoke of above; perhaps now we are nearer to understanding it more clearly. As is so often the case, my thought has been moving in a spiral path in the course of this chapter.

If we now focus our attention on the passion for knowing (we could as well take the passion for justice) we see that it involves something which can be expressed in the simple words "at any cost." However strange it may seem, there appears to be a task marked out in history or in the world, to which certain people find it imperative to dedicate themselves without caution and even without discretion. This is very important for our thesis. For if we remain on what we have called the level of arbitration, the words "at any cost" are meaningless. One does not work out a deal at any cost; beyond certain limits it becomes disastrous to try further for a deal, and the attempt must be abandoned. But in the passion for truth, or justice, we are dealing with something mysterious, for gaining truth or justice is in no way like working out an acceptable deal.

Yet we must proceed carefully, for often enough the expression "at any cost" can be heard in technocratic circles, whether communist or not. For example: "This dam must be finished by such and such a date no matter what the cost." The apparent coincidence in attitude here may well be disquieting. At any rate it forces us to inquire what are the limits beyond which the words "at any cost" become both an insult to reason and an outrage to humanity. For this we shall have to bring in some considerations which are of the order of wisdom. Thus, having dealt with the notion of passion, we return to the consideration of another essential element in the title of this essay; and with some remarks suggesting the pertinence of existential philosophy I shall have brought together the main lines of this study.

Today the word "wisdom" is in disrepute, for it is heavily mortgaged, so to speak. Is wisdom really the *ne quid nimis* of the Latin poet? Is it the spirit of moderation carried to the point where we are almost forced to call it mediocrity? I believe that considerable reflection has to be spent in a fundamental reevaluation of "wisdom." And such reevaluation seems to me possible only in the light of a fresh awareness of what man *is*, of what he *can be*, and at the same time of the abuses he has to avoid. But here we may be in danger of falling into contradiction.

On the one hand it is as true for us as for the Greeks that *hubris*, which is pretension, excess, and defiance, should be condemned. But on the other hand, have I not said that the direction of unchecked technological thought is irreversible? I see one solution to this contradiction, and it lies in recognizing the obligation to somehow overtake the activity of technology itself through a reflection which can be called existential in that it must focus on the implications of the "I exist" and must aim to unveil what is hidden behind those simplest and most mysterious of all realities—birth, life, and death. It is only on the basis of a reflection of this order that a wisdom worthy of the name is possible. The question remains whether this wisdom can be of a strictly humanist character, and to speak frankly I do not think so. I have in mind the humanism of which Anatole France and Renan were perhaps the last representatives—both of them a bit pretentious. We might add the names of Duhamel and even Giraudoux if you wish. At any rate I think that this humanism is a thing of the past. Marxism seems to have taken over humanism, and taken it over, incidentally, in a way that an impartial mind cannot fail to find seriously alarming.

When I say that the wisdom I have in mind is not properly speaking humanistic, I mean that it appears to itself, if it reflects on itself, as grounded to some extent in an action emanating from what many of us would call the Holy Spirit, or if one prefers not to use so theological an expression, from spiritual powers which are not at all situated within the orbit of the human world as it appears even to the most careful observer. All my own thinking has aimed at such a wisdom, at least since my conversion to Catholicism—though many notes dating from an earlier time unquestionably point there as well. I think this is important for anyone who wants to understand the development of my thought. In the beginning my thought was oriented toward what might be called a premysticism, that is, it tried to mark out certain preliminary approaches to mysticism properly so-called. But little by little, for a long time without my being aware of the way I was drifting, or rather inclining, I began to concern myself with discovering the conditions beyond which any wisdom worthy of the name tends to disappear, to be replaced by a madness particularly insidious because in certain circumstances it can take on the appearance of rationality.

Now to respond to the question implicit in the title—and this will be my conclusion—I would say without hesitation that a wisdom which does not include passion, which does not acknowledge the subterranean justifications of exaltation and sacrifice, is not worthy of being called wisdom. For passion ought to be a fact as fundamental as life or death. The job of the philosopher is to bring passion itself to light, and above all to cast light into the abysses in which passion can lose its way, in which it is blinded to the point where it takes itself as a law unto itself.

14 / Toward a Tragic Wisdom and Beyond

WORDS GET TIRED and worn out just as men do. For both, some relief may become necessary. Has the word "sage," which has made a timid appearance in French official and institutional language, been assigned to take over for the word "expert"? It was "sages," or at least men so designated by the public powers, who were given the job of making a comprehensive study of the wage problem when there was a strike of mineworkers in France some years ago. Their job was to determine what wage increases would have to be given under the circumstances, while taking full account of the continual price increases and the necessity of avoiding anything which might compromise financial security and open the way for inflation. A serious and difficult problem to be sure, but after all a job exclusively for technicians of the economy.

Now if we look at the history of human thought we cannot help seeing that wisdom is of an entirely different order, that it is metatechnical or metatechnological in the sense that it often involves a critical questioning of technology, of the very notion of technique. Thus the fact that it is precisely in virtue of his known or supposed technical competence that a man is assigned to try to solve a problem of the kind outlined above is enough to show that the word "sage," which implies wisdom, is the wrong word to describe him.

"But isn't that really only because the word 'sage' expresses an obsolete idea which belonged to a pretechnical age?" someone may ask. "Is not society, equipped with the instruments provided by the sciences, encroaching further and further on the realm of inwardness, of the *bei sich Sein*, where the words 'sage' and 'wisdom' hold their citizenship?"

Indeed I am afraid that this objection indicates what really is happening to the inviolability or impregnability so long attributed, especially by the Stoics, to the inner life. This is true at the level of knowledge, but also, tragically, at the level of life itself. More than fifteen years ago, in an address at the Convention for the Freedom of Culture held in Berlin, I said the following, and I hardly need remind you of the tragic experiences that lay behind my fears.

> Each of us, if he is honest with himself and not hopelessly naïve, must admit that there now exist concrete methods that could be used against him tomorrow to deprive him of that sovereignty, or to put it less dramatically, of that self-control, which in former times he was perfectly justified in regarding as inviolable. We cannot even say with the Stoics that a man retains the consoling possibility of suicide. This is no longer true, since he can be put in a situation where he will no longer even wish to kill himself, where sucide will appear to him as an illegitimate recourse, where he will think of himself as obliged not only to endure but to desire his punishment as retribution for faults of which he accuses himself, perhaps without even having committed them.[1]

These sinister possibilities (which no doubt become realities most often in countries under the Soviet yoke but perhaps elsewhere as well) are linked in a certain way with the fact that, especially since Nietzsche, the reality of inwardness has been radically thrown into doubt. It is more than doubtful that today any human being could succeed in isolating a certain core which he could call his essential self. This kind of fragmentation of the self serves as an indirect invitation to every form of interference and intrusion by society.

Perhaps here it would be well to anticipate and deal immediately with a question which might arise. It might be asked: "Isn't there good reason to simply speak of a decentralization of wisdom, and to recognize that in today's world society itself is taking on the characteristics traditionally thought of as belonging to the sage?" In fact it is probable that the somewhat confused idea of such a transfer has been fluttering before the minds of doctrinaire socialists for a long time, and probably this was also true for the utopians of the last half of the nineteenth

1. My translation.

century. But the idea of this transfer rests on an almost insane illusion, for society, whatever perfection it achieves in the technical sphere, can never become a genuine subject; it will always be only a quasi- or pseudo-subject. At best its behavior is to the being and acting of the sage what an electronic brain is to a thinking person.

But have we not been imprudent in seeming to admit so easily, as if it were perfectly obvious, that wisdom as defined by moralists was linked to a situation that no longer exists for man today? Actually it would be more precise to say that what seems no longer capable of maintaining itself in our time is a certain assurance, an assurance which is always in danger of degenerating into presumption and self-satisfaction. Thus we find ourselves drawn along one of many paths to enter a zone of insecurity whose visible or symbolic expression is the mortal danger our species is facing as a result of the presence of nuclear weapons. In such circumstances the so-called wisdom of the retired judge or military officer who translates Horace to fill up his time can only have for us the somewhat touching but nonetheless ridiculous quality we would find in old photographs discovered in a drawer in an ancient farmhouse. Certainly we must completely resist the temptation to think that wisdom is reducible to this kind of daily regime or spiritual diet happily practiced by those who, while they may still be living physiologically, have nonetheless actually said good-by to the responsibilities, risks, and temptations of life.

I should now like to present in positive form the idea whose negative side I have just shown. For man today, it seems that wisdom can only be tragic wisdom. Here of course we meet Nietzsche on our way, and it must be admitted that this encounter is hardly reassuring. For if at one time Nietzsche's thinking could qualify as wisdom—and perhaps this cannot be denied—still it can be asked whether it is by accident that it finally ended in insanity. At least this question is enough to force us to examine very closely the limits within which a wisdom that calls itself tragic, or wishes to be tragic, can remain wisdom.

It must also be acknowledged that these words "tragic wisdom" have a romantic ring to them, and this can hardly fail to awaken some disquiet. No doubt there is some good reason for thinking that contemporary man, if he wishes to reach a certain depth, cannot simply ignore the experience lying behind romanticism, even if he rejects this movement as a *Weltanschauung*. I think he must acknowledge this experience as part of himself, at least as a temptation overcome, though not, of course, overcome once and for all. The words "once and for all" are applicable only in the domain of rationality or of the technology in which rationality is embodied, not in life itself with its continual reversals, repetitions, and nostalgic appeals arising from the past, especially from the world of childhood. I would say that this permanent temptation, which each of us must fight against, is one aspect of a fundamental insecurity which must remain continually present to our consciousness, bestowing on the only wisdom which remains accessible or at least meaningful to us its authentically tragic character.

This view is sound, I think, but still much too vague and abstract. It will be truly worthwhile only if it can help bring at least the beginnings of answers to the burning questions we face today as a result of the accelerated and hyperbolic development of technology and the possibly mortal dangers to which this development exposes our species.

The supposed wisdom of Gandhi meant to oppose this development not only verbally but practically, and there are still men attempting to embody Gandhi's ideas. The writer Lanza del Vasto, for example, has founded a little community which is trying as far as possible to be self-sufficient. The intentionally anachronistic clothing worn by the community members, for example, is made by hand. But I am afraid that here we are in the presence of a false wisdom, an unwitting caricature of the genuine wisdom whose principles at least I am trying to bring to light.

I spoke above of the risk of complacency, and that is precisely the reef on which a community like Lanza's inevitably founders. It is exemplary only in its own eyes. It is exposed on all sides to the charge of an aesthetic hypocrisy. It seems that such a community is involved in the following dilemma: either its self-sufficiency is an illusion in that the community actually depends for its material life on an infinitely larger community which is set up on principles opposed to its own; or else it is actually autonomous but at the price of being without everything from the outside that could enrich and nourish its substance, so that very likely it is doomed to perish of pernicious anemia.

I think it is evident that the rejection of technology, of the world of techniques, is a kind of childishness which is worse for being artificial. At best a community like the one I have just referred to can be compared to the Indian reservations which are maintained at great expense in some remote areas of the United States. But these reservations look like nothing but carefully maintained wings of some natural history museum. Their purpose is to preserve the witness of an irretrievable past, whereas someone like Lanza surely means to be building something like a model for small societies of the future.

An exactly opposite attitude toward technology is possible, and the planetary optimism we find in the writings of Teilhard de Chardin illustrates this attitude quite clearly. Above all it is the enthusiastic affirmation of technology and, I am tempted to say, of its redemptive value. Here, however, it would be well to stay clear of a possible confusion which Teilhard himself took pains to denounce openly. "At this time," he wrote,

> what most discredits faith in progress in the eyes of men today, over and above its reticences and its helplessness in meeting the cry of the "last days of the human species," is the unfortunate tendency still shown by its adepts to distort into pitiful millenarianisms all that is most valid and most noble in our now permanently awakened expectation of the future appearance of some form of "ultra-humanity." An era of abundance and euphoria—a Golden Age—is, they suggest, all that evolution could hold in reserve for us. And it is but right that our hearts should sink at the thought of so "bourgeois" an ideal.[2]

In place of well-being Teilhard proposes what he calls a thirst for being-more as the only thing which can save the thinking planet from *tedium vitae*.

But this progress Teilhard is so sure of can operate in two ways. One way is by an increase, through external force, of the coercion artificially exercised by stronger human groups against the weaker, which simply adds to the natural pressures resulting from physical causes.

The other method consists in setting loose among men a profound force of mutual attraction, of unanimity, whose moving principle can only be in the last analysis the common attraction exercised by the same Someone. In a lecture in Peking on February 22, 1941, which is now included in *The Future of Man*, the author declares that "the more I strive in love and wonder, to measure the huge movements of past Life in the light of

2. Pierre Teilhard de Chardin, *Hymn of the Universe*, trans. Simon Bartholomew (New York: Harper and Row, 1961), p. 109.

palaeontology, the more I am convinced that this majestic process, which nothing can arrest, can achieve its consummation only in becoming Christianised." [3]

Thus nothing could be further from the spirit of Teilhard's thinking than a technocratic optimism which would find in technology as such the ability to solve all human problems. As a matter of fact the hope animating Teilhard is founded on a mysticism. I fear only that this mysticism is even more difficult to communicate than the optimism which it so far transcends. And that is why one can see certain Marxists showing some sympathy for this thinking, which is in fact completely irreducible to their doctrines and which they purely and simply decapitate when they adopt it.

Moreover it should be recognized that in Teilhard's own work this mysticism is very tenuously linked with some views of an entirely different order which are nonetheless presented as simple extrapolations. In the text I just quoted, for example, the sentence about the "process which nothing can arrest" either must be attributed to pure rhetoric or else it implies a fatalistic view of progress which is in flagrant contradiction to the very principles of Christianity. Of course it is just because the unity of Teilhard's thought is so fragile that it is almost inevitably destined to have its most superficial and I must say most seductive elements adopted and eventually exploited for partisan ends by men incapable of sharing the ardent faith which is the heart of his work.

Is Teilhard's thought a wisdom? It seems to me that if it is considered in its entirety, ignoring the contradictions it harbors, it appears situated beyond what could be called wisdom, in a zone that is obscure and hard to reach, where science and religion attempt to unite. But on the other hand, in the schematized and even caricatured expressions in which it is presented by the Marxists, it must be said to fall short of wisdom properly so-called.

This long parenthesis can serve to clear our path somewhat, for the remarks about Teilhard's work, whose historical importance cannot be seriously questioned, allow us to see more distinctly the limits we must respect in our groping search to discover the nature of a wisdom for today.

3. Pierre Teilhard de Chardin, *The Future of Man,* trans. Norman Denny (New York: Harper and Row, 1964), p. 76.

I think we may posit in principle that purely scientific and technological progress would not by itself be enough to bring about the harmony among men necessary to any happiness worthy of the name. This does not mean that we have to distrust science and technology, but it does certainly mean that we have to denounce the illusion that they can in any way confer a meaning on our life.

But it is precisely this meaning, this value, if you wish, which wisdom has the job of uncovering and safeguarding, without, of course, appealing to the assurances offered us by Revelation. I choose not to deal with the important problem of determining what wisdom would mean in a life centered on the assurances of Revelation. It is quite possible that in such a context wisdom properly so-called would have to undergo a substantial transformation.

In any case, the problem that interests me here concerns those who are not bolstered by such assurances. Surely it would be inexcusably superficial to suggest that these nonbelievers, most often neither belligerent nor militant but merely skeptical and uncertain what to believe, are doomed to fall into the idolatry of the technocrats. It does seem to me, however—and here we return to the idea I was trying to make clear earlier—that the spiritual equilibrium of a tragic wisdom can in no way be confused with the static character we find among those who have retired from life. On the contrary it must be an always precarious victory, not necessarily over insecurity itself, but over the anguish which seems to be the almost inevitable consequence of insecurity.

But is not this anguish intimately linked with mortality, and do we not find here, merely transformed by contemporary conditions, an ancient problem Plato and Spinoza dealt with so profoundly that perhaps no further progress in its solution is possible?

If we consider the matter closely, however, we shall see that circumstances have been so thoroughly modified, especially by the march of history and of historical consciousness, that it no longer seems possible today to formulate the problem in the same terms we find in the *Phaedo* or the *Ethics*, for example. Whatever weaknesses there may be in Heidegger's notion of *zum Tode Sein*—I have presented my own objections to this notion, and as far as I am concerned they remain unanswered—the author of *Being and Time* was right to point out, more forcefully perhaps than any thinker before him, the immanence of death in life. Because life, through a kind of verdict placed on it, carries death within itself like that "dreary half of shadow" Valéry speaks of in "The Graveyard by the Sea," we can neither accept the idea of preparation for death as Plato formulates it, nor can we, with Spinoza, put this idea beyond the concern of the sage. Once more it seems we are simply unable to get away from the tragic. It is by reference to this essentially ambiguous datum, of which life and death are inseparable aspects, that the sage must work out his position.

I do think it may be necessary to give up the traditional idea of the sage as some privileged kind of man who characteristically possesses some special quality of being. The sage thus conceived is too likely to strike us today as being a laicized and no doubt ridiculous version of the saint. But I would remark that true sanctity can in no way be considered a possession; it is and remains itself only through a grace to which one must unceasingly respond, while temptation in every form looms as a threatening possibility to be thwarted only by the most tenacious vigilance. As for wisdom, it is much less a state than a goal, and here we must draw attention once more to the *experience* of our fundamental insecurity. There seems to be a paradoxical proportion between the increase in fundamental insecurity and the development of the technical means designed to protect man against all the dangers threatening him (threatening his health, his possessions, and so on). This is not a matter of causal relationship, but rather of associated aspects of a certain situation which might be called historical in the broad sense. To aspire to wisdom is to aspire to achieve a kind of mastery over this situation, but as we know already the foundation of this mastery is eroded from within by forces which seem to join in rejecting the very possibility of wisdom.

Here I would like to sum up what I have been saying, but this summary will surely bring to light the inadequacy of the position I have reached. For does not wisdom appear now as something like a flickering flame, perhaps destined for early extinction?

I propose, however, that we look for a direction in which to go beyond this attitude, which may well represent a kind of apostasy.

I know that here I am on a terrain full of hidden traps, where one can travel only with the greatest caution. But I would consider it a lack of integrity not to speak my thoughts as I first formulated them at the end of the First World War—thoughts which remain the background of all that I have written since. This going-beyond can occur only if reflection sets about questioning an entire situation which until now has been regarded as requiring no investigation. This situation may be characterized as a practical anthropocentrism, but one which carefully avoids recognizing itself as such because of the troublesome associations ordinarily surrounding that word. The following lines of Maxim Gorky, which appear at the beginning of the French translation of his complete plays, present with a kind of naïve arrogance the quiet presumption which is at the core of such a position.

> As for me I am interested only in man: man and man alone, in my opinion, is the creator of all things. It is he who accomplishes miracles, and in the future he will be master of all the forces of nature. Everything most beautiful in the world has been created by the intelligence and the work of man. . . . I bow before man because I feel nothing and I see nothing on the earth except the evidences of his reason, his imagination, his inventive spirit.[4]

Let us contrast this affirmation with these golden lines of Gerard de Nerval.

> Man, free thinker! do you believe that you alone think in this world where life bursts forth in everything? Your freedom has power to use the strength you possess, but the universe is absent from all your councils.
>
> In the beast respect an active soul; every flower is a soul unfolded to Nature; in metal sleeps a mystery of love; "Everything is sentient!" And everything has power over your being.
>
> Fear a glance watching you in the blind wall: a Word is connected even with matter. . . . Do not make it serve some impious purpose!
>
> Often in the dark being dwells a hidden God; and, like an eye born covered by its lids, a pure spirit grows beneath the surface of stones![5]

Shall I be called unreasonable here for juxtaposing the ringing declaration of a storyteller with the witness of an orphic poet?

4. My translation.
5. English translation from *The Penguin Book of French Verse*, ed. Anthony Hartley (Baltimore: Penguin, 1958), III, 107–8.

But the whole question—and it must be acknowledged that this question is generally evaded in our time except by Heidegger and those who draw their inspiration from him—is one of knowing whether wisdom, if it is taken as something more than a mere catalogue of utilitarian guidelines and techniques, can take root anywhere but in the same soil from which poetry originates and draws its nourishment. This may at first seem to be a wholly gratuitous suggestion, but I think that it will be clarified and justified by what follows. The aggressive anthropocentrism I mentioned can obviously only encourage a spirit of immoderation irreconcilably at odds with the constant teaching of traditional moralists. And here we return to a new form of the question underlying this entire inquiry: must this traditional teaching be considered out of date? The main objection to upholding the moralistic view could perhaps be enunciated in the following way: "Is not what you call anthropocentrism actually the tendentious and pejorative expression of a truth which stands above all others and which could be denied only in the name of some supposed assurance arising simply from the domain of affectivity? This central (or primary) truth actually determines the very conditions outside of which the word "truth" loses all meaning—for are not these conditions exclusively found in the intelligent effort of man?"

This may seem obviously true, but from such a general observation one can deduce nothing resembling anthropocentrism. I think that Heidegger has seen into this matter with perfect clarity, although his language, as is so often the case, tends to hide the thought he wants to reveal (admittedly he reminds us that for him to hide and to reveal are inseparable aspects of the same act). Perhaps we would not wholly misrepresent the essential thrust of his thought if we put it this way: On the one hand the fact of being man, if not man himself, outstrips all the specifications or definitions which classical philosophers have usually been content with since Aristotle. The fact of being man, especially as this fact appears in language (from which man is inseparable) cannot be thought without reference to being. For my part, however, I propose to avoid using the word "being" here, at the risk of deviating somewhat from Heidegger's thought, since I am less interested in reproducing what he says than in showing to what extent his thought is capable of being clarified, and above all, of clarifying our own problem. Thus, in place of what I consider to be the radically suspect distinction between *being* and *beings* I propose to substitute that of *light* and *what is illuminated*. Of course it goes without saying that by "light" here I do not mean a physical agent. When we come to understand— whether gradually or all of a sudden—something that was initially obscure to us, light floods our minds, and this is as true for the blind man as for those who can see.

Now there would obviously be no sense in saying that man *produces* this light, and trying to define or describe the production. At least for the moment we can set aside the question of whether light thus understood has a source, or even whether there is any precise meaning in asking such a question. But if I reflect on my condition as man (or as a thinking being) I come to see that this condition cannot be defined without reference to that intelligible light. Reflection shows us, moreover, that this light invades me the more I become forgetful of myself—not only of my individual self, but also of the very fact of being a self in general, precisely the fact that culminates in anthropocentric pride. It is not hard to see that it would be sheer folly to claim that man produces light in the way that a factory produces electricity. It is certainly absurd to imagine that the hyperbolic development of technology serves in the least to modify the fundamental situation of man with regard to this light. Indeed this situation will always be very difficult to clarify, because the clarification would inevitably have to be brought to bear on the illuminating light, and there is no sense in saying that light can be clarified.

In going beyond anthropocentrism in this way, are we getting near our goal? It may at first seem doubtful that we are. For what has been said up to now has to do with truth, with man in the presence of truth. But is there an obvious relationship between truth and wisdom? If we do insist that there is such a relationship, do we not *ipso facto* subscribe to an intellectualism which can only be maintained by misunderstanding certain essential aspects of human reality?

Here it seems to me that we must introduce the notion of a certain truth of life. Indeed it may well be that if someone denies that the words "truth of life" have any meaning, he implicitly refuses at the same time to admit any content in the word "wisdom." I think that here we are very close to the thought of Simmel:

In the same way that life at the physiological level is continual procreation, so that living is also more than merely living, so too at the spiritual level life gives birth to something more than life, namely objectives which in themselves have value and meaning. This way life has of raising itself to more than itself is not something given from without; it is rather its own being grasped in its immediacy.[6]

Now one may have some reservations about Simmel's terminology, particularly his use of the word "objectives." But nonetheless he is making the essential point that a philosophy of life is always in danger of forgetting, namely, that it is the essence of life to *culminate* in something which is in some way its own beyond, and in this way the words "truth of life" take on their real meaning. Let me try to clarify this still further.

Earlier, in a quite different context, when I was trying to bring to light the connection between life and the sacred, observing that this connection seems to be abolished in the naturalistic view, I proposed that it is only to the extent that we take life in its spontaneous upsurge, in its freshness, and thus in a kind of referential quality—the reference being to a primordial, secret, and, as it were, inviolable integrity—that we can, as in a flash of lightning, once again see its sacred value. But now, in speaking of the "truth of life," do we not encounter precisely that integrity? Incidentally it seems to me that the *Heil* of Heidegger corresponds closely to what I am here calling integrity, and the French translator was wrong to render it by the word *indemne* [uninjured, undamaged]. I think that on this point the thinking of Simmel and that of Heidegger complement each another, although the difficult idea I am trying to bring to light here would not be wholly acceptable to either one of them. It seems to me that life, in the sense in which each person speaks of *his own* life, cannot be thought of wholly apart from light, taken as an ultimate ontological given—a given which is ultimate in that it is at the same time *giving*. But here language fails us, for it is evident that life and light cannot be treated as distinct givens between which one could try to establish a connection. Nor can it be said that life produces light, any more than the reverse relationship can be affirmed. These would be crude and unacceptable schematizations. It would be better to bring out with all possible concrete precision the way in which the nature of life is illuminated for someone who has lived much and who is trying to find

6. Georg Simmel, *Lebensanschauung* (Munich and Leipzig: Duncker und Humblot, 1918), p. 94; my translation.

some order in what, as he was living it, perhaps appeared as complete confusion. Here the example of Goethe comes easily to mind, or perhaps the "ripeness is all" of Prospero.

At this point in our inquiry, however, we cannot forget what we said previously about the radical insecurity enveloping man today. It seems that now perhaps we can formulate distinctly the problem that has remained at the center of our concern: is not that insecurity quite incompatible with the ripening that seems to be involved in any wisdom worthy of the name? For a sage is not something one *is;* rather one *becomes* a sage. And with that have we not simply returned to the anguish we described at the beginning of our inquiry? Was it worth the trouble of all this arduous travel to come out with such a negative conclusion? But perhaps after all a positive conclusion does result from our reflections. We said that it is an inexcusable mistake for man to see the ordering principle of the world in his own ego and in the powers of technology he controls; the new anthropocentrism is even less justifiable than the old, which, after all, depended on a previous theocentrism. Now I would say without hesitation that this new man-centeredness presents the challenge which is the beginning or principle of wisdom as it must be defined today. What is demanded is a humility grounded in reason and linked to the illumination accompanying every act of genuine understanding, a humility which regards as a temptation or danger the affirmation "It is I who . . ." I do not mean that we ought to accept the radical thesis of a Simone Weil, according to which the use of the "I" is somehow sinful in itself; but I do advocate a more subtle view in which the "I" must be given the place belonging to it in a certain hierarchy of powers. I am using the word "powers" here in the sense in which Schelling uses it.

I would say that insecurity (which is linked to the threat of nuclear weapons I spoke of above) seems to diminish to the extent that man truly reestablishes the relationship joining him to the original light. But if we do put this concern at the center of our lives, are we not in danger of returning to a kind of Spinozism, and thus of forgetting the dimension of the tragic which, I have insisted, must be emphasized in the contemporary world?

Here I come to what I think is the most important point, but one which is also sure to provoke the sharpest opposition. For here I depart most resolutely from Heidegger's thought as it is commonly interpreted. Indeed, I am brought back to the criticism I felt I had to make of *Sein zum Tode:* that this notion radically minimizes the importance of the death of the other, the death of the loved person. In my opinion this defect seriously affects Heidegger's entire work, and ends by imprisoning him in an existential solipsism (itself enclosed, moreover, in a purely lyrical ontocosmology). In such a view, what becomes of *agapē* and all that it implies? The problem certainly cannot be solved by bringing in, as Binswanger has done, an extra category called "love." For love is simply not a category; it is the very destiny of each of us as creatures, and any category, whatever it may be, is only meaningful insofar as it is in the service of or at the disposition of that destiny. Our task is to understand what I have called the original light (which certainly should not be taken as a kind of Aristotelian, depersonalized nous), given this tragic world we live in where each of us participates in being-toward-death—not only toward his own death, in virtue of a *Drang*, an instinct of preservation, but much more profoundly and intimately toward the death of the being whom he loves and who for him counts infinitely more than himself, to the point of his being, not by nature but by vocation, decentered or polycentered.

But here the problem is put in terms which seem to suggest a return to some gnostic speculation reminiscent of Jacob Böhme. In fact that is not the direction I would take, although I am far from misunderstanding or underestimating the importance of Böhme's thought or that of his modern disciples. My aim will be less ambitious, yet I would not reject the terms "gnosis" or "orphism," so long as this renewed gnosis is understood to be centered in a widely elaborated experience. Here I am very close to what I wrote immediately after the Liberation in an article called "Audace en métaphysique," which I think was scandalous to certain people, though for the most part it went unnoticed. Actually I was simply drawing out certain ideas which had first appeared in the second part of the *Metaphysical Journal*. I think that each of us is invited, as it were, apart from any appeal to faith, which does not concern us here, to restore the traces of a world which is not superimposed from without ours, but is rather this very world grasped in a richness of dimensions which ordinarily we are simply unaware of. And here I do not mean only the world as *Umwelt* or *Umgebung*, but the world as it merges with those depths of ourselves of which psychoanalysis can only show us a small and inessential part.

Though I shall certainly cause some dismay and scandal among philosophers and theologians, I would say that in this age of absolute insecurity we live in, true wisdom lies in setting out, with prudence to be sure, but also with a kind of joyful anticipation, on the paths leading not necessarily beyond time but beyond *our* time, to where the technocrats and the statistic worshippers on the one hand, and the tyrants and torturers on the other, not only lose their footing but vanish like mists at the dawn of a beautiful day.

Conversations between
Paul Ricoeur and Gabriel Marcel

Conversation 1

PAUL RICOEUR: We are at the beginning of a series of six conversations, in which I will have the pleasure of asking you some questions, just as I did some thirty years ago when I was your student in this same house.

I expect a good deal from these conversations. For I will be asking you not just for a recapitulation of your work but for a critical review, something which in former times would have been called a retraction, that is, a revision or correction. Perhaps we will even find ourselves brought to the advancing frontier of your work, for a philosophy takes on new aspects when it is projected into new landscapes. And perhaps we will be able to explore in your work those new possibilities which the new philosophical situation can bring forth.

We have agreed to regard this first conversation as an exploration. I believe, M. Marcel, that this word "exploration" has been fraught with meaning since your childhood.

GABRIEL MARCEL: Yes, it is true that even as a young child I felt a confused desire to be an explorer later on. It can be said that in a way this vocation has been preserved and yet also transformed.

But first of all I would like to respond to what you said at the beginning. I would like to say how happy I am to have you as an interlocutor. I recall with some emotion the time when you used to come to my home—yes, it must have been thirty years ago—with Maxime Chastaing, Roger Arnaldes, and others, when we

[217]

used to work together and reflect on the problems that were our passion. That time has remained for me an infinitely precious memory, and not least because of the presence there of my wife, that admirable companion who used to follow our conversations and note down what we were saying.

Yes, it is a great joy for me to see you today truly arrived, one might say, at the summit of your career. For you are, at the moment, one of the outstanding philosophers at the Sorbonne, one of those who have truly earned the respect and affection of all their students.

PAUL RICOEUR: Let me recall, Mr. Marcel, that time when as students we used to come to your home. We met in the hopes of getting to the very quick of experience and exploring its meaning. At the time we were reading your *Metaphysical Journal,* written from 1914 on and published in 1927. We were also reading "On the Ontological Mystery," which you had just published in 1933 as an appendix to *Le Monde cassé.* And you were in the process of preparing *Being and Having* which was to contain the lectures you were then giving.

You were an explorer in everything that we know of your work. But the form this exploration took raises certain questions.

When we open the *Metaphysical Journal,* we see an obvious difference between the two parts. The first part astonishes us with its extremely dialectical form, as I believe it astonished even you from very early on. The work is a struggle against the systematic spirit, but a struggle carried on with systematic means. Hence it can be asked—and this will be my first question—if from the very beginning your work, by the very excess of its dialectic, has not given hostages to a kind of irrationalism. How do you read this first part of the *Journal* today?

GABRIEL MARCEL: When you say that the first part of the *Metaphysical Journal* astonishes me, I think you are being euphemistic; I would say that it exasperates me. To be sure, I can understand retrospectively what this kind of drilling meant to me—I think that "drilling" is really the right word here. For me it was a matter of sinking a shaft, as in a mine. I had to rid myself of certain dialectical paraphernalia. But how? It is thus that we meet the strange contradiction in the first part of the *Journal,* the fact that it was by dialectical means that I was striving, very awkwardly it seems to me, to free myself from dialectic.

PAUL RICOEUR: What were your philosophical points of reference at that time?

GABRIEL MARCEL: It is rather easy for me to recall them. I believe it is necessary first of all to recall what the Sorbonne was like at that time. I remember especially the situation in the history of philosophy. I am thinking of a man I spoke to you about recently, who has remained for me an exemplary figure of what the historian of philosophy can be: I mean Victor Delbos. The other professors of philosophy were interested in critical reflection, but in their presence little was felt of that kind of affirmation I needed. Of course it was just the other way around with Bergson. I had the good luck to attend his lectures for two years at the Collège de France, and I will never recall that experience without emotion. Every time one went there, it was somehow with a beating heart and with a kind of hope of hearing a revelation. And here we get back to the word "exploring," the idea of exploration which you are focusing on in this first conversation. Yes, the feeling really was that Bergson was in the process of discovering something, that he was in the process of revealing to us certain deeper and more secret aspects of our own reality.

But the paradox for me was that this admiration I had for Bergson coincided, or more exactly coexisted, with a very different disposition which was in general a kind of cult of the most abstract and most dialectical thinking.

PAUL RICOEUR: You were reading Schelling . . .

GABRIEL MARCEL: Yes, I was reading Schelling and a little Hegel. And I was reading especially and more deeply the English Neo-Hegelians, particularly Bradley. At that time, there was a kind of split in me between this preoccupation with an abstract rigor and a simultaneous taste for philosophical adventure. And I would say that this contradiction could only be resolved very slowly and perhaps always partially.

PAUL RICOEUR: Perhaps the first part of the *Metaphysical Journal* is today more readable for us than for you. You may think that the results of the struggle that you carried on both with and against concepts were somewhat trivial. But in fact its results were like stores put in for the winter, or like an investment at compound interest. It is in the second part of the *Metaphysical Journal* that the fruits of your early work are enjoyed. Here the most concrete analyses are the true fruit of dialectical conquest. You recall, moreover, in the preface to the *Metaphysical Journal* that mysterious encounter between the conclusions of your initial dialectic and the results of your subsequent meditation. And to-day, after the ebb of the existentialist wave, at a moment when the demand for rigorous thinking is being newly affirmed, would you not say that the conceptual analysis of the first part of the *Journal* deserves to be recognized?

GABRIEL MARCEL: Yes, I agree. What irritates me when I reread the first part of the *Metaphysical Journal* or the earlier *Philosophical Fragments*,[1] which were published in Belgium three or four years ago with the preface by Père Blain, is that I find a certain looseness, a certain lack of precision and rigor in the vocabulary. I find it to be a thinking which has not yet benefited from the conceptual equipment that would be necessary for the work to be done in a fashion that would seem to me today satisfactory. I believe it is this above all that irritates me a little when I reread these texts, all the while recognizing once again that it was a kind of preliminary undertaking that I was unable to exempt myself from. I do not regret at all having devoted so much effort to this enterprise.

PAUL RICOEUR: As a matter of fact, it is the adversary of the *Journal* which has disappeared today, idealism, or, as you used to say, "idealist postulates."

But let us turn to the second part of the *Journal*, which you wrote between 1915 and 1923. It is there that the real breakthrough is made.

I am reading from the preface: "I was inclined always to concentrate my reflections even more on those anomalies brushed over or avoided by every rationalism." But this winding and fragmentary research crystallized in the notion of *existence*. It is

1. *Metaphysical Journal,* trans. Bernard Wall (London: Rockliff, 1952); *Philosophical Fragments 1909–1914,* trans. L. Blain (South Bend, Ind.: University of Notre Dame Press, 1965).

this notion that I would like to discuss with you. But first of all I want to say that when the essay "Existence and Objectivity" appeared, the essay in which you gathered together the principal results of your inquiry, we had the impression, just as we did a little later with "On the Ontological Mystery," of being in the presence of one of those great programmatic texts, the kind of text Bergson's *Introduction to Metaphysics* and *La Perception du changement* had been for the previous generation. But this notion of existence poses certain problems for us today. You opposed it to the notion of objectivity in order to fight against the tendency to give primacy to analytic knowledge. Would you today justify in the same way the antithesis of existence and objectivity?

GABRIEL MARCEL: It does not seem to me that I have changed on this point. I think I might have to correct some details, to rectify certain assertions. But the basic position remains the same for me, and it is this position which appears in many of my later works.

I believe that what I saw clearly at that time is what I call the indubitable character of existence. It is the consciousness of the impossibility of reducing existence to anything else whatsoever, of even putting existence into question. That is to say, I have never been able to understand the question that certain philosophers have asked, notably Schelling and more recently Heidegger, the question that goes, "How is it that something exists, that an entity is?" From the beginning my answer has been that this question today makes no sense at all because it implies a possibility which is not granted to us, the possibility of abstracting ourselves in some way from existence or of placing ourselves outside existence in order to behold it. But what we are able to behold are objects, things which share in objectivity. Existence, however, is nothing of the sort; existence is prior. Of course, when I speak of the priority of existence, I do not mean the priority of existence with respect to essence—perhaps we will have to come back to this point with reference to Sartrian existentialism. But what is more important for me is the affirmation that existence is not only given, it is also giving—however paradoxical this sounds. That is, existence is the very condition of any thinking whatsoever. And there, of course, I am putting myself right on the margin of traditional idealism.

PAUL RICOEUR: Yes . . .

GABRIEL MARCEL: Well, you know as well as I how this thought is detailed and specified in the analyses dealing with sensation and with what is often today called the body-subject, that is, my body precisely as mine.

PAUL RICOEUR: Your reflections on "feeling" and on "receiving" in the *Metaphysical Journal* really inaugurated a kind of analysis which was to have great success in French philosophy. You are the one who made the connection between the philosophy of sensation and that of existence. Sensation was no longer just the business of psychophysiology. According to you, sensation testified to our participation in existence, the participation of my own self in the world of existing things. When you criticized the conception of sensation as a message passing between one thing and another, between a transmitter and a receiver, you laid the foundation of what Merleau-Ponty and others later called phenomenology of perception.

GABRIEL MARCEL: Yes, very likely. But don't you think that in a certain way Claudel anticipated this in his poetic art, in his idea of *co-naissance*? I am always careful to credit my sources—I have a horror of ingratitude and amnesia—and I believe that here I owe a rather specific debt to Claudel, even though Claudel does not seem to us to be a philosopher in the technical sense of the term. But in a man of genius, don't these barriers and divisions break down, so that poetry and philosophy are joined? So I don't think I am being unfair to myself in pointing out here what I owe to Claudel's theory and practice of poetry.

PAUL RICOEUR: With one small difference: Claudel was looking in the region of speech, of the word, for the key to this insertion in being, in existence. You are the one who has brought back to the level of feeling itself this "absolute presence." You have taken the body, rather than language, as the primary focus of your reflection on existence. Perhaps we should not forget this today when French philosophy is suffering from a kind of fascination with the problems of language. In joining a criticism of sensation as message to your criticism of the body as instrument, you opened the way to a philosophy of the body-subject, and gave philosophy the means for thinking embodiment.

Conversation 2

PAUL RICOEUR: Our first conversation brought us to a reflection on the close link in your thought between the concrete description of sensation and of the body-subject, and the philosophical theme of existence. But the reader who passes from the *Metaphysical Journal* to *Being and Having* may be surprised to see the question of being replacing the question of existence. The turning point was reached, I believe, in that magnificent text dating from 1933, "On the Ontological Mystery." Why this change of front?

GABRIEL MARCEL: I think we ought to set these things straight. The problem of being arises in the middle of the *Metaphysical Journal*, toward the beginning of the year 1919, toward the spring. But it is perfectly accurate to say that until then when I thought about metaphysics I didn't think about being or the problem of being. And it is interesting to ask why. I believe it's because my entire formation had been idealist, and the word "being" conveyed to me something of its ambiguous scholastic connotation. For me "scholastic" could only be pejorative. Remember that at that time there were only a few specialists who were interested in the philosophy of the Middle Ages. The rest of us, at least the philosophy students, did not in general know medieval philosophy and were hardly even curious about it. There was a quite respectable M. Picavet who used to give courses on the philosophy of the Middle Ages. But I don't think he had very many listeners. And I wonder if these listeners were even students. At that time, that is, during the years immediately preceding the war and even perhaps at the beginning of the war, I remained faithful to a certain distinction, one might even almost say a certain opposition between so-called philosophies of being and philosophies of freedom. And all my sympathy was with the philosophies of freedom. I am thinking, for example, of the very real sympathy with which I read certain pages of Secrétan. Moreover, here we come back to Schelling, whom you spoke of the other day. It can be said that Secrétan, like Ravaisson on another level, continued Schelling's thought without perhaps being very faithful to what is essential in Schelling's doctrine. But this is not important here.

Hence, certain circumstances which are rather difficult to specify were necessary in order for my thinking to be concentrated on being. And I believe that this could not have taken place until after I was able to develop in a precise or *relatively* precise way what I shall call the phenomenological perspective. This was the moment when I began to ask myself *what we mean* when we speak of being, what is our intention, what is our aim. This appears quite clearly in the *Metaphysical Journal,* if I am not mistaken. Perhaps it would be good to read several lines from this section.

PAUL RICOEUR: Here is the passage: "Being is that which does not frustrate our expectation; there is being from the moment at which our expectation is fulfilled—I mean the expectation in which we wholly participate. The doctrine that denies being can be expressed by the phrase: 'All is vanity,' in other words that we must expect nothing, and only the man who expects nothing will avoid being disappointed. I believe that it is only on this basis that the problem can be stated. To say: 'Nothing *is*' is to say 'Nothing matters.' I must make a deeper examination of the meaning of this kind of nihilism. Take care not to confound 'to be' with 'to exist.' " [1]

GARBIEL MARCEL: And here does not Claudel come to mind again? Remember that nihilistic character in *La Ville* who declares at one point, "nothing is." Here it is certain that Claudel's influence, his mark on my thought, has been profound. I have

1. *Metaphysical Journal,* trans. Bernard Wall (Chicago: Regnery, 1952), p. 179.

very often had the opportunity in later texts to cite this passage from *La Ville*. It seems to me extremely revealing.

PAUL RICOEUR: But at the same time you are introducing perhaps a certain equivocation. You write several years later in *Being and Having:* "The uneasiness I feel on these subjects is partly due to my old difficulty in seeing the relation between being and existing. It seems obvious to me that existing is a certain way of being; we shall have to see whether it is the only one. Perhaps something could *be* without existing. But I regard it as axiomatic to say that the inverse is not possible, except by an indefensible juggling with words." [2] Don't you think that the two notions of being and existing, even if they easily overlap one another, nevertheless can be distinguished from one another insofar as they arise out of different preoccupations of yours? As we were saying the other day, you raised the question of existence in relation to the question of objectivity. It was a matter of reaching a zone where it was no longer possible to doubt. Existence is indubitable; but at the same time existence is reached in opposition to objectivity. But you raise the question of being with a different concern in mind, ontological *exigence;* we shall have to take up this notion of *exigence.*

You had been oriented, I believe, toward the problem of being by an extremely concrete preoccupation deriving on the one hand from your experience of the war and on the other from certain reflections on the spirit of the times, on the course of the world.

GABRIEL MARCEL: Yes, that is beyond doubt. That, I believe, is the really essential point. In fact it is in the meditation entitled, a little heavily, "On the Ontological Mystery" that this opposition is made completely precise, I would even say almost this polarity between what appeared to me as something given in a world more and more technologized, more and more functionalized on the one hand, and on the other this aspiration, this *exigence* which bears us toward a fullness, toward something which is totally resistant to these functional and abstract determinations.

PAUL RICOEUR: Yes, "On the Ontological Mystery" begins with a reflection on the sense of a world centered on what you call the "function," the biological function, the social function. . . .

2. *Being and Having*, trans. Katherine Farrer (New York: Harper Torchbooks, 1961), p. 37.

GABRIEL MARCEL: That's it. It is a world where man is dealt with only as a bundle of functions. And hence, a distinction is made between vital functions and psychological functions; the status of the latter is rather uncertain since they are situated between the vital functions and the social functions properly speaking. Nothing seems more awful to me than this reduction of man, of a human being (and here it is necessary to accent the word "being" and man's dignity) by such distinctions. It is all too clear that what I said at that time, around 1930, has become infinitely more detailed in the world we are in today. We will have to reconsider at greater length this central theme in our fifth conversation. . . .

PAUL RICOEUR: In brief, the word "being" helped you at a certain time to mobilize a protest that came from the depths. The ontological *exigence* is thus no longer simply that indubitable character we were speaking about in connection with existence; it designates the recovery of a forgotten foundation.

GABRIEL MARCEL: This *exigence* seems to me to go against the facts, if you will, like the foundation of a protest.

PAUL RICOEUR: But what is astonishing is that you raised your protest at that particular time, not only against the reduction of existence to a bundle of functions, but also against a basic philosophical tradition, the tradition of the *cogito*, which other philosophers today are again disputing. In turning the ontological *exigence* back against the *cogito*, do you not risk weakening the core of resistance to this tendency of the world which you condemn?

GABRIEL MARCEL: This is perhaps one of those points where I would have to revise what I wrote at that time. It seems to me now that I would not put the emphasis where you do. I do not want to say that I am against the *cogito;* that would be absurd. What I wanted to say was that Descartes seemed to me precisely to have mistaken the indubitable character of existence, a character which in general seems prior to any determination or to any intellectual act whatsoever. I think we would have to examine— but I have never undertaken this—the relation between what I outlined at that time and have doubtless elaborated in my later works, and what Karl Jaspers has written against the *cogito*. I believe that there our positions are extremely close.

PAUL RICOEUR: Yes, but both of you have read Descartes in Kantian terms. For you the *cogito,* I think, is the epistemological subject. When you call the *cogito* "the guardian of the threshold of the valid," you reduce the *cogito* to a pure function of watchfulness over a world of pure mental objects. But Descartes himself saw in the *cogito* essentially the affirmation, "I am." In this sense, perhaps, you recover in your work Descartes's forgotten intention by taking the "I am" in all its density.

GABRIEL MARCEL: Yes, I believe there was much more in Descartes's thought than my critique of the *cogito* might suggest. Indeed, I have often said that there is infinitely more in Descartes than in Cartesianism. On this point you agree with me, don't you? In any case, a certain kind of Cartesianism has resulted in a narrowing of the field of Cartesian thought. The idea of absolute freedom, as Descartes conceived it, obviously goes well beyond a formalism of the *cogito*. I think you are probably right when you say that I had too much of a tendency to read Descartes in Kantian terms. Moreover, it is probable that the idea of the transcendental ego correlative to the Kantian object is much more central to all my reflections. In any case, I am sure that your reservations are from the historical point of view absolutely justified.

PAUL RICOEUR: Inversely, it could be said that your "On the Ontological Mystery" is not sufficiently critical from another point of view. Let us reread the text we were alluding to just a moment ago. "Being is—or should be—necessary. It is impossible that everything should be reduced to a play of successive appearances which are inconsistent with each other ('inconsistent' is essential), or, in the words of Shakespeare, to 'a tale told by an idiot.' I aspire to participate in this being, in this reality." [3] Would not critical reflection come to question the value, the soundness of this protestation? Will it not be brought to denounce this "being is," or even more this being "should be," as the expression of *wishful thinking,* of a confusion between desire and reality?

3. "On the Ontological Mystery," trans. Manya Harari, in *The Philosophy of Existentialism* (New York: Citadel Press, 1963), p. 14.

GABRIEL MARCEL: This is certainly a question we have to raise. In fact I did raise the question at that time and I have come back to it quite often. But the answer should have been much more rigorously formulated than in fact it was. What I was trying to show was first of all that a philosophy that neglects ontological *exigence* or that repudiates it is strictly speaking possible. A philosophy of despair is possible. I don't believe it can be seriously said that such a philosophy entails contradiction. What strikes me as false is pretending, as certain pessimists do, that this philosophy of despair in fact is required by a certain objective reality, by a certain structure in things, which could be considered apart from every form of desire. I believe that in fact there is an assumption there and that this assumption needs to be explored from the viewpoint of a philosophy like mine.

PAUL RICOEUR: But in that case, everything is a matter of our being able to link critical reflection on adverse "assumptions" with . . .

GABRIEL MARCEL: That's it . . .

PAUL RICOEUR: . . . with what you have called "concrete approaches." . . .

GABRIEL MARCEL: Yes.

PAUL RICOEUR: How would a critical thinking today link these concrete approaches—for example, the analysis of having, of autonomy taken as stoic constancy or as the will to be in agreement with oneself—with ontological *exigence*? Your method consisted then in somehow mining these experiences in order to recover there that reference to being which you call fidelity. . . .

GABRIEL MARCEL: Yes . . .

PAUL RICOEUR: What would it mean today to relate the criticism of assumptions to the retrieval of these ontological experiences?

GABRIEL MARCEL: Well, I believe that what intervenes here is what Schelling, in probably a very different sense, called a higher empiricism.
In other words, it is a recourse to a certain type of ex-

perience which must be recognized first of all and which in some way bears within itself the warrant of its own value. In fact, if there has been a real transformation in my thinking, it is in my way of appreciating experience. I must say that I smile a little when I think of the scorn which empiricism and even the notion of experience roused in me at a certain time of my life. I have come to understand that this refusal of experience, this kind of systematic apriorism, actually betrayed a lack of reflection, and that it was necessary to rediscover experience, but at a level beyond that of traditional empiricism. Moreover, as I mentioned in a communication to the Institut, my friend Henry Bugbee introduced ten years ago the notion of experiential thinking as opposed to empirical thinking. It seems to me that we will have an opportunity later on to see this kind of thinking, for it is precisely this experiential thinking which is at work in this investigation, where we are dealing with themes you were speaking about a moment ago, particularly with fidelity, which, as you know, ultimately plays a pivotal role in my thinking.

PAUL RICOEUR: In brief, we would have to say that these cardinal experiences bear in themselves the critical function. They are critical experiences to the extent that they are experiences which effect in the same movement the retrieval of the ontological aim and the criticism of the modalities which conceal it from us.

GABRIEL MARCEL: And these experiences in fact accommodate what I have called secondary reflection, as opposed to primary reflection, which is purely critical or analytic. Secondary reflection is a reconstructive reflection, and the practice of this reflection has been my concern from the moment when, toward the 1930s, I became fully aware of what I wanted to do.

It has been my aim to bring about this reconstruction, but to bring it about in an intelligent and intelligible way, and not by some kind of appeal to purely subjective intuitions.

Conversation 3

PAUL RICOEUR: Our last discussion brought us to an important threshold in your work, drama. Everything in your work comes from drama and everything leads to it as well, especially the analysis of those experiences you have called "ontological," insofar as these experiences have a dramatic character.

In *Being and Having* you write: "the fact that despair is possible is a central datum here. Man is capable of despair, capable of embracing death, of embracing his own death." And elsewhere: Metaphysics ought to take up its position just there, face to face with despair: metaphysics as an exorcism of despair." [1]

How do you consider your plays now? How do you see the relation between your dramatic work and your philosophical work?

GABRIEL MARCEL: I am very glad you are asking me this question because I believe it is the most important one, and it is one of those points where there have probably been the most serious misunderstandings, particularly among theater people who have not taken the trouble to really read my work. The truth is that the connection between philosophy and drama in my case is the closest, the most intimate possible.

Briefly, I would say that my philosophy is existential to the

1. *Being and Having*, trans. Katherine Farrer (New York: Harper Torchbooks, 1961), p. 104 (translation modified).

[230]

degree that it is simultaneously drama, that is, dramatic creation. What has struck me very much these last years while reflecting on my work is the fact that existence, or, if you will, the existing subject can be adequately thought only where the thinking subject is allowed to speak. If we speak of this existing subject in some other way, we insist *in the words* on its subjective character, but by the very fact that we are speaking of it we inevitably objectify it and consequently distort it.

Of course this is an a posteriori viewpoint. Chronologically, I did not proceed this way at all. And besides—I will have a chance later on perhaps to repeat this—I was thinking about drama a great deal before I knew or suspected what philosophy is.

But if you ask me how I understand this relation today, I would refer to a text that appeared last spring where I developed a comparison which strikes me as quite accurate. Taken as a whole my work can be compared, I think, to a country like Greece, which comprises at the same time a continental part and islands. The continental part is my philosophical writing. Here I find myself to some degree in the company of other thinkers of our time like Jaspers, Buber, and Heidegger. The islands are my plays. Why this comparison? Well, just as it is necessary to make a crossing to get to an island, so to get to my dramatic work, dramatic creation, it is necessary to leave the shore behind. The reflecting subject in some way must leave himself behind, forget himself in order to yield completely, in order to be absorbed in the beings he has conceived and whom he must try to bring to life. And it might be added—I don't think this would be superfluous—that the element which unites the continent and the islands in my work is music. Music is truly the deepest level. In a certain way the priority belongs to music.

PAUL RICOEUR: I think that if drama has had the influence on your philosophy you say it has, then this is so because it has allowed you not only to acknowledge subjectivity by letting the subject speak, but also to encounter individual subjects. In your plays the striking thing is the permanent exercise of what you have called somewhere "that higher justice which resembles charity." Destinies remain intertwined, unseparated. You yourself are never in the position of a judge when you are exercising what I would call the dramatic act.

GABRIEL MARCEL: This seems completely correct to me, and I have attempted elsewhere in recalling my childhood and adolescence to discover the roots of this disposition. There would be more we could say about this.

The Dreyfus affair, which I will have a chance to speak about again in another context, played a definite role here.

But there were also family circumstances, in this case a divorce, which were important. I became aware that members of my own family had clearly diverging positions. Each seemed a prisoner of his own viewpoint. So I think I experienced at a very early age the need to raise myself up to a certain level where everyone would be included, where each one would have his place, where each one would in some way be justified.

Moreover, when I consider my first plays, I notice that almost all of them imply the condemnation of the judge, the condemnation of the one who condemns. I think—here I am also anticipating something we will have to talk about later on—that it was in this context that I was first drawn to Christian ethics.

PAUL RICOEUR: If your plays are wholesome and purifying, this is so because they are in no way apologetic. I am very much struck by the fact that in plays like *La Grâce, Le Palais de sable,* and later on *Un Homme de Dieu, La Chapelle ardente,* and *L'Iconoclaste,* the tragedy consists in the fact that nothing is solved for the characters. And nothing is resolved because the bearers of meaning or hope are always challengeable, or even suspect, sometimes even unbearable. I spoke of the wholesomeness of your plays. Actually, your plays serve to get rid of phantoms, to exorcise them, preparing the way for what the philosopher is not yet able to say. . . .

GABRIEL MARCEL: Yes, several times I have even asked myself —and I would like to know what you think of the matter—if there might not be a certain unexpected analogy between the role of drama in my thought and indirect communication as Kierkegaard conceived it. What strikes me is the interest Kierkegaard had in the theater. The theater is often mentioned in his *Journals,* and I have asked myself occasionally if, in uniting philosophical and dramatic thinking so intimately, I have not in some way accomplished something that Kierkegaard was straining toward. What do you think?

PAUL RICOEUR: I think you are right. But what is characteristic of your particular viewpoint is this justifying comprehension of all the characters. You assume them all simultaneously, without ever being their judge. Now, do you think that all your plays are equally significant in this respect? I am very much struck by a certain alternation between those plays which seem to close in darkness and others where at a certain moment a kind of spark, a kind of lightning flashes out. It seems to me there is something like a pulse in your plays. Sometimes it is that possibility of despair we were speaking about earlier which invades everything; at other times all is swept up in a kind of witness and vague recognition of a mystery which can never be apprehended or possessed. It seems to me then that your plays, besides representing an unresolved tragedy, also express the existential pulse of your philosophy.

GABRIEL MARCEL: I believe that there actually is an alternation, but that it is no more deliberate than it is regular. As a matter of fact, in the book entitled *Le Secret est dans les isles*, this kind of opposition can be found. The first two plays, *Le Dard* and *L'Emissaire*, close with the discovery of a certain light, an obscure light, while the third ends in despair.

La Fin des temps is one of the darkest plays I have written. Probably by looking at the web of events we have lived through, one could find something which could help explain this kind of alternation. But I don't believe that a rigorous explanation of it could be given. Of course I would be somewhat distrustful of these plays if in fact each one closed on a happy note: they would seem to me a little mechanical and, because of that, quite suspect.

Among the plays you mentioned, *La Chapelle ardente*, for example, there are some which are certainly very dark plays. I think the spectator can draw something positive from the plays, but this positive element remains implicit. The spectator has to make an effort, a kind of work of reflection, which can be suggested but cannot be insisted on.

PAUL RICOEUR: I think that the theme of death is the one that crystallizes your own inquiry just as it crystallizes the inquiry of the protagonist, of the spectator, and of the reader. You write somewhere that death is "the test of presence," and also that death is "the springboard of an absolute hope." The movement that bears your plays along is that of an "in spite of . . .": in spite of all the denials and the disavowals, despite everything.

. . . And why? Because in your dramatic work death is taken seriously, not just *my* death but, as you say insistently, *your [ta]* death. Death then is truly the crisis which completely shatters all faith in existence, all certitude of presence. Your drama, then, is purifying; but even more than purifying, your drama bears witness.

GABRIEL MARCEL: The role of death in my plays is absolutely primary, and so too in a certain way is the role of sickness. Incidentally, this is one of the things which, rather unusually, Pierre Aimé Touchard has reproached me for in his book *Dionysos.* He says I have given much too much importance to sickness and death. I confess that this made me smile because I do not believe that one can give too much importance to sickness and death. It is in facing them, in fact, that we are at the very heart of our destiny and of our mystery.

Now there is another point I would like to insist on with regard to this relation between my dramatic and my philosophical work. This is the fact that the dramatic vision, what I see with the help of my characters, has very often been an anticipation of what could appear to me only later on at the philosophical level. A number of examples could be given. You referred to *Le Palais de sable,* which is one of my first published plays. *Le Palais de sable* was written in 1912–13, and what strikes me is that it is clearly in advance of what I was writing at that time in the philosophical register. One sees here, actually, a kind of criticism, from an existential standpoint, of that idealism of faith that I was still somewhat clinging to, a criticism which appeared again a little later on in the first part of the *Metaphysical Journal.*

Already in *La Palais de sable,* without my being able at that time to formulate it for myself in a precise and philosophically rigorous way, the fundamental idea of intersubjectivity appeared, the fact that we are not alone, that whatever we do we are responsible for what happens to others.

Another play often mentioned in books about my work is *L'Iconoclaste.* In the last scene the idea of mystery as clarifying appears in a dramatic context, mystery as a positive value which comes to be set in opposition to what remains merely problematic.

PAUL RICOEUR: But if the drama anticipates your philosophy, what happens to the autonomy of the philosophical act, of philosophical reflection? Could we accuse your philosophy of being a philosophy of the theater? You have insisted on the importance of what you call "secondary reflection." What place has the reflective moment in this meditation on drama and on the tragic in thinking?

GABRIEL MARCEL: I believe that the autonomy of the philosophical act, which is actually an act of reflection, must be recognized absolutely and safeguarded completely.

Moreover, I think you are right in recalling here what I have written about secondary reflection. What did I want to say exactly? I wanted to say that surely there is a primary reflection which, roughly speaking, is purely analytical and which consists, as it were, in dissolving the concrete into its elements.

But there is, I think, an inverse movement, a movement of retrieval, which consists in becoming aware of the partial and even suspect character of the purely analytical procedure. This reflective movement tries to reconstruct, but now at the level of thought, that concrete state of affairs which had previously been glimpsed in a fragmented or pulverized condition. It is quite certain that it is this secondary reflection which is at work in all my philosophical writings, starting from the moment when I truly became fully conscious of my task. Perhaps this is not yet sufficiently clear in the *Metaphysical Journal*. But it becomes perfectly clear in *Being and Having*, and even more so in the later writings.

PAUL RICOEUR: I am ready to concede the autonomy of philosophical reflection in your work, particularly because you never refer, or almost never, to your dramatic writings. Your philosophical reflection generally begins with examples, with situations, with concepts already elaborated which you then analyze. In this sense your philosophy finds and follows its own path.

GABRIEL MARCEL: Yes, I think that is absolutely correct. Moreover, I am happy you have spoken of the role of examples in my work. Actually, I believe this role is very important.

How many times have I said that thinking which does not deal seriously with examples always runs the risk of losing itself, of letting itself be deluded by a kind of antecedent linguistic structure? For me, giving an example is a way of justifying myself to myself, and also of proving to my interlocutor that I am speaking of something, that my words are not empty. I would almost say that examples serve as a kind of irrigation.

PAUL RICOEUR: Could we say that the philosophical example is like the dramatic character whose significance is not wholly revealed without some kind of existential confrontation?

GABRIEL MARCEL: Yes, but perhaps we should make this more precise by remarking that the character is like an embodied example. It is an example that enjoys a kind of autonomy and can thus be very stimulating philosophically. In this way the comparison is possible. Actually, what strikes me now after so many years is that I still find in my plays a kind of living interest or freshness which seems to be somewhat lacking in my philosophical writings to the extent that they are in some way too explicit, too summary, or have occasioned too many commentaries which are often mere repetitions rather than creative reflections. If I can make use of a histological comparison, I would say that drama for me is like living tissue; it is more capable of internal regeneration than is properly philosophical thinking. This, at least, is true for my own work.

Conversation 4

PAUL RICOEUR: In this fourth conversation, M. Marcel, I want to ask a question we cannot put off any longer. A tag—there's no other word for it—has been attached to your work, the tag of Christian existentialism. People like to say that there is an atheistic existentialism, that of Sartre and Heidegger, and a Christian existentialism, that of Jaspers and Gabriel Marcel. What do you think about this?

GABRIEL MARCEL: I must say that I'm completely against this classification. You know as well as I do that Sartre was the one who started it in his well-known lecture on existentialism as a humanism. I cannot protest enough against this way of putting the matter. In fact I have never spontaneously used the word "existentialism." It was in 1946 at the Rome Congress that I found out that someone had used the word to characterize my work. At the time I was rather unconcerned. But shortly afterward I did become concerned when someone came to ask whether I would agree to the title *Christian Existentialism* for a commemorative volume which was to be dedicated to me in the collection *Présence* which Plon publishes.

I have to say that on the whole I did not find the idea very agreeable. I made it a point nevertheless to ask the advice of a man I had a great deal of confidence in, Louis Lavelle. I said to him: "You know my work. I have a great deal of confidence in your judgment. What do you think of the matter?" He answered: "I understand very well that you don't like the phrase 'Christian existentialism.' I don't like it either. It seems to me nonetheless that you can make a concession to your publisher." So I yielded. But very soon when I became aware of the inanities the word "existentialism" led to, and especially among society women, I was sorry to have been so accommodating. Since 1949 I've said on every occasion that I reject this tag, and more generally that I'm repelled by labels and "isms."

PAUL RICOEUR: Nevertheless, that summary characterization included an adjective, the adjective "Christian." We can't get away without some discussion on this point.

GABRIEL MARCEL: Certainly not.

PAUL RICOEUR: How do you see the relationship of your philosophy to Christianity? I'm asking the question because, without any ill will, someone might object to your thinking along these lines. When you speak of the ontological mystery, you are using a word taken from the language of Christianity, the word "mystery." But the word "ontological" belongs to the language of philosophy. Doesn't the expression "ontological mystery" really say too much for the philosopher, and not enough for the believer or at least for the theologian, inasmuch as you make no specific reference to the person of Christ as such? What do you think of this line of reasoning?

GABRIEL MARCEL: Here we have to go back quite a bit. What has to be seen is how I came to Christianity. You know I was raised without any religion and that, nevertheless, from the moment I began to think philosophically for myself, it seemed I was irresistibly drawn to think favorably of Christianity. That is, I was drawn to recognize that there must be an extremely profound reality in Christianity and that my duty as a philosopher was to find out how this reality could be understood. The problem I had then was truly a problem of intelligibility. That was when I used to hand in my writings to Victor Delbos, and I used to feel what a great interest he had in this inquiry. But over the years I found myself in the quite unusual situation of someone who believed deeply in the faith of others and who was completely convinced that this faith was not illusory, yet who could not acknowledge the possibility or the right of taking this faith absolutely on its own account. There was a paradox there—I saw this very clearly—which lasted a long time. I might also say that I walked a tight rope for a long time, and that at a certain moment I needed some outside intervention, that of Mauriac, to help me face this anomaly, to question, to ask myself: "Do I really have the right to stay any longer on this path?" No, I felt drawn to profess my allegiance openly. This happened at a time in my life when I was at peace with myself and when there was no special anxiety. For me this was a reason for thinking that the invitation Mauriac addressed to me should be taken absolutely seriously. I have probably told you that I hesitated for some moments. I said to myself: "I must become a Christian, I must enter a church, but will this be the reformed church?" My wife was Protestant and we were extraordinarily close. I have the greatest affection for her family. I have a brother-in-law who is a minister and who is really like a confidant to me. But I chose Catholicism. The influence of du Bos was certainly the major one. It seemed to me that choosing Christianity meant choosing Christianity in its fullness, and that I would find this fullness more in Catholicism than in Protestantism. It seemed to me that Protestantism offered only partial, variable, and sometimes inconsistent expressions of this fullness, and that it would be very difficult to choose among these expressions. That's exactly how things happened.

You referred to that essential text on the ontological mystery which came after my conversion. My conversion was in 1929 and that text was written in 1932. I don't believe it is easy to specify exactly what the relationship was between this kind of experience—I can use the word properly here—this lived experience which accompanied and followed my conversion, and what is said in this text. I believe that even at the time I was writing those reflections on the ontological mystery I experienced the need to reach a level universal enough to make what I was saying acceptable or understandable by non-Catholics and even perhaps by non-Christians, so long as they had a certain apprehension of what seemed to me essential.

PAUL RICOEUR: You speak somewhere about the peri-Christian zones of existence. It's these you wanted to touch on in your work. But the question remains. When you take up the themes of hope and fidelity, aren't you exploring theological dimensions?

GABRIEL MARCEL: Of course . . .

PAUL RICOEUR: You've refused the title "Christian existentialist." But if the bond between "I believe" and "I exist" is constitutive of your philosophy, if it contains the principle for every refutation of despair, don't you have to accept the term "Christian philosophy?"

GABRIEL MARCEL: Strictly speaking yes . . . perhaps I would accept this term to the extent that I reject the position Bréhier took when he denied—which seems completely absurd to me— that life or Christian experience could include elements capable of nourishing and enriching philosophical thought. In this way, that is, as a negation of a negation, I would accept the idea of a Christian philosophy. But let us return to what you were just saying, something which is very important. I consider myself as having always been a philosopher of the threshold, a philosopher who kept himself in rather uncomfortable fashion on a line midway between believers and nonbelievers so that he could somehow stand with believers, with the Christian religion, the Catholic religion, but also speak to nonbelievers, make himself understood by them and perhaps to help them. I don't think this kind of preoccupation is an apologetic one—that word would be completely inappropriate—but I do think that this fraternal concern has played an extremely important role in the development of my thought. Thus the questions or objections you've brought up are certainly legitimate, and I am not dismissing them. But I must somehow specify and locate the place where I have always stood, where perhaps I continue to stand. . . .

PAUL RICOEUR: This threshold position links you with Jaspers and Heidegger. I would very much like to discuss this with you.

GABRIEL MARCEL: Certainly.

PAUL RICOEUR: I am letting myself draw you onto this ground because some years ago when I wrote about you I was myself much more aware of your kinship with Jaspers than with Heidegger. But today I think I would emphasize the distance and even the opposition I've since noticed between you and Jaspers, and on the other hand I would underline everything which, despite very strong appearances to the contrary, draws you closer to Heidegger.

GABRIEL MARCEL: I think you're completely right. It's certain that when I read Jaspers' *Philosophy*—that must have been in 1933 if I'm not mistaken—I was extremely impressed. In many ways this reading seemed liberating. I am alluding especially to volume two, *Existence.* I found there masterly analyses, particularly of what Jaspers calls limit situations, and you remember that I wrote a study then which first appeared in the *Recherches philosophiques* and which afterwards was included in the book *Creative Fidelity.*

I was attracted much less by volume three, *Transcendence.* It seemed to me that there the idea of cipher which Jaspers used so copiously remained equivocal. It was impossible to get a firm grip on it.

PAUL RICOEUR: My own tendency would be to view Jaspers' second volume with the same reservations you just mentioned. His philosophy of freedom stresses choice so much, that is, self-choice in anxiety, whereas I see a more Claudellian strain in your philosophy of freedom. For you, the freedom of response goes beyond the freedom of choice. By way of contrast I am much more aware now that in Jaspers' philosophy of freedom the major emphasis is on exile, solitude, and refusal. This is what moves all his thought toward a kind of romantic speculation on failure, something that runs throughout his thought. I'm thinking of texts like the doctrine of the night in which everything that has an order must be destroyed, where the night is seen as the thrust of existence toward its own ruin. I don't think that you could have written that kind of text.

GABRIEL MARCEL: Certainly not. Romantic and, if I remember well enough, Wagnerian strains can be detected in his philosophy, don't you think? No, I think you're completely right.

PAUL RICOEUR: What place does the theme of anxiety have in your philosophy?

GABRIEL MARCEL: Yes, this question has to be met head-on. Certainly for me the theme of anxiety is not the central theme of what I would call, *grosso modo,* my philosophy of existence. Perhaps this is what makes a very great difference between myself and, for example, Heidegger. It has become more and more clear to me—and here in fact we meet Claudel again—that there could be an existential experience of joy and of fullness. And I believe also that what you pointed out about freedom is perfectly correct. The identification of freedom with freedom of choice was a mistake. Just this morning I had to make a somewhat painful decision. It was a matter of my recalling from a publisher a certain text that he had asked me for, because I realized that if this text were published it would put someone else in danger. I didn't hesitate. I said: "The text has to be recalled, even suppressed." I had made no real choice there, and yet I had never felt more free than at that moment. Why? Because there was nothing resembling an outside necessity. There was just this certainty that I would be betraying myself, be wanting in my own person, be putting myself in contradiction with everything I had always thought and said yes to, if I failed to recall the text and as a result exposed someone else to serious danger. This example seems to me quite revealing.

PAUL RICOEUR: I want to come back to the theme of anxiety because it has been a source of misunderstanding between Heidegger and you. Heidegger's texts on anxiety have too often been read by way of Sartre. Actually, for Heidegger the anxiety provoked by the contingency of everything is the result of a disengagement from what you would call the ontological dimension. This brings me back to the suggestion I just made, that perhaps you are very close to Jaspers in appearance, but under the surface very close to Heidegger. What Heidegger calls the forgetfulness of being has an echo in your analysis of having, of *indisponibilité*,[1] and of despair. Similarly your use of questioning, which we will have to come back to in our sixth conversation, seems to me close to Heidegger's use of interrogation. I would locate the difference between Heidegger and you in another area, that is, in your relationship to the Judaeo-Christian tradition. I am always somewhat disturbed by what I might call the prudence with which Heidegger circumvents this tradition.

GABRIEL MARCEL: Heidegger is a Greek!

PAUL RICOEUR: It is only to the extent that your philosophy is more peri-Christian or pre-Christian than Christian that your

1. Mr. Marcel has suggested keeping this word in French, since previous attempts to translate the terms *disponibilité* and *indisponibilité* have, in his judgment, not been successful. The idea is something like being at the disposal of others, openness, availability.—Translator.

standpoint as a philosopher of the threshold approximates Heidegger's.

GABRIEL MARCEL: Yes, probably so. I think that what Heidegger's position and my own have most fundamentally in common is the sacred sense of being, the conviction that being is a sacral reality. This seems to me extraordinarily important, and I believe it is sufficient to dispel any illusions one might have about the closeness between Heidegger and Sartre. I'm glad that you are giving me a chance to express myself on this point, because the satirical play I wrote about Heidegger could be misleading here. The French title of the play is *La Dimension florestan,* but the actual title is the German one, *Die Wacht am Sein.*[2] Actually the criticism in the play is directed essentially at the use of jargon and a kind of pretension. But it doesn't exclude—and I've taken pains to say so, once in a lecture delivered at Oberhausen and another time in Berlin—it doesn't at all exclude the possibility of a metaphysical kinship between Heidegger and myself.

Of course I am still a little doubtful as to how, when all is said and done, the well-known distinction between being and a being is to be interpreted. For example, I asked Henri Birault the following question: "Do you think Heidegger would accept my program of substituting for being the light, the illumining, and for a being, the illumined? Do you think Heidegger would go along with this?" Birault seemed rather skeptical. I don't know what you think of the matter. For me it's extremely important, because Heidegger's terminology is a problem for me here. I find it suspect because on the whole it depends too much on grammatical analysis. Yet it can't be denied for a moment that for Heidegger, who in certain respects is an inspired thinker, this terminology corresponds to an experience that is spiritual, speculative, and extremely deep.

PAUL RICOEUR: I would tend to minimize this disagreement about terminology and to emphasize a difference in the use of metaphor: Heidegger's metaphors are Greek, your own are biblical.

2. "Die Wacht am Rhein" is the title of a German nationalistic song.—Translator.

Conversation 5

PAUL RICOEUR: Our fourth discussion led us through a confrontation with Christianity, with the different kinds of existentialism, and finally with Heidegger, to the threshold of your ontology. At this point someone might ask whether your philosophy could be accused of evading certain fundamental problems about the modern world. Could it be said that your philosophy is a philosophy of the interior life, and therefore ultimately a thought which is out of contact with reality, or perhaps that it only deals with the world in order to insist on the value of interpersonal relations like fidelity—which you have written some magnificent pages about—so that strictly social relations are ignored? This objection brings us to a consideration of what you like to call "the human in man." What place does this theme have in your philosophy?

GABRIEL MARCEL: I think this theme has become more and more important in my thought over the last twenty years. I would even go further. When I think back and remember even my own formation, I discover that, very early and in circumstances I shall shortly describe for you, I became aware of the problem of justice. I think I have already alluded—that must have been in our third conversation—to the fact that the Dreyfus affair impressed me very much as a child. I don't have the time to go into all the details. But it so happened that my music teacher was a relative of Captain Dreyfus, and I remember how avidly I used to follow the conversations about this matter. I remember also my emotions and those of my aunt, who had a preponderant influence on me in this matter, when at Burjenstoek—that must have been in 1899—we learned the verdict of Rennes. I think this affair established a certain attitude in me. It seems to me that throughout my life I have behaved as a Dreyfusard. When I decided to participate in a protest meeting on the subject of the Maurras trial, for example, I began by saying: "It is as a Dreyfusard that I come today to speak in favor of Maurras in his trial." I did not even think of trying to justify Maurras himself because I had never been one of his followers.

The war of 1914 too, and the conditions in which it began, have had a very great influence on my deeper development. I remember how anxiously I perused the diplomatic documents which were available to us at that time. I wanted to be sure that on our side the war of 1914 was a just war. Today however, in the light of many documents I did not know about then, I have come back to my initial feeling of anxiety. I think today that French responsibility at the outbreak of the war was considerably clearer and much heavier than I believed it to be at that time. But this is of secondary importance. What I want to say is that this event seemed to concern me in the most direct way. I started to follow the development of the military situation much more closely than most intellectuals did. The result is that I watched the remilitarization of Germany with irrepressible anxiety and I deplored the inertia the allies showed in the face of this remilitarization.

I think I can say then that it would be a profound error, an extremely serious error, to claim that my thought is concerned exclusively with the interior life.

It is true that it was only at a certain moment that these other constant concerns began to take philosophical form; this process became more pronounced in the course of the Second World War and afterward. With regard to the problem of the technological world, I would reply similarly: this too was a matter that occupied my attention more and more. In this regard I would point to a certain evolution in my position.

At first perhaps I took an overly hostile view of technology. Today this seems to me absurd. I would no longer condemn a single instance of technology. I believe that technology is good in itself. On the other hand I think that technology can be put to the wrong use and that too little importance can be attached to the question of what ends technology ought to serve.

PAUL RICOEUR: Yes, it's striking that in "On the Ontological Mystery" the theme of mystery is introduced by way of a criticism of the reduction of man to "function," to biological and social functions. There you set up a fundamental opposition between the world of technology and the philosophy of existence. More recently however, in 1960, you delivered a lecture at Frankfurt entitled *Searchings,* which was also the title, I believe, of a collection of essays published in Germany in 1964.[1] Surely here is the crux. A certain insistence on the value of the human takes precedence over your criticism of the inhuman. Hence my question remains: at what level of your philosophical reflection is this concern for the human situated?

GABRIEL MARCEL: Your question is quite legitimate and I want to attempt a reply.

The difficulty here, as you well know, is that I have never thought in an absolutely systematic manner. Thus I could not point to a rigorously defined matrix in which this reflection would have a determined position.

What has played the essential role here, as I was saying a moment ago, has been my reflection on current events. It has seemed more and more clear to me that the problem of justice is the supreme problem, as Plato saw in his own way, and that a state that does not maintain justice in the supreme position it deserves will be a degraded state.

PAUL RICOEUR: I would say that the connection between this sense of justice and the rest of your philosophy is everywhere established through negative themes. Your 1951 work, *Man against Mass Society,* sets out to denounce every form of inhumanity. The crux, as I see it, is the continual criticism in your philosophy of the spirit of abstraction. Between your speculative philosophy, if this word is even suitable, and your judgments about the modern world, this criticism has a cardinal

1. The exact title of the book is: *Auf der Suche nach Wahrheit und Gerechtigkeit* (Frankfurt a.M.: Knecht, 1964); English translation (anonymous) as *Searchings* (Westminster: Newman, 1967).

position. It appears in your attacks on technological excesses and the wrongs of the partisan spirit, and in your criticism of every attempt to "problematize" the question of existence or of being.

GABRIEL MARCEL: You're entirely right. I can perhaps be reproached for not having sufficiently clarified what might be called the positive foundation for this denunciation, for not having sufficiently explained the kind of thinking I use as both a model and a means to condemn the spirit of abstraction. However, I think a review of my writings would show that it is precisely on the basis of ontology, of a reflection on being, that this denunciation of the spirit of abstraction becomes not only possible but necessary. I wonder, too, whether on this point—this is a question I put to you—there is not a certain profound agreement between Heidegger and myself, even though our modes of expression certainly remain quite different.

PAUL RICOEUR: In a certain respect I think you are right. In your denunciation of the techniques of debasement one word returns incessantly, the word "sacrilege." Whether you are speaking of propaganda or of certain aspects of the mechanization of human life resulting from man's mastery over nature, you always come back to this point: a certain core of the sacred in man has been violated. It is this concern for the integrity of man as sacred which profoundly unifies your philosophy and your commitments.

GABRIEL MARCEL: Yes, it is really for that reason that in my recent lectures I have come back so often to the question of the sacred, asking myself what might happen to the sacred in a world more and more delivered up to technology. It is here, I think, on the question of the sacral dignity of being, that Heidegger and I are in agreement.

Naturally this is something very difficult to express, something that can hardly be reached except by successive approximations. And I think that the lectures collected in that small book you were just talking about, which has not yet appeared in French, are so many approaches to a grasp of being as sacred and of being in the human person as sacred. Actually, this is also the principle of those lectures I gave at Harvard in 1961, *The Existential Background of Human Dignity*, which have appeared in France under the annoyingly abridged title *La Dignité humaine*. There, basically, I was trying to recover the traditional notion of the person, of personal dignity, but at the same time to avoid giving this notion a purely rational basis, in the Kantian sense of "rational."

PAUL RICOEUR: Yes, even when you speak of justice, you don't speak of it on the level of judicial thought, because this would call attention to an intellectualism you reject. For you justice is also propriety, respect not merely for man's rationality but for his capacity for the sacred.

GABRIEL MARCEL: That's it . . . an acknowledgment which at bottom is connected with piety. I am taking the word "piety" here in a sense which has absolutely nothing to do with the Christian sense. It is closer to the meaning the Greeks gave the term.

PAUL RICOEUR: But if this is the case, then the connection with political and social behavior becomes more difficult. What kind of political commitment does seem to you compatible with the mission of a philosopher?

GABRIEL MARCEL: I have often insisted on making a distinction between a fundamental commitment and a contingent one. To me a fundamental commitment seems linked to the vocation of the philosopher. The philosopher must never refuse this kind of commitment. But there is also a partisan and contingent commitment which I do reject.

Fundamental commitment has to do with—how shall I say it?—with the structural conditions of personal existence. For example: for me it would be wholly out of the question not to condemn absolutely every kind of racism. Likewise, religious intolerance is absolutely out of the question. Here are two examples of situations where I think a philosopher must take a truly militant position.

Partisan commitment is something else altogether. It truly is commitment in the name of a party. And you know very well that in certain of my works, especially in my plays, I have set up a very stark opposition between the partisan and the human, understanding by "the human" here the attachment to properly human values. This is the deep sense of my play, *Le Dard*, which was just republished several months ago and which I consider among the most significant of my writings.

PAUL RICOEUR: I find the same distinction between fundamental commitment and partisan commitment in your magnificent response to Professor Carlo Schmidt when you were awarded the Prix de la Paix on September 20, 1964. In this German context I see you as being close not only to Heidegger, as we were saying a while ago, but perhaps also to Max Weber with his distinction between an ethics of conviction and an ethics of responsibility (what he also used to call an ethics of force). Would you say that there are actually two levels of morality, one which expresses a commitment in depth and which must continually exert pressure on the political and social order, and another which is measured by the possible and the reasonable?

GABRIEL MARCEL: I don't know Max Weber's thought very well, but I would not be at all surprised if you are right in making this comparison. On the other hand, it is here, isn't it, that we must come back to Heidegger. We have to remember that Heidegger at one point was more than indulgent to a nascent Hitlerism, and for me this remains his indelible fault. It seems to me that this indulgence could not have been possible without a certain philosophical deficiency, whereas we know very well that Max Weber always had an irreproachable attitude on every essential matter.

PAUL RICOEUR: The phrase which might best serve to suggest your own attitude here is "the vigilant philosopher," "the watchful philosopher."

GABRIEL MARCEL: Yes, that is the expression I used in the lecture at Frankfurt you mentioned a moment ago. I think this is an essential function—but I don't very much like the word "function." Let us say, rather, that the philosopher has the task of watching over current events, and also watching over the development of certain habits of thought, because as we know very well each of us is always in danger of falling back into a kind of crowd morality, a purely irrational morality. On this point I fully agree with certain past philosophers, certain men I have known and profoundly esteemed, such as Léon Brunschvicg. Whatever may be the differences between his thought and mine, he is a man I shall always think about with a certain feeling of veneration.

Conversation 6

PAUL RICOEUR: With our sixth and last conversation, M. Marcel, the moment has come to make our most strenuous effort to grasp the profound unity of your work. Certainly, as we have remarked, there is no Marcellian system. Yet perhaps we can discern the living unity governing all the themes of your philosophy. What we are looking for is the ridge common to all those slopes of your work which we have considered separately—the ontological, the dramatic, the existential, and the ethical. Do you think that this unity can be expressed in the only designation you have accepted, I believe it was in the preface to *The Mystery of Being,* that of Neo-Socratism?

GABRIEL MARCEL: Yes, but notice that this term wasn't mine. Joseph Chenu, who is now professor in Morocco, suggested it once when he was coming regularly to participate in my seminars. That was just after the Second World War. Actually I think this characterization is perhaps the least misleading one, although of course I strongly dislike all "isms." The expression "Neo-Socratism" does seem to emphasize the central role interrogation plays in my thought, the fact that often my primary concern has been to find an adequate way to pose problems before attempting to solve them.

This expression also indicates the fact that despite the illusions of my adolescence, I eventually found it necessary to renounce absolutely the idea of building a system. My way of

[251]

thinking seemed incompatible with systematic form. I might add that I have reflected critically on the equivocal and at times disquieting character of the relation between the subject and his system. Something about the phrase "having a system" has always bothered me.

From the moment someone has a system, it seems to me he is concerned with exploiting it and managing it. And these verbs which apply so well to the material level lose something of their meaning, or at least their meaning is distorted, on the spiritual level.

To this extent I believe you are right in saying that the expression "Neo-Socratism" can be retained. I notice that, in one of the most profound books written about my work, my friend Xavier Tilliette has himself used this expression. Perhaps I could go a bit further. I have found it less and less possible to situate myself at some central point of view which would be like that of God. This would be a pretension completely incompatible with our status as creatures, it seems to me. That is why I have always emphasized the importance of humility on the philosophical level, the humility directly opposed to pride, to *hubris*. Naturally there are difficulties here, because humility can also become pretension and then it is destroyed. But I am convinced—and it is probably in my plays that this is most noticeable—that we simply have to recognize the ambiguity connected with everything that we are, insofar as we are equals, subjects.

Let me read you a few lines from the third act of *L'Emissaire*, which illustrate precisely what I have in mind here. Here is one of the characters I sympathize with, Antoine Sorgue, who says: "Yes and no: this is the only response possible where we ourselves are in question. We believe and we don't believe, we love and we don't love, we exist and we don't exist. But if this is so, it is because we are on the move toward a goal which we both see in its entirety and don't see." [1]

PAUL RICOEUR: This fine text brings us to consider the place and the importance in your work of the theme of "man underway," of journeying. *Homo Viator*, that's the title of one of your works. But I wouldn't want these expressions to give the impression that you have in mind a voyage whose goal is known;

1. In *Le Secret est dans les îles* (Paris: Plon, 1969); my translation.

that would be to misunderstand your notion of experience (which we shall come back to in a moment). It is actually the detours, the twistings, the meticulous and wary steps of a journey which make it important as a theme in your work. In the excellent study you mentioned a moment ago, Tilliette describes very well the alert but toilsome activity that characterizes your thought. With this analysis in mind I suggest we explore what I would call the reverse side of your philosophy of hope, that is, the theme of journeying. Perhaps this will bring us to a center which we could not find and would not care to look for in systematic thought. I think it could be said that a hidden fissure divides your thought. On the one hand there is an alarmed diagnosis of the signs of the time, and on the other a reflective celebration of incarnation, of concrete being. In your philosophy as a whole you are antidualist, and yet there are two tonalities, one bitter, the other reassured, even joyous. I would even say that in your work a metaphysics of light and a sociology of shadows confront each other incessantly. Where is the link between the two, where is the connection? I would say it is in a certain interpretation of experience. This answer may seem odd at first, but if we succeed in taking experience and journeying as a whole, perhaps we will approach the center we are looking for.

GABRIEL MARCEL: I think you're right. As I look back over the path I have traveled, I see that I have gradually revalued my notion of experience.

I remember, and I must say this stirs up an old irritation, the scorn I used to have for empiricism when I was an adolescent. It is true that this empiricism was particularly the English brand; I was thinking of Locke and, even more, of Hume. Later, when I came into contact with American thought, particularly the thought of William James, I revised my judgment. But I believe my thinking about empiricism became more precise not simply because of contact with other philosophers. No, I think this precision was above all a result of life. By "life" I mean life with others, reflection about others, about personal relationships, about intersubjectivity, which perhaps we haven't talked enough about and which is nonetheless so essential to me. I think it could be said here that intersubjectivity is openness to the other, an openness which is perpetually threatened because at every moment the self may close itself again and become a prisoner of itself, no longer considering the other except in relation to itself. But the possibility of opening to others (that is, in a completely different language, charity) is clearly one of the key certitudes I have come to. I think that it is on the level of *agapē*, on the level of charity or intersubjectivity, that experience undergoes a certain transformation in that it takes on the value of a test.

PAUL RICOEUR: Yes, and it is in this way that your meditation on mystery differs as much as possible from any movement of flight or of exile. We have spoken of Socrates. You are Socratic but certainly not Platonic, if "Platonism" means being carried off to an "elsewhere" or to an "over there." The problem of intersubjectivity, the problem of others, has ceaselessly brought you toward the inexhaustible wealth of the concrete. It is the act of *recognizing* others which ceaselessly leads us to experience and makes experience a test.

GABRIEL MARCEL: Yes, I think you are right to use the term "recognize" [*reconnaissance*]. It seems central to my thought, and the term must be allowed to echo in all its senses. It might mean reconnaisance as in the military sense, or it might mean an acknowledgment, similar to gratitude. For me what is essential for man is to recognize but also to admit his faults, to recognize his errors.

PAUL RICOEUR: It is to this act of recognition that we must also look for the true sense of hope; we must not regard hope as contrary to experience, but rather discern hope in the very richness of experience. I have right here another speech of Antoine Sorgue who, as you remarked just a moment ago, is so close to you. This is from that same third act of *L'Emissaire:* "There are not only those unfathomable waters. There is also the world of light, into which we do not draw ourselves but are drawn, because this world is a world of grace. It becomes more and more distinct, more and more consistent as we believe in it more." [2] This text certainly would demand a long commentary, but I think it roughly expresses the main thrust of your reflection. At the same time it immediately raises a doubt, an objection. Doesn't the recourse to grace arbitrarily close off the process of question-

2. *Ibid.;* my translation.

ing we just spoke of? How can you attribute this Christian recourse both to grace and to a kind of Socratic thinking?

GABRIEL MARCEL: Let us remember first of all that this Socratism is not a skepticism. It is a search, a groping search, as you have said, but a search that does not imply that one need close himself off from any light he might see.

Grace has to be conceived thus. The temptation so many theologians have succumbed to, in my opinion, is to have imprudently objectified grace, to have treated grace, for example, as a cause. But then grace ceases to be grace and becomes a kind of pseudo-knowing. There's no question of anything like this in what Antoine Sorgue says. His remark is simply the word of a believer, a believer who is looking for his way, who feels himself illumined, but who knows very well that his inconsiderate acts and his faults can extinguish the light that guides him.

PAUL RICOEUR: Yes. We have to come to see that hope and journeying are not two different things, but that hope is what makes the passage something more than just simple wandering. I like very much one of your expressions, the one where you say "being is being underway." That's hope. It's hope that gives all your research a tempo, a groping and yet confident rhythm. The unity of your concrete philosophy is the conjunction of two ideas, the labyrinth of existence and the rays of hope that cross it. I am thinking also of another of your formulations: "I hope in you for us." Hope is always coming back, but *beneath* our experience and not above it, if I may put it that way.

GABRIEL MARCEL: Perhaps we could add that hope is connected with *disponibilité* just as it is connected with patience. Here too are values which all the great spiritual masters have recognized but which the philosophers, particularly contemporary philosophers, are not sufficiently concerned with.

PAUL RICOEUR: Perhaps here is the connection between the themes which, when treated abstractly, are so difficult to situate in relation to each other, the themes of being and existence. Being and hope have to be put on one side and existence and journeying on the other. If we understand the profound unity between hope and journeying, then we understand also the inextricable link between the two questions of being and of existence. You are of the same breed as Péguy, Emmanuel Mounier, and all those who have grasped the profound unity of the body and the spirit. All your thought, despite the fact of the inhuman we were speaking about in an earlier conversation, testifies to the extreme proximity, the strict continuity between incarnation, which is like the *basso continuo* of all our wanderings and quests, and hope, which is nothing other than a continual getting underway again.

GABRIEL MARCEL: I believe you are quite right to mention Péguy. Surely there are few writers whom I feel so close to in so many ways. On the whole I feel much closer to him, for example, than to Claudel. In any case I am much closer to his way of thinking, his particular kind of commitment, than to Claudel's, even though I greatly admire Claudel's genius and I acknowledge the influence he had on me around 1912–14.

PAUL RICOEUR: Well, I don't think our recalling Péguy at the end of these conversations takes us far from Socrates, because the Socratic spirit is always the spirit of "risk," the "magnificent venture." Doesn't he leave the scene at the end of the *Phaedo* with a vow and an invocation? Perhaps we may do the same.

Here is the conclusion of *Homo Viator:* "Oh, spirit of metamorphosis! When we try to obliterate the frontier of clouds which separates us from the other world guide our unpractised movements! And, when the given hour shall strike, arouse us, eager as the traveller who straps on his rucksack while beyond the misty window-pane the earliest rays of dawn are faintly visible!" [3]

3. *Homo Viator,* trans. Emma Craufurd (Chicago: Regnery, 1961), p. 270.